Militainment, Inc.

Militainment, Inc. offers provocative, sometimes disturbing insight into the ways that war is presented and viewed as entertainment—or "militainment"—in contemporary American popular culture. War has been the subject of entertainment for centuries, but Roger Stahl argues that a new interactive mode of militarized entertainment is recruiting its audience as virtual citizen-soldiers. The author examines a wide range of historical and contemporary media examples to demonstrate the ways that war now invites audiences to enter the spectacle as interactive participants through a variety of channels—from news coverage to online video games to reality television. Simply put, rather than presenting war as something to be watched, the new interactive militainment presents war as something to be played and experienced vicariously. Stahl examines the challenges that this new mode of militarized entertainment poses for democracy, and explores the controversies and resistant practices that it has inspired.

This volume is essential reading for anyone interested in the relationship between war and media, and it sheds surprising light on the connections between virtual battlefields and the international conflicts unfolding in Iraq and Afghanistan today.

Roger Stahl is Assistant Professor of Speech Communication at the University of Georgia. His work has appeared in publications such as *Rhetoric and Public Affairs*, *The Quarterly Journal of Speech*, and *Critical Studies in Media Communication*. He wrote, produced, and narrated the 2007 documentary film *Militainment, Inc.: Militarism and Pop Culture*, which is distributed by the Media Education Foundation.

"Roger Stahl is a one-man bomb squad, painstakingly disentangling the complex cultural circuitry that wires our entertainment consumption habits to US military hardware. This richly sourced, vividly illustrated page-turner will recast your next cinema, stadium, or virtual world visit in a startling new light."

—**Gordon Mitchell**, University of Pittsburgh and author of *Strategic Deception: Rhetoric, Science and Politics in Missile Defense Advocacy*

"While many have written about militarism, and many more have written about the entertainment industry, I do not know of a book that ties the two together in such an insightful argument. *Militainment, Inc.* is a smart and engaging book about how US citizens relate to and engage with US military actions, and how the increasing integration of militarism and the entertainment industries limits democratic commentary. I can't imagine anything more timely."

—**Susan Jeffords**, University of Washington and author of *Remasculinization of America: Gender and the Vietnam War*

"Roger Stahl has systematically researched US popular culture and recent military history and has provided a highly illuminating study of how recent wars have been produced as media spectacles, and processed by audiences as entertainment, hence the term *Militainment*. Providing illuminating studies of the media, sport, video games, TV reality shows, and other forms of militainment, Stahl's book should be read by everyone concerned with the intersection of war and entertainment in the contemporary era."

—**Douglas Kellner**, UCLA and author of the forthcoming *Cinema Wars: Hollywood Film and Politics in the Bush/Cheney Era*

"From the thrills of virtual war worlds to macabre fascinations with deadly killing fields, Roger Stahl tracks a culture where war and its horrors are transformed into a landscape of entertainment. This new geography of militainment is mapped with great skill in an original work that is essential reading for those who would like to see beyond the battlefield to a world of peace and stability."

—**Robin Andersen**, author of *A Century of Media, A Century of War*, winner of the Alpha Sigma Nu Book Award 2007

Militainment, Inc.

War, Media, and Popular Culture

Roger Stahl

Routledge
Taylor & Francis Group

NEW YORK AND LONDON

First published 2010
by Routledge
270 Madison Avenue, New York, NY 10016

Simultaneously published in the UK
by Routledge
2 Park Square, Milton Park, Abingdon, Oxon OX14 4RN

*Routledge is an imprint of the Taylor & Francis Group,
an informa business*

© 2010 Taylor and Francis Group

Typeset in Perpetua by RefineCatch Limited, Bungay, Suffolk
Printed and bound in the United States of America on acid-free
paper by Edwards Brothers, Inc.

Library of Congress Cataloging in Publication Data
Militainment, Inc.: war, media, and popular culture / Roger Stahl.
    p. cm.
  Includes bibliographical references.
  1. Mass media and war—United States.   2. War in mass
media—United States.   3. Popular culture—United States.
4. War and society—United States.   5. Militarism—Social
aspects—United States.   6. United States—Social
conditions—1980–   7. United States—Social life and
customs—1971–   I. Title.
  P96.W352U5574 2009
  070.4'49355020973—dc22   2009010701

ISBN10: 0–415–99977–4 (hbk)
ISBN10: 0–415–99978–2 (pbk)
ISBN10: 0–203–87960–0 (ebk)

ISBN13: 978–0–415–99977–9 (hbk)
ISBN13: 978–0–415–99978–6 (pbk)
ISBN13: 978–0–203–87960–3 (ebk)

Contents

List of Figures

Acknowledgments

Though there is only one name on the spine, this book was a collective project. I would like to first and foremost thank a visual artist, Ted Heine, for drawing my attention to the phenomenon of militainment and planting the initial seeds of the project. Thanks to the members of The Streets Project at Penn State University, especially Doug Morris and Lee Rensimer, for generally raising my consciousness regarding foreign policy. Thanks to my mentors at Penn State— Rosa Eberly, Thomas Benson, Stephen Browne, Charles Scott, and Alphonso Lingis—for their inspiration and nurturing. Thanks to Christine Harold and Pat Gehrke for being the smartest people within earshot during the formulation of my ideas. Thanks variously to my colleagues at the University of Georgia, especially Barbara Biesecker, Kevin Deluca, Jennifer Monahan, and Thomas Lessl, for your judgment and encouragement at various stages of the project. Thanks also to those who have affected this book probably without knowing it, including Marita Gronnvoll, Gordon Mitchell, Richard Doyle, Jon Leon Torn, Michael Butterworth, Nick Maradin, Brett Robinson, Kelly Happe, Mitch Reyes, Martin Medhurst, and Linda Steiner. I am grateful for a Willson Center for the Humanities grant that allowed me to travel and speak with artists and activists in person. I am grateful for these artist and activists themselves— Wafaa Bilal, Anne-Marie Schleiner, and Joseph Delappe—who creatively provoke the world to consider what war means. Thanks to all of the thoughtful students in my media and war classes for their inestimable contributions to the book. Thanks to Sut Jhally of the Media Education Foundation, who took a chance on a video I produced also called *Militainment, Inc.* that helped bring critical thinking about war and media to the classroom. Thanks to the editors at Routledge—Matthew Byrnie, Siân Findlay, and Susan Dunsmore—for their care and thoughtful manuscript suggestions. On a more personal note, thanks to my late grandfather, James Lade, and my father, Duane Stahl, who worked in military communications during WWII and Vietnam respectively, a combination that seems to have unpredictably resurfaced in a new generation. Thanks to my family, who do not shy away from political discussion at the dinner table and who has always made me think about things. Finally, thank you, Kate Morrissey, for keeping my fire lit and feet on the ground with your intelligence, wisdom, patience, and love.

Introduction
Step Right Up!

From the theaters to malls, on every shore,
The thin line between entertainment and war
The front line is everywhere, there be no shelter here . . .[1]

For a Westerner, a typical vacation visit to Southeast Asia includes an excursion into Cambodia to see the majestic Khmer temple at Angkor, commonly listed among the wonders of the world. Trips of this kind must be made by riverboat or airplane as many of the roads have been destroyed by years of war. En route from Bangkok, the comparatively wealthy Thai countryside gives way to Cambodia's desolation, still recovering from losing one-third of its population to the ravages of the Khmer Rouge and other conflicts. Here, the immense assuredness of Angkor Wat and the surrounding temples stands in contrast to the seemingly fresh bomb craters, throngs of orphans and amputees, and the Toul Sleng democide museum. Thousands of headless Buddha statues, decapitated by the Khmer Rouge, sit as silent witnesses to the violence, which continues to pulse just below the surface of the earth. In this country the size of Ohio, left-over landmines continue to take hundreds of lives every month. The threat is ever-present. Signs warn people to stay on the road.

Due to the bustling tourism industry, a common sight is a procession of air-conditioned black Mercedes taxis laboring over potholes on the road to the temples. The taxis contain tourists who gaze like monarchs out of the window at the blazing countryside squalor. A local woman walks alongside the caravan and greets each passing taxi in turn with a smile and a stack of merchandise. The woman knows her ideal customer well, and proceeds to unfurl a red T-shirt depicting one of the land mine warning signs whose ubiquity has made them iconic. The shirt reads "I Survived Cambodia" in jagged script. A few of the taxis stop, roll down smoky windows, and meet the woman with protruding arms and cash. Most drive on. Here, the mines constitute a tourist attraction, produced by the simple economics of alienation on the part of the buyer and desperation on the part of the seller. The exchange, especially on such personal terms, must be a surreal transaction for both parties.

Back in the town's cafés, one may witness another facet of the war tourism business: advertisements for the chance to fire high-end military hardware. Squeezing off a round on a grenade launcher, for example, costs around fifty dollars (listed in US currency). These appeals hang alongside flyers for mountain trek adventures and historical tours. In a land rife with the signs of war's fallout—amputees, orphans, and landmines—the business of selling the experience of war can catch a person off guard. Reactions vary. One might look at the ads and try to picture the typical patron: the thrill seeker who found a site on the Internet or an ad in *Soldier of Fortune*, goateed with blade sunglasses; the sex tourist who had wandered over from Bangkok; the college backpacker wearing a red T-shirt reading "I Survived Cambodia." Or perhaps one might look at the ads and think: I have fifty bucks and would love, just once, to fire a rocket-propelled grenade.

As it turns out, this phenomenon is not so exotic. In the midst of the occupations of Iraq and Afghanistan, an American would only have to travel to Sherman, Texas—alone or with a corporate retreat group—to a private "military amusement park" called Tactical Tanks. At Tactical Tanks, one could spend an entire day running "missions" in an actual tank for $8,500.[2] On a budget, one might have caught up with the Army's traveling "Special Operations Adventure Van," a recruiting effort that offers the chance to hop aboard a tank, a helicopter, and variety of other weapons simulators. One might take the family to the local fairground to try out the 19,000 square-foot "Army Virtual Experience," located near the tilt-a-whirl, which includes rides in Humvee and

Figure 0.1 (left) Landmine warning sign, Cambodia; (right) the US Army's traveling Army Virtual Experience offering itself as another ride at the fairgrounds.

Sources: Photo courtesy of Heico Neumeyer. The Virtual Army Experience page at http://www.vae.americasarmy.com/.

helicopter simulators. Such exhibits will likely be a permanent fixture at the local mall in the coming years. As of 2008, Philadelphia's Franklin Mills Mall houses the prototype "Army Experience Center," a 12 million dollar military theme park for leisured shoppers wandering out of the nearby Dave & Buster's.[3] In 2013, such a facility will be a part of the National Museum of the United States Army scheduled to open in Fairfax, Virginia. The proposed museum will contain theme park-style simulator rides designed with the help of Universal Studios, the folks who built the King Kong railcar ride and the Jaws live-action fright cruise.[4] A feature attraction will be the proposed simulator ride, "The Grenade," which will take museum-goers on an ear-splitting jeep ride through a battleground. Generally, however, it has not been necessary to leave home to experience such thrills. Beginning in 2002, one could play the Army's new recruiting video game, *America's Army*, or any of the other war-themed games developed in concert with the televised invasion of Iraq. One might have fantasized about hopping aboard a tank or armored Humvee through an array of military-themed reality television shows that appeared in proximity to the 2003 invasion of Iraq. The so-called "embedded reporting system" offered a similar set of pleasures, even billing itself as the ultimate in reality television. In the new century, it seemed that the US had become a nation of virtual war tourists.

This book is about the changing civic experience of war in the United States at the turn of the twenty-first century. Numerous scholars have noted that Desert Storm in 1991 represented a moment where the event of war became a fixture in the entertainment landscape, a feature of popular culture, and an object of consumption. The dominant perspective has been to regard the presentation of war in terms of the "spectacle," that is, to argue that these discourses tend to function to control public opinion by distancing, distracting, and disengaging the citizen from the realities of war. Subsequent decades, however, introduced a new set of discourses and practices that invaded the home front experience of war in the United States. The intensification of the relationship between the Pentagon and the entertainment industries brought about the crystallization of platforms that invite one to project oneself into the action. During the 2003 invasion of Iraq in particular, opportunities abounded for the citizen to play the "interactive war," which appeared across a range of fields, from military recruiting to journalism to consumerist practices. This interactive mode modified the usual narrative filters to promote first-person fantasies of war. Certain legal, institutional, economic, and technological trends have also redrawn the landscape of information circulation and thus have rewired the citizen's relationship to the soldier. At its core, however, this new orientation toward war is a symbolic shift, described by dominant narratives of war, ways of imaging war, and the integration of the experience of war with established entertainment genres.

Describing the shift to the interactive war is ultimately an exercise in describing changes in the construction of the citizen subject. The evolving quality of this citizen is vitally important to the quality of contemporary war, especially in an ostensibly democratic system where one has a say in the approval and authorization of war. Sam Keen writes, for example, that "before the weapon comes the image. We think others to death before we invent the battle-axe or ballistic missiles with which to actually kill them."[5] In order to "think others to death," we assume identities willing to commit large-scale acts of collective violence. Judith Butler argues that we ought to pay close attention to how journalistic discourses position and constitute the "imperialist subject."[6] Caren Kaplan similarly notes that discourses and communication technologies constitute "circuits of power," that serve nationalist interests. "War can be ended," she notes, "only when we recognize our attachments to its subject-making potential."[7] In other words, understanding the citizen's relationship to war is crucial to understanding how power functions to manufacture war itself. This book argues that by inviting the citizen to "play the war," the interactive mode works to rewire those "circuits of power" to craft the "imperialist subject" in important ways.

Before examining the transition to the interactive war, it should be acknowledged that the line between war and entertainment has always been permeable and negotiable, especially in a world saturated with electronic media. To use a different metaphor, this relationship has become something of a political fulcrum. It may not be such a stretch to say that every representation of conflict must wrestle with the ethics of its own entertainment value. The classic Cold War suspense film *Fail-Safe* (1964) offers a lucid parable for navigating this peculiar cultural compulsion. In an early scene, a political science professor played by Walter Matthau amuses a cocktail party by speculating about the aftermath of a hypothetical thermonuclear war. After the party a guest back-handedly congratulates him on his performance. She tells him, "We all know we're all going to die. But you make a game out of it. A marvelous game that includes the whole world ... You make death an entertainment, something that can be played in a living room." This is not only a condemnation of the good professor. The film unmercifully congratulates us too on our willingness as movie-goers to comfortably assume an indefensible position. By virtue of our own spectatorship of this nuclear disaster movie, we have willingly entered the marvelous parlor game that stages our own mass destruction as the evening's entertainment. The symmetries of the theater itself seem to have been tailor-made for such an experience: the all-consuming fireball spilling across the darkened, awe-struck worshippers of a vengeful god. After all, what could be more fail-safe fodder for a "blockbuster," a term that originally referred to a large aerial bomb?[8]

A highly stylized dream sequence bookends the film and drives home our complicity as watchers. One of the US Generals, known as "Blackie," has a recurring nightmare of being a spectator at a bull fight. As the matador plants the *banderillas* and issues the final mortal lancing, Blackie undergoes the bull's agony and delirium. His head lolls and his eyes roll while the fans seated around him cheer. When he wakes from this nightmare, Blackie tells his wife that when he meets that bullfighter "it will all be over." Near the end of the film, after US planes have nuked Moscow by accident, the president selects Blackie to fly the jet that will drop a nuclear bomb on his own New York City, a good faith offer to the Soviet premier to forestall a more destructive retaliation and escalation. After Blackie releases the bomb, he commits suicide by poisonous injection. His life fading, the scene of the bullfight again appears behind his eyes, the black bull twitching in its final death throes on the arena floor. In the end, this image suggests, spectatorship is only an illusion of security.

Some version of this moral has become a mainstay of the American experience of war, particularly since Vietnam. Michael Arlen's description of Vietnam as a "living-room war" or General Norman Schwarzkopf's warning at a press conference in 1991 that Operation Desert Storm was "not a Nintendo game" have taken their place among the well-worn clichés of the age, appearing either as righteous indignation ("You make death an entertainment . . .") or more mundane platitudes for navigating the persistent relationship between entertainment media and post-industrial war. On the other hand, such pronouncements have been curiously absorbed into the media that bring us the "television war" and the "video game war." Just as *Fail-Safe* begins by reeling in the viewer with a feigned slap on the hand, so too is news coverage replete with cautionary asides reminding us that what we are about to see is not, in fact, a video game, a fireworks show, nor a Hollywood blockbuster. The necessity of such warnings assumes a default reading of the mediated war as entertainment, which is significant in itself. These warnings do not simply represent the moralistic impulse, however. In the same breath, they serve to morally inoculate the act of consumption while conjuring a forbidden fruit. They are, in a sense, precise instructions on how to transgressively consume the scene.

The contradictions between war and its consumption gathered a critical mass in 2003. That year, unique in world history, began as Earth's lone superpower, whose arsenal eclipsed the rest of the world's military capacities combined, was well on its way to an unprovoked overthrow of a small sovereign nation. Though invasions had been conducted in the past, none were so ostentatiously executed, so brashly demonstrative, and none had captured the attention of the world in quite such a manner before. Events played out on 24-hour, real-time, round-the-world television, gloriously and excruciatingly "live," certainly well beyond the imperfect liveness of reporters in tent cities and hotels a decade prior. This time the war featured the liveness of a hundred satellite-uplinked cameras fanned out through a hundred armored vehicles racing across the desert floor, a liveness that sold itself like a drug, a liveness that threw news anchors into fits of breathless anticipation. In its build-up and execution, the invasion fully integrated itself into the entertainment landscape, providing a constant stream of action-packed footage punctuated with a steady rhythm of must-see TV pseudo-events.

The year 2003 also marked the moment when the word "militainment" entered the public lexicon. Princeton's online dictionary WordNet was first to document the term, defining it as "entertainment with military themes in which the Department of Defense is celebrated," apparently a predominantly American experience. This definition is likely based on a *CNN.com* article that claimed a new television genre for the term: the multitude of war-themed reality TV shows that materialized in early 2002.[9] A few days after 2003's Shock and Awe blitz of Baghdad, "militainment" came up again, this time defined by Steve Ford of the Raleigh, North Carolina *News and Observer* as "news coverage, particularly on the tube, that seems almost to revel in the suspense and excitement, and inevitably the violence and suffering, of combat."[10] The flood of Pentagon-sponsored reality television that opened the century and the three new military-themed cable television channels that appeared in 2005 drew the term further into the public view.[11] In the same year, the tenor of war news and the embedded reporting system earned the title of "militainment" in former *ABC News* producer Danny Schechter's critical documentary, *Weapons of Mass Deception*. For the purposes of this book, we will define the word simply as state violence translated into an object of pleasurable consumption. Beyond this, the word also suggests that this state violence is not of the abstract, distant, or historical variety but rather an impending or current use of force, one directly relevant to the citizen's current political life.

"Militainment" is thus a term at war with itself, taut with its own centrifugal force, and loaded with the brisance of contradiction. The term melds the martial with the mercurial, two previously incommensurable aspects. Jonathan Burston outlines the binaries: grit/glamor, action/representation, real/fake, public/domestic, masculine/feminine, patriotic/cosmopolitan, homophobic/gay-friendly, conservative/liberal.[12] The term seemingly contains its own critique, whether lending a propagandistic aura to entertainment or cheapening both the sacrifices of the military and the tragedy of war. Like previous critical oxymorons, however, it is perfectly reasonable to assume that the term will be naturalized. Half a century ago, Theodor Adorno and Max Horkheimer chose "the culture industry" specifically to convey a sense of absurdity of what they viewed as an art factory.[13] Now "The Culture Industry" is a large brand marketing and consulting firm based in Los Angeles with clients like Microsoft and General Electric.[14] During the 1990s, the term "infotainment" fell from grace as a critical term and instead came to describe the new quotidian genre of soft news. There is no reason why "militainment" will not be naturalized in the same way. Certainly we will need a word to describe the entertainment frenzy that swarms around the war-of-the-week. The term's life is destined to be volatile and its acceptance will likely require philosophical shifts. If or when "militainment" becomes just another generic marker, whatever critical prophesy the word contained will have been fulfilled.

While "militainment" may be a neologism used to describe some fairly recent developments, the contradictory spirit of the word has deep roots in the twentieth century. In the epilogue to his famous essay, "The Work of Art in the Age of Mechanical Reproduction," Walter Benjamin wrote that the very being of German fascism depended upon "the introduction of aesthetics into political life."[15] The one predictable result of this process, he concluded, is the exaltation of war. Benjamin directed this critique not only to the emerging cult of the *Führer* but also to Filippo Tommaso Marinetti and his 1909 Manifesto of Futurism. The Italian Futurist art movement unreservedly celebrated the triumph of industrialism, speed, and the obliteration of time and space as the highest achievements of humankind. To the Futurists, there was nothing so marvelous as the union of man and machine, especially in the pure act of war. The Manifesto's ninth plank reads, for example, "We will glorify war—the world's only hygiene—militarism, patriotism, the destructive gesture of freedom-bringers, beautiful ideas worth dying for, and scorn for woman."[16] The Futurists, Benjamin argued, were perhaps the real progenitors of fascism. Hitler and Mussolini were only figureheads, cut with Marinetti's severe prose in a style that held up the romance of techno-war as the highest aesthetic.

With some assurance, we can say that Benjamin more than Marinetti resonates with contemporary sensibilities. This is likely due to the fact that Benjamin had the benefit of seeing the devastation of WWI in hindsight and German fascism at close range, events that surely turned many a budding Futurist toward Dada. The echoes of this contest, however, continue to reverberate into the twenty-first century. Benjamin and the Futurists come to blows particularly around the politics of the camera. On one hand, we accept the conventional wisdom that war is, to coin a phrase, the "consummate unconsumable." That is, it takes some work to render war an aesthetic object. As Air Force doctor William Burner famously said in the aftermath of the 1989 US invasion of Panama, "Two things people should not watch are the making of sausage and the making of war."[17] If there is one human event or activity that, in itself, defies easy digestion, it is war, with its wailing mothers, fetid hospitals, devastated neighborhoods, walking wounded, hasty graves, and lifetimes of quiet pain. Benjamin captured this sensibility best when he wrote that the aestheticization of war depends on a self-alienation so extreme that we approach the possibility of suicide or the annihilation of the species, that is, the possibility of experiencing "our own destruction as an aesthetic pleasure of the first order."[18]

On the other hand, war paradoxically appears as the consummate object of the eye. The history of photography is very much a history of the war photographer—from Matthew Brady to Robert Capa to Yahoo News's "Kevin Sites in the Hot Zone," a webcast of a wizened former embedded reporter who in 2005 purported to tote his camera to "every armed conflict in the world within one year."[19] Convention, too, holds that the highest order of television journalism is the war correspondent, that most celebrated of news reporters. This compulsion hearkens back to the invention of the moving picture itself. The precursor to the Lumières' moving picture camera was Etienne-Jules Mary's chronophotographic rifle, which both resembled and was inspired by the machine gun.[20] The same year the Lumière brothers began exhibiting the first short films in Paris, Thomas Edison showcased his *Barroom Scene* (1894), arguably the first fight on film. The first war film, *Tearing Down the Spanish Flag* (1898), fanned the flames of the nascent Spanish-American war already stoked by William Randolph Hearst. The war film genre gained momentum through WWI which not only pressed war film fully into the service of war but also debuted newsreel footage from the front lines.[21] Susan Sontag notes in *Regarding the Pain of Others* that "Ever since cameras were invented in 1839, photography has kept company with death."[22] Photography, she notes elsewhere, carries with it an essential prejudice toward fostering "emotional detachment," creating a world "in which every subject is deprecated into an article of consumption, promoted into an item of aesthetic appreciation."[23] Thus, when the camera encounters the battlefield, another battle rages in the background between the twin photographic purposes of beautification and truth-telling.[24] The history of war photography is a history of image-combat between war's aestheticization and an entire canon of Antietams, Dresdens, and My Lais. This dialectic is not simply limited to the still camera or even the documentary idiom. Writing in *Harper's Magazine* in 2005, Lawrence Weschler extends this theme to wonder if there can be such a thing as an anti-war film "or whether any depiction of war in film necessarily lends itself to military-pornographic exploitation."[25] Weschler paraphrases the director Samuel Fuller's remark that for a film to show the true nature of war, "bullets would have to be spraying out from the screen, taking out members of the audience at random, one by one, in scattershot carnage."[26] Otherwise, it is just another evening out.

This basic contradiction of war's beautification has intensified as war "comes home." A shrinking world continues to erase the lines between home front and battlefield. The camera's saturation of the social field has drawn together the actual scene with its representation both spatially and temporally. A major theme of contemporary life is the need to navigate the shrinking zone between the consumable image and the event itself, a volatile combination in the case of violent conflict. Perhaps the September 11, 2001 attacks on the World Trade Center illustrate this state of affairs best. Americans experienced a contest between the magnitude of the falling towers and the magnitude of the image in its multiple filmings, its instantaneous dissemination, and its infinite repetition on television. The trauma cut both ways. For those on site, a common appraisal was that it was "just like a movie"; those at home, on the other hand, felt compelled to visit ground zero to prove to themselves that it was not.[27] Slavoj Žižek, in his typical style of chiasmus, notes that while 9/11 is normally said to have shattered our naïve illusions, "It is not that reality entered our image: the image entered and shattered our reality."[28] Jean Baudrillard draws attention to the numerous disaster films that predicted the cinematic quality of 9/11, suggesting that, as a culture, the West participated in the attack by repeatedly dreaming it into existence far in advance: "It is they who did it, but we who wanted it."[29] Though utterly repulsive, what gives this statement its power is that it cannot simply be rejected.

The September 11 attacks thus cast into sharp relief the American public's schizophrenia regarding war's consumption. Even while Vice President Dick Cheney and Bush advisor Karl Rove met with Hollywood heavyweights to explore how the industry could be mobilized for the ensuing "war on terror," the conventional wisdom in Hollywood held that all references to terrorism or the Twin Towers, war films, and perhaps all images of realistic violence, ought to be tabled for an indefinite grieving period.[30] Because an entire army of war films had gone into production after the success of Stephen Spielberg's *Saving Private Ryan* (1998), this meant a sizeable bite of the industry.[31] The Schwarzenegger-takes-on-the-terrorists film *Collateral Damage* (2002), due in October 2001, was put on hold as was John Woo's WWII action-drama *Windtalkers* (2002), originally due in November of 2001. At the time of the attacks, a number of films were in production that uncannily anticipated 9/11, adding gravity to Baudrillard's suggestion that is "we who wanted it." These included Jackie Chan's *Nosebleed* (about a plot to blow up the Trade Towers), James Cameron's *Deadline* (terrorists hijacking a plane), and *WW3.com* (featuring a plane skidding through Central Park on the way to a Simon and Garfunkel concert). After 9/11, of course, these three were never to be seen again.

This initial hesitancy did not last long, however. Studios quickly learned that the US invasion of Afghanistan and the patriotic backlash following September 11 primed audiences for the heroic depiction of state violence on film. Several war films set for 2002 were even pushed forward to satisfy this craving. *Black Hawk Down*, based on the 1993 debacle in Somalia, moved from March 2002 to early January. *Charlotte Gray*, a film about an Englishwoman working with the

WWII French Resistance, moved from 2002 to late December 2001. The bloody Mel Gibson Vietnam saga, *We Were Soldiers*, moved from late 2002 to March. Of this spate of films, *Behind Enemy Lines* was the first to take advantage of the new wave of war film fever. The film's original release date was January 2002, but after wildly successful test screenings, the studio bumped the film to November 2001. The president of domestic distribution at Twentieth Century Fox remarked, "I think 'September 11' may have influenced the scores and made people love the film a little more." This was an understatement. The film received some of the highest focus group scores in the studio's history, with audiences reportedly standing to cheer and applaud at the end.[32] The line between entertainment and war is thus a highly charged political space which has come to function as a barometer for public attitudes about war.

Arguably, entertainment has been part and parcel of military propaganda from the invention of mass media forward. In this most literal sense, "militainment" is nothing new. It is useful, however, to distinguish between discourses of militainment and what has been classically understood as propaganda. In the world wars, for example, the primary locus of social control was the message itself—an argument, a set of narratives, depictions of the enemy, practical ways to help, and so on. The Committee for Public Information (CPI), created by the Wilson administration to initiate and manage US involvement in WWI, worked to affect public opinion through journalism, feature films, and other more direct message systems. The committee included such public relations pioneers as George Creel, Walter Lippmann, and Edward Bernays, all of whom considered industrial society to be so complex that public opinion could no longer be left to the people but rather needed to be manufactured by paternalistic elites.[33] World War II yielded the much more pervasive but arguably less manipulative US Office of War Information (OWI), established in 1942. The OWI designated Hollywood an "official wartime industry."[34] After the war, the newly christened defense establishment permanently set up the new Pentagon Hollywood Liaison Office for doing business with the major film studios.[35] One of the OWI's leading planners, Archibald MacLeish, also recognized the centrality of public opinion, famously noting that "The principal battleground of this war is not the South Pacific. It is not the Middle East. It is not England, or Norway, or the Russian Steppes. It is American opinion."[36] While these institutions came to view the civil sphere as an adjunct to the military apparatus—one battlefield among many to be managed through public relations, propaganda, psychological operations, and information warfare—they did so mainly through direct appeals to public opinion. This approach is captured in the title of the *Why We Fight* series of propaganda films directed by Frank Capra and others with assistance from the Disney Corporation, films originally screened for troops but later released to the general public. This approach can also be heard in Jack Benny's radio plea to buy war bonds: "When we buy those bonds, remember we're not doing the *government* a favor. *We're* the government! This is *my* war, and *your* war! So let's get rolling . . . hard and fast."[37] The kind of military-entertainment collusion here was one aspect of the classic propaganda approach, which was to use the entertainment industries as arteries through which persuasive messages could be channeled.

Prominent critics of propaganda at the time also conceived it primarily as a persuasive (and sometimes coercive) process. Perhaps the most eloquent observer of wartime propaganda was the American sociologist Harold Lasswell. Writing in 1941 in reaction to the likes of Lippmann and Bernays (both of whom were his close contemporaries), Lasswell outlined what he saw as a tendency of modern society he called the "garrison state," a politics where every aspect of civic life becomes a function of the military. Rather than promoting the participatory integration of the citizen into matters of state and defense, the garrison state relies on the exclusion and management of the citizen. Alongside a highly regulated workforce and the diversion of money to the military machine, in the garrison state rulers seek to curtail liberal democratic elements through the elimination of participatory rights, the manipulation of public opinion, and perhaps, in a brave new world, the administering of drugs ("to deaden the critical function of all who are not held in esteem by the ruling elite").[38] As Lasswell and others theorized it, the garrison state deploys a set of techniques for managing public opinion as an extension of the war machine.[39]

Similar critiques persisted into the postwar era after the establishment of the standing army. In 1956, sociologist C. Wright Mills wrote that alongside the "permanent war economy" had come a sophisticated apparatus to influence popular opinion. The fallout from these trends, he contended, was an anti-democratic transformation of the "public" into "the masses." Mills suggested that while discussion animates publics, one-way messaging of mass media characterizes the masses, a sphere where "far fewer people express opinions than receive them."[40] The task of the propagandist, publicity expert, or public relations strategist, is to manage mass opinion.[41] In 1961, President Eisenhower delivered this warning in his farewell address, famously coining the term "military-industrial complex" to describe a shift in the political landscape.[42] This term described an influential new bloc that, alongside economic power, could wield propagandistic power, what Eisenhower called "spiritual" influence.[43]

This same period, however, produced other critics who began to rethink the means by which power exerts influence over public opinion. Rather than carpet bombing public space with pointed appeals, these theorists described the restructuring of civic space and civic identity. In his lifelong attempt to grapple with the militarism that gripped Nazi Germany, Frankfurt School critic Jürgen Habermas described a process where active public citizens had been gradually transformed into individuated "receptors" of consumer culture, mainly through the commercial colonization of leisure time. While still acknowledging the powerful role of public relations and advertising, Habermas saw this manipulation of "public opinion" as an effect of the privatizing of public life. Where there once had been public deliberation, now there was a sensationalist press and the privatization of politics as personal "taste."[44] Hannah Arendt similarly lamented the loss of the public citizen, suggesting that the public memorializations to the "Unknown Soldier" bear testimony to this loss and the "need for glorification, for finding a 'whom,' an identifiable somebody whom years of mass slaughter should have revealed."[45] For Arendt, such sites memorialized the citizen who went missing in action, functioning as a shadow memory of an agential public erected to cope with the realization that "the agent of the war was nobody."[46] Walter Benjamin's observation of the close relationship between war and the aestheticization of politics seemed to suggest something similar—that the social control lay not in saturating the public sphere with the right messages in the hope of fostering the right opinion, but rather extracting the citizen from a deliberative role in the first place.

This subtle shift in perspective coincided with a number of legal and institutional changes that detached the citizen from the military sphere in the late twentieth century. Apart from the establishment of a new permanent military made of professionals, WWII was also the last time Congress would officially declare war, what amounted to a *de facto* abdication of this constitutional prerogative to the executive branch.[47] In 1973, President Nixon abolished the draft and introduced the all-volunteer force, removing a linchpin that connected the citizen to the military apparatus. These trends toward professionalizing the military continued with the Persian Gulf War of 1991, where the US military began to replace regular forces with armies of internationalized private military contractors (PMCs). Following the 2003 invasion of Iraq, the military's use of mercenary forces exploded.[48] In 2007, the number of mercenaries in Iraq and Afghanistan matched the number of enlisted public soldiers one to one.[49] On this point Michael Hardt and Antonio Negri note: "There is no way to conceive of the US military at this point as 'the people in arms.' It seems rather that in postmodern warfare, as in ancient Roman times, *mercenary armies* tend to become the primary combat forces" (emphasis original).[50]

These changes gradually dismantled the central political character that had animated American civic ideals since the revolutionary war: the citizen-soldier. From its Renaissance origins, the citizen-soldier represented a departure from the aristocratic practice of using mercenary forces and toward the investment of citizen identity in the military apparatus.[51] With this investment came political power and a voice in a republic composed "of and for the people," that usually goes by the name of "civic republicanism."[52] The citizen-soldier ideal is behind the notion that legitimate citizenship—full participation in politics as an individual or group—depends on a history of military service.[53] The institutional separation of the citizen from soldier thus signaled a general divestment of the citizen from a deliberative role in the state and especially decisions regarding the use of the military.[54]

Indeed, separating the citizen from soldier has been a very successful strategy in releasing the executive branch from democratic accountability in matters of war. Nixon's decision to abolish the draft, for example, functioned to safeguard future wars from mass public protest. By the time of Desert Storm in 1991, the citizen had been radically disconnected from a deliberative role. As Elaine Scarry observed of Desert Storm, the citizen had no role in authorizing (through congressional declaration of war), funding (as the standing army was already in place), or fighting (as the draft had been abolished).[55] In committing troops to this conflict, President George H.W. Bush assured the public and policy makers that it would not be another Vietnam. Among other reasons, he noted that "the motivation of our all-volunteer force is superb."[56] More recent efforts to revive the citizen-soldier have predictably been viewed by those in power not as patriotic gestures but rather as threats to the unbridled use of the military. In January 2003, for example, three Democratic representatives introduced a bill that would have required universal military service.[57] They argued that universal service promotes not only a more equitable racial and economic arrangement, but also a more enlightened public dialogue that acknowledges the gravity of the decision to make war.[58] Congress soundly defeated the measure by a 402–2 vote in late 2004. Above the grumblings of his generals who were short on personnel, President Bush repeatedly reassured a docile population that the draft would not return on his watch, let alone universal service. Even those who had sponsored the bill voted against it, playing the bill down as a purely symbolic anti-war statement.[59] The public predictably showed resistance to the bill given its introduction during an unpopular war. For powerful interests in Washington, however, the real objection to universal service was precisely that it threatened to activate the deliberative citizen. Such a law would have reversed the long process of uncoupling the military from public accountability. In all likelihood, universal service would catalyze dissent just as the draft had done during Vietnam. The bill was therefore "anti-war" insofar as it reintroduced the notion that the citizen should have deliberative involvement in matters of state violence.

The same trends carried over into the more immaterial realms of media and discursive practices. Complaining that the television war brought civilians too close to the battlefield, the Pentagon initiated a decade of experimentation that eventually engineered a symbiosis between news providers and the executive branch of government. By the Persian Gulf War in 1991, the Pentagon has successfully positioned journalism as a real-time extension of military public relations. Journalistic institutions, realizing that war sells, drew closer to these public relations organs, demonstrating that an interest in "access" to the Pentagon's war could not readily be distinguished from a willingness to be programmed. Settling into the commercial context, the television war event took on the complexion of entertainment media, establishing its own flow and main attractions. The presentation of war took the form of mass spectacle—from sports to cinema—while at the same time reframing the citizenry as an audience of war consumers. This absorption required that the programming assume certain features harmonious with the traffic of toothpaste and car commercials. Dominant among these was the development of war coverage fastidiously scrubbed of images of death, references to death, and the language of death. In its place, the new television war substituted an obsession with the power and pleasures of high-tech war machinery. Combined with an increased political alienation from war, these factors delivered the highest gratification-to-guilt ratio possible. Such a scene implied the ideal witness, the *citizen-spectator*, who was now invited to consume war, perhaps with a tub of popcorn.

The Persian Gulf War thus renovated conflict from a negative to a positive political phenomenon—from an event that *must be sold* (legitimated via propaganda) to an event that *could be sold* (integrated into the economy of commercial entertainment, leisure time, and pleasure). Such alliances between war and entertainment had been attempted to some degree during the World Wars.[60] The level of real-time, daily integration of entertainment and conflict during the Persian Gulf War, however, was unprecedented, leading to a wealth of commentary on the subject. The 2003 invasion of Iraq added further momentum to these trends, integrating the mediated war into a ubiquitous aspect of consumer capitalism. Journalistic depictions of war took on the conceits of spectator sports coverage, reality television, video games, and other entertainment genres. Pentagon and State Department public relations strung together public relations spectacles into larger "war movie" plot chains, expansions on the multi-generic "war miniseries," as Robert Stam called the television blitz of Operation Desert Storm in 1991.[61] These public relations events were often spun further into based-on-a-true-story, made-for-TV films produced with cooperation between the Pentagon and entertainment studios. Such spectacles reverberated into wider circles of consumerist activity from toys to collector's sets.

Much of the attention that has been paid to the term "militainment" has been to track the *level* of cooperation between the Pentagon and the entertainment industries. In 2003, Jonathan Burston noted that "one does not have to be a rocket scientist to have noticed a growing compatibility between the military and the entertainment industry over the last decade or so."[62] Tonja Thomas and

Fabian Virchow recognize a similar economy of "banal militarism" where official military entertainment organizations like the USO have bled into civilian culture.[63] Nick Turse's popular 2008 study describes entertainment as just one aspect of "the complex" whose tendrils have wandered far beyond anything that Eisenhower could have imagined, colonizing nearly every sphere of social and material production.[64] These approaches generally view militainment as an issue of quantity, existing on an axis of presence and absence, as in the conventional meaning of the word "militarism." Mark Andrejevic, for example, suggests that these new connections signal a revival of classic propaganda, arguing that the Bush administration used stateside propaganda to sell the war just as it used top advertising talent to market the US foreign policy "brand" to the Muslim world after 9/11.[65] From this perspective, the entertainment industries become the vehicles through which power reinforces dominant justifications for war.

The political economy of this "militainment machine," as Burston calls it, is an important part of the puzzle. On one level, we can acknowledge that the saturation and control of public life by such interests leads to "militarism." Scholars generally argue this happens in one of two ways. The first is that militainment simply gives the government an additional platform (among many) from which to conduct classical propaganda, thereby keeping the population in tune with official justifications for war. The second comes from an analysis of political economy. Rather than identifying straight-out propaganda, this approach applies to entertainment media the "propaganda function" that Noam Chomsky and Edward Herman apply to the news: entertainment media have become subject to an invisible hand, a network of corporate and governmental interests that nudges cultural narratives toward the profitably bellicose. The effect on entertainment is something akin to the "spiritual influence" that Eisenhower claimed the military-industrial complex has on the legislature.

This book approaches the subject through a third lens by asking how the consumer war works to construct the citizen's identity in relationship to war. In so doing, this book primarily seeks to describe two related aspects of the evolving phenomenon of militainment. The first might be described as the "wiring" of the citizen's relationship to war, the material arrangement of technologies and institutions that make war a phenomenon available for consumption. These interfaces normalize certain practices, habits, and dispositions toward war. Closely related is the second aspect, the symbolic construction of military activity. This includes the dominant generic alignments, narratives, images, and language choices that not only paint a picture of state violence but also work to articulate the citizen subject within it. Together these two aspects work in what Gilles Deleuze and Félix Guattari call an "assemblage" of content and expression, an integrated machine of hardware and software interfacing the subject with the military apparatus in particular ways.[66] It is through this variety of channels, practices, and discourses that citizen identity and military power continue to co-evolve.

At heart, this book challenges the notion of the "spectacle" and its place as a dominant means of accounting for the control function of media in wartime. This conventional account considers the ways that media discourses work to exclude, distract, and ultimately *deactivate* the political subject. The critique of the spectacle has stood as one way of describing the "propaganda value" of contemporary military-media couplings—how they control populations, marginalize dissent, and suppress the citizen's deliberative function. This book does not argue that the critique of the spectacle has become irrelevant, however. The spectacle remains a powerful critical tool for understanding a still prevalent mode of mediated politics that invites the citizen into a position of voyeuristic complacency. Rather than disparage a highly productive strand of critique, this book tracks the entry of a new discourse of the consumer war in the new century, what can be described as a turn toward the interactive. The interactive mode presents myriad ways for the citizen to plug in to the military publicity machine, not only through new media technologies but also through rhetorics that portray war as a "battlefield playground." Here the citizen has been increasingly invited to step through the screen and become a virtual player in the action. This book contends that rather than acting to exclude and deactivate, these trends signal a transition toward the absorption of citizen identity into the military-entertainment matrix. This is a curious development indeed considering that the relationship between citizen and soldier has historically been one of increasing separation and exclusion. To make sense of this seeming reversal, this book begins by charting the migration of civic identity from the spectacle to the brave new world of the interactive war. Chapter 1, "All-Consuming War," not only examines how the citizen has been brought into close proximity to the battlefield through electronic media, but also what this apparent reconnection of citizen and soldier means. The chapter gives an historical and theoretical account of this transition with an eye on how the prominent discourses of "citizen-spectator" translate into the emerging subject of the "virtual citizen-soldier."

In exploring this transition, this book confines itself, with some exceptions, to the decade or so between the 1991 Persian Gulf War through the aftermath of the 2003 US invasion of Iraq. The analysis draws its four main case studies from this period. Chapter 2, "Sports and the Militarized Body Politic," examines sport as a perennial metaphor in discourses of war. Having such a close historical relationship to war, the quality of sports discourse plays a significant role in texturing the quality of citizen's relationship to war, especially at the points where sport and war metaphors comingle explicitly. The television coverage of both Desert Storm in 1991 and Iraqi Freedom in 2003 illustrates the prominent place of sports metaphors, events, pre-game shows, countdown clocks, and other transplanted signs of spectator sports in the coverage. During this period, "extreme sports" began to displace traditional spectator sports as a primary means of mapping the meaning of war. This chapter thus seeks to describe the features of the extreme sports metaphor and its relationship to changes in the global political scene. Extreme sports provide an entirely new set of pleasures, competitive relationships, and identifications that have come to inform and mediate the citizen's relationship to global conflict. In particular, extreme sports meld pleasure and death into a new amalgam that begins to function as a primary consumable feature of the new war discourse. Moreover, extreme sports' visual aesthetic reorders the viewer into a first-person relationship with the endangered body, providing a means of virtually projecting oneself into that body. This chapter examines venues such as film and military recruiting where the codes of extreme sports have been mapped onto a discourse of war.

The embedded reporting system deployed during the 2003 Iraq invasion relied on the pleasures of the extreme sports idiom for much of its effect. The system made for incredibly compelling television precisely because it provided a venue for the viewer to safely fantasize about entering the battlefield through a fellow "ordinary" civilian journalist. Embedded reporting, as many commentators noted, resembled a reality TV extreme sports challenge of a sort. This was not simply a metaphor. Chapter 3, "Reality War," describes the progressive integration of established reality television genres and the military, beginning in the late 1990s. During this period, reality television became a preferred venue through which the Pentagon constructed the public face of the military. The embedded reporting system grew directly from these efforts, itself inspired by an actual reality television show. This new kind of journalism marked a new dynamic between civic and military spheres. As a surrogate citizen, the embedded reporter stood as a powerful symbol for the assimilation of the citizen by the military apparatus. In addition, this new journalist—rather than the soldier or the enemy—became the primary focal point of war coverage, a celebrity character who mediated the pleasures of citizen playing soldier.

This interactive urge naturally penetrated the fourth wall of the television screen. When commentators from across the spectrum noted that the Persian Gulf War in 1991 "looked like a video game," they may not have suspected that it would soon "play like a video game." The interactive war has thus been facilitated by the increased presence of interactive technologies. Chapter 4, "War Games," investigates video games as both a medium and metaphor for the new politics of integrative war play. Games have "crossed over" between military and civic spheres in significant ways, creating perhaps the most integrated "complex" of them all. The military has become quite adept not only at modifying a number of commercial games for their use as training simulators but also releasing official training simulators on the commercial market. Commercial war-themed games have evolved increasingly in concert with the television war, extending its pleasures through a truly interactive medium. Thematically, games have shown a trend toward integrating the "realities" of war as seen on TV. Temporally too, the lag time between an event on television and its appearance in a game has progressively shortened. While television coverage of war has reciprocated by adopting a certain gaming aesthetic, some games have strived toward reproducing the television war as a real-time, playable event. Finally, this chapter examines the role of an Army-produced recruiting video game, *America's Army*, that has added a level of significance and authenticity to the broadening cultural practice of "playing the war." Taken together, training, war coverage, and recruiting have produced the video game as a primary interface governing the civic experience of war.

The practice of merchandising war with real-time themes has only accelerated since the 1991 Gulf War. Like video games, war toys crossed into the official discourse of war, even feeding back into military operations by showing up in insurgent propaganda. The US Army issued its own line of action figures as well. Here the gap between the television war and the ability to play it collapsed into a new, real-time, interactive war toy market. These were not simply generic toy soldiers and board games but rather explicit attempts to reproduce the "realism" of the television war. Chapter 5, "Toying with Militainment," examines the conflation of politics and consumption that infused American culture immediately following 9/11. Perhaps due to their perceived frivolity, war toys have historically existed at the front lines of public criticism. The proliferation of television war-themed toys in the Iraq War period provoked a visible cultural reaction to the blending of war and play. This discourse provides a useful starting point for thinking about the various resistant practices for engaging, critiquing, and even playing with the military-entertainment complex. Indeed, the very nature of the interactive war provides new tools for responding to militainment culture. Rather than resisting from the outside, these strategies take advantage of the new milieu by working from within the medium and sign system. For example, one of the main selling points of interactive war culture is "realism," or the ability to accurately reproduce the battlefield. For the sake of conscience-free playing, certain realities of war are not part of this realism. Simply introducing unconsumable realities of war into the scene has thus become a major weapon of critique. Other resistant techniques work by hyperbolizing the interactive war, accelerating its logics to the point of absurdity. Still others play with militainment through a strategy of reversal, turning the tables and denaturalizing the dominant position that allows one to play the war. This strategy forces the culture to confront the question of why it is harmless fun to play war with one set of characters, but barbaric to reverse these positions.

Militainment, Inc. concludes with Chapter 6, "Debriefing: Previews to Postviews," stepping back to gain perspective on the period that might be called the "militainment bubble" that appeared in the early years of the Iraq War. This chapter marks transitions in the consumable war, tracks its enduring aspects, and speculates on what the future may hold. From theoretical inquiries and case studies through this final reflection, *Militainment, Inc.* continues a conversation. In many ways, this conversation is as old as conflict itself, as it deals with a seemingly perennial set of forces. These forces have developed, however, to encompass the home front, the mass media, and the economy of the interactive. This book hopes to engage the voices along the way that have attempted to understand these migrations so that we may better understand the process by which war "becomes us." Ultimately, this book asks how we can engage in a productive critique of militainment in order to foster a civic culture with a solemn responsibility toward the armed services, the use of state violence, and those who have had their lives shattered by conflict. This requires that we become a certain kind of warrior rather than risk the disarmed life of "the conquered," in the poet Allen Ginsburg's words, "drafted into shadow armies, navy'd on shadow oceans, flying in shadow fire."[67]

Chapter 1

All-Consuming War

From Spectacle to Interactivity

When the term "militainment" arrived in 2003, it was really only a late-coming symptom of trends already in motion. The 1991 Persian Gulf War made it abundantly clear that war has entered into the system of consumption. In the years following Operation Desert Storm, critics widely understood these processes to function as a mode of social control, as a way to dampen deliberation and dissent so that the polity better fell in line behind official pronouncements. Among these commentators, traditional propaganda no longer held its place as a dominant explanation for how this control worked. Scholars began to understand war discourse not in terms of attempts to change the citizen's beliefs (either consciously or unconsciously) but rather in terms of the "spectacle," a critical term meant to describe a political and media environment characterized by alienation and distraction. This perspective holds that a "spectacular war" does not work through appeals, explanations, and justifications to a citizen acknowledged to be in a decision-making position. Rather, the spectacle is a certain kind of discourse that dazzles the citizen subject into a submissive, politically disconnected, complacent, and deactivated audience member. The most insightful commentary on the period uses the critical language of the spectacle explicitly, though many others hold some implicit version of the spectacle at the center of their critique.

In contrast to Desert Storm in 1991, the 2003 invasion of Iraq represented a dramatic surge in cooperation between the military and culture industries. The major innovation, however, was not necessarily in the level of cooperation but rather in the introduction of discourses that repositioned the citizen subject in reference to war. In particular, a new interactivity began to challenge the spectacle as the primary quality of the home front experience. To be sure, the spectacle still held a prominent role in the rituals and rhetorics of the mediated war. The post-9/11 environment, however, began to offer a variety of channels and discourses by which the citizen could step through the screen and virtually participate in the action. This shift was consistent with trends in the late twentieth century marked by a transition from so-called "lean-back" to "lean-forward" media technologies. During this period, the viewer has taken an increasingly active role in viewership, pushing buttons, surfing, and generally crafting the scene. Interactivity gave birth to the avatar, a facsimile of the self projected through the screen, pointing toward the future moment of perfect projection, a controlled lucid dream that immerses the entire sensorium. The mediation of war has traversed such a path, from a third-person to a first-person consuming position. In contrast to the deactivated citizen-spectator, the interactive war presents war as something to be played by a new character, what may be called the "virtual citizen-soldier." Though challenging the spectacle in many ways, the interactive war also represents a distillation and intensification of its modes of control. After gaining a foothold in the spectacle, this chapter asks what it means to make the leap into the interactive pleasures of the first-person, virtual battlefield.

Citizen-Spectator

On March 1, 1991, the day after the US declared victory and a ceasefire in the Persian Gulf War, President George H.W. Bush held a press conference. As a reporter on the scene noted, the president stood at the podium "exulting not so much in the battle triumph but in the public opinion back home."[1] President Bush explained the nature of this victory. "No question about it, the country's solid," the president said. "There isn't any anti-war movement out there. There is pride in these forces."[2] Earlier in the day in a separate meeting with state legislators, Bush celebrated in language geared more toward the political elite. "It's a proud day for America," he said prefacing the primary reason for this pride. "By God, we've kicked the Vietnam syndrome once and for all."[3] The "Vietnam syndrome" had been a code word for what some in the administration saw as the public relations failure of the Vietnam Conflict, which, as the metaphor implies, culminated in a particular disease of the body politic. This "disease" was a resistance to authorizing war, represented by a lack of trust in federal government during this period, which plummeted from 75 percent to 25 percent between 1964 and 1980.[4] With the Vietnam Syndrome "kicked," a certain velvet revolution had evidently transpired. Bush's pronouncement signaled not only the reversal of decades of aversion to war, but also that the locus of battle had migrated from the battlefield to home front. The ingredients necessary for victory (or, in the updated language, for the US military to "prevail") increasingly meant building a sophisticated public relations apparatus, fostering a more compliant press, and placating a nervous and reticent population.

Indeed, the civic relationship to the military changed dramatically between the Vietnam War and Operation Desert Storm. During this period, political, economic, and cultural forces reconditioned the civic experience of war into one governed by the logic of the spectacle. This meant first the construction of a citizen progressively purged of political connection to the military, and second, a civic experience of war thoroughly choreographed for privatized consumption. The citizen had been legally distanced from the military both by the legislature's relinquishing the power to declare war and the abolition of the draft. The Persian Gulf War, however, unfolded on a changing media landscape to further sculpt the citizen-spectator into being. The changes included economic and institutional shifts toward the integration of Pentagon, journalism, and the culture industries.

Structurally, the spectacular war developed out of changing alliances between the Pentagon and the media, both in terms of journalism and entertainment. In large part, this meant the integration of war with commercial television. This process arguably began during Vietnam with what *New Yorker* critic Michael J. Arlen famously called the "living-room war." This term did not merely identify the presence of a new medium. Arlen pointed out that the appearance of war had fundamentally shifted. The television had smoothed and contained war's brutality, introducing almost imperceptibly into everyday life as something to be habitually consumed at six o'clock along with supper. In the guise of bringing the home front closer to the conflict, Arlen argued, television news paradoxically alienated the citizen from war, rendering the repetitious and chaotic banality of nightly footage a normal part of domestic existence.[5]

Tamed as the "living-room war" might sound, many in positions of power decided it needed further discipline. Policy planners placed much of the blame for the US failure to "pacify" Vietnam on its ad hoc system of roving, unsupervised reporters. Alongside the press, the novelty and ubiquity of the television medium, especially its emotional image power, became a primary scapegoat. By its very nature, went the conventional wisdom, the medium had helped to lose the "war at home," playing a fundamental role in nurturing public dissatisfaction and the subsequent Vietnam syndrome.[6] Between Vietnam and the Persian Gulf War, the executive branch thus experimented with how best to manage the medium. The immediate reaction was to order a total press blackout as in the Reagan administration's approach to the interventions in Lebanon and Grenada in the early 1980s. Predictably, the blackout strategy meshed neither with the business demands of news outlets nor the citizens' perceived right to know. In response, the US government experimented with ways to tune television's potential as a centralized gatekeeper, beginning with a very limited press pooling system during the 1989 Panama invasion. This structure was by no means an improvement on press freedom. Rather, Panama represented an attempt to open up a controlled channel between the home front and the battlefield while satisfying public demand for war news. The officially sanctioned news that did happen to trickle through this bottleneck did not entirely satisfy either. The public greeted this military–press setup with a mixture of anxiety, suspicion, and a sense of privation rather like the home front reaction to the 1982 British invasion of the Falkland Islands. Here, the setup featured a similarly restricted pool of officially selected reporters who stood close to military advisers but far from the action. The executive had yet to discover the potential of television to serve as an arsenal of image power, viewing the press as something that must be negatively suppressed rather than positively channeled. These experiments by the Pentagon taught that the solution to the "Vietnam syndrome" could be found neither in total press freedom nor total press exclusion, but rather in large-scale press integration into a system of Pentagon public relations.

The eventual ability to align the media as an extension of military public relations was made possible through changes in the economic landscape already in motion in the 1980s. Regan-era deregulation initiated the steep consolidation of corporate media holdings from approximately fifty major news media outlets in 1983 to what would eventually be a bare five only twenty years later.[7] The field of competing perspectives dwindled and homogenized during this period. As larger corporations absorbed more independent news outlets, televised discourse became beholden to ever vaster corporate entities, large "media-industrial complexes" in their own right. This new concentrated model tended to cleave more to business prerogatives and less to the ideals of journalistic practice. This more corporatized news tended to jettison expensive journalism (such as investigative and international news) in favor of segments that delivered a higher ratings bang for the buck (such as opinion, entertainment, and health news).[8] Pre-fabricated official public relations material fell into the category of "cheap news," increasingly passed off as journalism by editors looking to cut costs and increase profits.[9] Growing accustomed to a diet of drip-fed public relations material due to merge-and-purge economics, corporate media was well prepared to pair up with the Pentagon in 1991.

The military institutionalized the press pooling model on a grand scale during the 1991 Persian Gulf War, hand-picking some 1,600 reporters for life in a Saudi Arabian desert tent city and a smaller number pooled with individual units. The Iraqi government granted a handful of reporters access to a Baghdad hotel from which CNN issued live broadcasts. These centralized points of access to the war necessitated very little overt censorship on the part of the Pentagon. Indeed, there was little actual newsgathering that could be censored. Moreover, a reporter who deviated from the official story might risk losing access to what had become that reporter's bread and butter, the steady stream of war programming issued from the official public relations apparatus. Both the military and participating news agencies fared quite well under these conditions. For the Pentagon, the relationship ensured a near monopoly of the news cycle in both agenda and language.[10] For journalists, the system provided compelling footage, access to officials, updates, and human interest stories for free and at virtually no human risk. This symbiosis was enormously successful in meeting the needs of corporate news, transforming 24-hour cable news from a failing idea into a resounding commercial success. The war boosted CNN's audience by a factor of ten, living proof that real money could be made in playing ball with the Pentagon.[11] The sacrificial lamb in this new military-media arrangement, of course, was the American public. Along with the diversity of perspectives, so disappeared the very oxygen of democracy.

Conditioned by the press, the posture of the citizen reflected these new relationships. The pooled press assumed the role of stenographer for military public relations, even serving as a conduit for so-called "black propaganda" and misinformation aimed at enemy ranks. For the most part, the citizen represented the final destination of this pre-packaged, one-way message stream. Live reports from journalists in the Al Rashid hotel in Baghdad, as Ernest Larsen puts it, mainly consisted of a "dramatized confession" of the reporter's "entrapment in ignorance." As such, Larsen argues that the coverage had a primary "anesthetizing" effect whereby one "tunes in in order to tune out."[12] While the press pools eagerly awaited daily briefings—often featuring impressive weapons footage, illustrated tales of brinksmanship, and military celebrities like General "Stormin'" Norman Schwarzkopf—the same display summoned the citizen to sit back and marvel as well. In doing so, Desert Storm maximized television's potential as a spectacular medium, one capable of packaging not just a contained war, but a compelling, real-time, main event. Having consolidated itself as ultimate gatekeeper, the Pentagon delivered a war that both satisfied its public relations interests and remained television-friendly. That is, the new symbiosis positioned war as a dramatic screen production increasingly at home amidst the usual menagerie of televised consumables and amusements.

The televised consumption of the spectacular war cannot be separated from larger trends in global US power. The outsourcing of the US manufacturing sector in the late twentieth century was made possible by a sprawling global network of military bases, which functioned to maintain "stability," ensure constant access to resources and trade routes, and to generally protect global economic hegemony.[13] As such, the prime metaphor for war during this period migrated from "defense" (of a geographical nation state) to "security" (of a worldwide network of capital).[14] These changes in overseas power had their domestic counterparts. Economically, the nation migrated from an industrial society to a consumer society, a receptor of low-wage overseas production.[15] Whereas the industrialism had focused on the manufacture of products, the consumer society took upon the more immaterial task of manufacture of consumers. Advertising moved from a secondary role of extolling the virtues of products to a primary role in consumer capitalism as a mechanism for creating so-called "brand identities."[16]

The reception of overseas military operations operated along similar principles. Traditional propaganda, like the relationship between traditional advertising and its product, still maintained a role in legitimating war by addressing its merits. Consumer society, however, increasingly functioned to produce the war consumer—the passive receptor of overseas military operations—in much the same way that it produced the consumer of overseas manufacturing. This process differed from propaganda, which asked its target to make a judgment about a claim. The consumer war only asked that one assume the position of audience member and enjoy the show. The creation of this new subject required presenting a war that implied disengaged spectatorship as a natural response. Operation Desert Storm thus completed the circle, transforming a war "to protect our way of life," as George H.W. Bush described it, into an object of consumption itself, a channel of entertainment tailored to consumer-citizen.[17] Put another way, as the military carried out corporate energy policy overseas, the media mouthpieces of these same business interests served as conduits for conditioning the home front citizen. In this milieu, the term "military-industrial complex" increasingly failed to fully map the terrain of post-industrial war. The turn of the twenty-first century thus ushered in the "military-entertainment complex," the "military-industrial-media-entertainment network," the "military-information-entertainment complex," and others to describe broad changes in the 1980s and 1990s that drew mass media into alliance with military interests.[18] These trends challenged the meaningfulness of the active, legislative citizen, cultivating instead a citizen-spectator fed directly from executive branch public relations. Under these conditions, "war" opened itself up to become a much more malleable and plastic event, occurring as much on the screens of public perception as on the sands of the Persian Gulf. Such structural changes made way for rhetorics that came to typify the spectacular war. In particular, three foundational tropes emerged during this period: clean war, technofetishism, and support-the-troops rhetoric.

Clean War

The first of these tropes, the "clean war," is a manner of presenting war that maximizes viewer alienation from the fact of death in order to maximize the war's capacity to be consumed. Conventional wisdom among policy elites following Vietnam held that unsupervised roving reporters had corrupted the will of the body politic and lost the war. One of the primary causal factors of this Vietnam Syndrome, goes the conventional mythology, was the predominance of uncensored violence on the television. Media scholars have since persuasively exposed the myth of the blood-soaked television as for the most part exaggerated.[19] Regardless, by the time that the 1991 Persian Gulf War arrived, Pentagon planners had succeeded in spit shining what had been during Vietnam a relatively antiseptic screen. The clean war depended first on the disappearance of the dead American soldier, who topped the list of public concern. Conveniently, the near infinite imbalance of force during the first "war" in the Persian Gulf guaranteed that, statistically, three times as many US soldiers would have died in car accidents had they stayed home in civilian life.[20] The few soldiers who died overseas were rendered invisible by a new policy implemented by President George H.W. Bush, who in early 1991 disallowed press at Dover and Andrews Air Force Bases, the entry points for returning caskets.[21] Erasing Iraqi deaths proved to be a much bigger task as official counts reluctantly issued by the Defense Intelligence Agency ranged from 50,000–150,000 dead.[22] Even amidst this hundred-hour war's astronomical Iraqi body count, however, the clean war succeeded in virtually eliminating the visage of death from the television. In one instance, using bulldozer plows mounted on the front of M-1 Abrams Tanks, US forces buried perhaps two thousand Iraqis—many still alive—in seventy miles of their own defensive trenches. Later, massive Armored Combat Earth movers (ACEs) took on the job of smoothing away all the arms and legs protruding from the sand, a task that journalist Patrick Sloyan called a "metaphor for the conduct of modern warfare."[23]

This was a far cry from Vietnam's publicly touted enemy body counts, which were broadcast daily as a measure of success. In 1991, those in charge cited numbers wildly varying from a hundred thousand (an early Pentagon estimate) to "tens of thousands" (as General Norman Schwarzkopf finally conceded in 2000) to 457 (as in Secretary of Defense Dick Cheney's formal report to Congress, which remains the only precise number issued by the government.)[24] Subsequent wars cemented this evasive philosophy. In 2002, Secretary of Defense Donald Rumsfeld insisted that Afghani soldier and civilian deaths were immaterial when he told the press, "I don't do body counts. This country tried that in Vietnam, and it didn't work. And you've not heard me speculate on that at all, and you won't."[25] A few days later, Commanding General Tommy Franks repeated the policy.[26] This new media war, with its imperative to both physically and televisually hide the body, thus conformed more to the idiom of the "perfect crime" than to war. Here, perpetrators had successfully erased all trace of that which anchors war to the moorings of the real.

The clean war also eliminated the body from the language of warfare through the mobilization of euphemism. Operation Desert Storm initiated a lexicon that replaced bombing raids with "sorties," "campaigns," the leveraging of "assets," or the more neighborly "visits" that "deliver ordnance."[27] Munitions did not rip through buildings but rather performed "surgical strikes." Rather than a battleground, they did so as if in a sterile room, a "theater of operation" where violence is regrettably necessary in the service of life. "Collateral damage" depersonalized and legitimated the death of civilians, transforming destruction into a legitimate byproduct of a noble endeavor. Rather than terrorize, militaries "softened up" cities and "sent messages" with "psychological effects."[28] Writing about the literature of World War I, Paul Fussell charts the perennial euphemistic language of war: the dead were "the fallen," to die was "to perish," death was one's "fate," the enemy was the "foe," bravery was "gallant," to conquer was to "vanquish."[29] While carrying through with many of these conventions, the language of the spectacular war substituted the language of individual heroics with the language of bureaucracy. Elaine Scarry notes, for example, that a primary convention of modern warfare is the metaphorical abstraction of the individual soldier body into a larger machine colossus. Communications becomes the "nervous system" to be "shut down," supply lines become "arteries" to be "ruptured," reconnaissance are "eyes" to be "blinded," and the leadership a "head" to be "decapitated." As such, the individual body disappears into a depersonalized war machine.[30] The job of the clean war is also, predictably, a "clean-up job." Rather than "vanquishing the foe," armies "get the job done" by "mopping up resistance." Rather than emerge victorious, the clean war seeks to "secure," "neutralize," and "stabilize." In the language of extermination, insurgents are "smoked out of hiding," henchmen are "hunted," and enemy leaders are plucked from "spider holes." The clean war prosecutes with smooth, sterile, and smart weapons, while the weapons of the enemy are "dirty bombs" designed to spread poison or germs. Rather than destroy, the clean war seeks to "disarm," blessed with the moral authority of hygienic high technology. The disappearance of death represents the primary method of neutralizing the citizen's moral culpability in the decision to unleash state violence. Amidst the glow of the clean war, the citizen-spectator, like the pooled journalist, realizes that the process involves death. Such knowledge becomes immaterial, however, once death itself becomes unreal. This unreality makes possible a degree of "plausible deniability," where mass death both does and does not exist, suggesting that the limited war that had evolved since Vietnam had taken on characteristics of secret war.[31] As such, the spectacular war was something like Slavoj Žižek's notion of "war without war," a manifestation of the immoderate consumer society that joins the list with coffee without caffeine, cream without fat, sex without sex (pornography), and more.[32] This is a war that makes itself *unavailable* for critique: *unthinkable* not for its ghastliness but in its ghostliness.

Technofetishism

The second trope of the spectacular war—"technofetishism"—entails the worship of high-tech weaponary. This trope has much in common with the clean war. As Asu Askoy and Kevin Robins note, the deathless war borrows much of its credibility from the notion that high-tech weapons are inherently more ethical as a means of destruction.[33] The techno-spectacle sometimes works by eroticizing weapons, imbuing them with overt sexual symbolism. Other times, some blunt aesthetic conceit such as sunset backlighting turns the weapon into an object of beauty, a twilight dream equal to the somnambulant spectator. During the first Gulf War, one study found such sunset shots in an astonishing 38 percent of stories from Saudi Arabia, while CNN featured backlighting shots in four out of five of the segments that closed out news reports.[34] Photographers and television crews showed a particular preference for shooting weapons at night when the "rocket's red glare" most resembled a fireworks show or a Christmas tree.

The fetishism of technology goes beyond ascribing weapons an inherent virtue or beauty to positioning military hardware at the center of the television war drama. This rhetoric can be traced back to the massive success of the Pentagon-funded recruitment poster, *Top Gun* (1986). In anticipation of the post-Soviet "New World Order" announced by President Bush in 1990, *Top Gun* refigured public interest in the military from the axis of ideology to the axis of technology.[35] In the 1991 Gulf War, the Pentagon consummated this public love affair with the high-tech military by releasing smart weapons footage during news conferences. The new war dazzled audiences with tales of righteous and true technology (Patriot missiles) squaring off in the skies against wicked and errant technology (Iraqi SCUD missiles). Shortly after the Gulf War, Paul Virilio identified this worshipful reverence as a new religion—"technical fundamentalism"—and added it to the long history of disastrous radicalisms.[36] Technofetishism organizes the world according to the divine right of high-tech "civilization" to conquer and defeat low-tech "barbarism." The civilization/barbarism dichotomy is a time-tested one to be sure.[37] In this manifestation the specific difference is cast not in terms of culture but rather hardware. Weapons not only take center stage but also become the primary symbolic currency through which war negotiates legitimacy, righteousness, and a host of other related values. Such values would normally be the province of deliberation and debate. The repeated inscription of these values onto high-tech weaponry displaces the process of democratic deliberation with the material fact of the weapon in all of its self-justifying glory.

Support the Troops

The third major rhetorical feature of the spectacular war—the call to "support the troops"—resembles technofetishism in that it functions to turn civic attention away from debates about legitimacy and toward the war machine itself. This rhetoric does so through a number of mechanisms. In one sense, this phrase is an entirely virtuous request, extolling mindfulness and gratitude for those volunteer servicemen and women who have been ordered into harm's way. The virtue of the phrase, of course, is part of what allows for its strategic use to suppress dissent, which it does by equating support for official policy with support for the soldiers. In its primary usage, "support the troops" relocates the decision to wage war from the air-conditioned Washington, DC, office to the tent in the desert.[38] As such, the phrase suggests the soldiers deployed themselves, acting also as a populist appeal to combat the notion that the soldier is being used to fight the proverbial "rich man's war."

By the same token, "support the troops" suggests that opposition to the policy shows opposition toward the soldier. This aspect, which implies that the protester has a fundamental antagonism toward the soldier, has a history that extends at least back to Vietnam. Late in that war, the Nixon administration worked hard to contain a new character that had joined the ranks of anti-war demonstrators: the protesting veteran. To minimize the symbolic power of the protesting veteran, the administration engaged in a series of strategies to rhetorically split the character and separate the soldier from the protester. This included mobilizing the stateside military for pro-war "counterdemonstrations" in response to large anti-war rallies, to create the appearance of opposition. In Nixon's parlance, the contest consisted of "campus bums" on one side and "tall and proud soldiers" on the other.[39] Nixon also created front groups like Vietnam Veterans for a Just Peace to debate members of Vietnam Veterans Against the War.[40] Finally, the administration adopted an alternate strategy after the Tet Offensive in 1968, when public support for the war began to rapidly fall. Nixon's rhetoric shifted from external justifications such as "containing communism" to redefining the war as primarily an operation to rescue American prisoners of war.[41] The new war to save our own soldiers increasingly positioned the anti-war protester as an enemy of the troops.

This rhetoric dovetailed with a narrative propagated in the 1980s that suggested Vietnam was lost not on the battlefield but rather on the home front by media, politicians, and protesters. The soldier had been stabbed in the back, or, in Ronald Reagan's words, had been "denied permission to win."[42] Such an orientation somewhat absurdly implied that those who opposed the policy bore more responsibility for endangering the soldier than those who ordered them to war. This rhetoric was given force through a popular myth that gained momentum in the 1980s alleging that protesters routinely spat on returning G.I.s during the Vietnam War. Though there is no documentary evidence that such an event ever occurred—much less that it was public and widespread—a mythology developed that dissent necessarily contained an element of antagonism toward the soldier.[43] The rhetoric of "support the troops" thus acted to confirm the stabbed-in-the-back account of Vietnam while offering an antidote to this supposed tendency to sabotage the soldier. Activated within this context, this rhetoric offered the citizen a choice: either stand with official policy or stand against the soldier. As a number of commentators have noted, the phrase "trapped" the citizen in a framework that coded dissent and deliberation as immoral.[44] This can be illustrated with a common argument often associated with support-the-troops discourse. The argument begins with the premise that the soldier sacrifices to protect civilian freedoms, chief among them freedom of speech and the prerogative to publicly disagree. Thus, goes the logic, it is a terrible irony that the protester would use those very freedoms to ambush the soldier. Of course, one can make a strong argument that it is the citizen's patriotic duty to engage in a robust debate regarding the use of the military, if only to serve as a check on the potential misuse of the soldier. In its dominant use, however, "support the troops" suggests that the citizen has no place in discussing the role of the military and that to do so is instead a direct threat to the besieged men and women on the front lines.

In addition to discrediting dissent, this rhetoric rewires the citizen's relationship to the soldier. From the standpoint of representative democracy, the military is a tool of state authorized by the Congress and ultimately beholden to "the people" who constitute government. The citizen's relationship to the military ideally works through legislative mechanisms that deliberate to arrive at policy regarding how to use the military. "Support the troops" short-circuits this route, substituting a quasi-personal relationship for a deliberative, public, and political responsibility to the soldier. Andrew Bacevich describes this change succinctly, that "support *for*" has replaced "service *with*" as the "new standard of civic responsibility" in wartime.[45] That is, rather than advocating an active role in the politics of war, this rhetoric suits the citizen-spectator with an ethic of depoliticized and distant veneration. Moreover, the use of "support the troops" as the ideal public expression diverts public attention away from the point of policy's creation and toward its point of execution. Rationales and objectives tend to fade into the background of a war stripped of political context. In place of these elements, the immediate battlefield plight of the soldier takes center stage. As such, the support-the-troops response to war is not so different from a response to a similarly apolitical event such as a distant natural disaster. Just as it makes little sense to deliberate the legitimacy of an earthquake, "support the troops" fosters an ethical universe where sympathy for the soldier and deferring to expert authorities are the only options. During the 1991 Persian Gulf War, this rhetoric aligned the citizen with the deactivation of the clean war and technofetishism central to the new television spectacle.

Spectacular War

The notion of the "spectacle" itself originates in Guy Debord's classic 1967 text *Society of the Spectacle*, where Debord describes a social condition infused by images and representations that serve to distract and politically deactivate the masses. The spectacle consists of panoramic illusion, a "pseudoworld" that replaces the actual world and uproots society from its real conditions, ultimately producing an alienation that pervades all levels. This process is not simply a type of "false consciousness" perpetrated by the centers of power. In the society of the spectacle, the image itself comes to occupy the center, a place of endless self-reproduction, where "deceit deceives itself."[46] Here, Debord writes, "The ruling order endlessly discourses upon itself in an uninterrupted monologue of self-praise. The spectacle is a self-portrait of power in the age of power's totalitarian rule over the conditions of existence."[47] The spectacle colonizes leisure time such that real engagement with actual political circumstances fades in its shadow. The book's first chapter, tellingly entitled "Separation Perfected," describes a citizen marked by a divestment, a profoundly anti-democratic mood brought on by the "permanent opium war" of the spectacle.[48] Debord writes: "The spectacle is the bad dream of a modern society in chains and ultimately expresses nothing more than its wish for sleep. The spectacle is the guardian of that sleep."[49] The more soporific this citizen, he suggests, the greater the potential for authoritarianism. "The dominion of the spectacle in its concentrated form means the dominion, too, of the police."[50] Debord's vision thus presents the spectacle as distinct from the conventional notion of "propaganda." Whereas propaganda rationally engages with argument and narrative, the spectacle forgoes persuasion in favor of fostering disengagement. Whereas propaganda addresses an audience that matters, the spectacle presumes an audience that does not. And whereas propaganda seeks to answer the question of *why we fight*, the spectacle loses itself in the fact *that we fight*. Thus, rather than mounting an argument or even the "big lie," the spectacle operates mainly through the disappearance of debate. As described above, both technofetishism and support-the-troops rhetoric most literally satisfy Debord's notion of the spectacle: "the dominant order's monologue of self-praise," where a seductive vision of the military apparatus itself begins to appear as the reason for its existence. If Debord's spectacle is a "permanent opium war," the bloodless, antiseptic battlefield could be said to be a quest for the cleanest opium, a dissociative designer drug prescribed to flat-line the democratic citizen. The spectacular war does not examine the legitim-acy of military action so much as it inserts itself into the momentum of an inevitable conflict. All obstacles cleared that might prick the deliberative con-science, this war asks the citizen to sit back and marvel at the glorious machine in motion.

The unreality of the spectacular war was probably most succinctly diagnosed by Jean Baudrillard in a 1991 essay provocatively entitled "The Gulf War Did Not Take Place."[51] Baudrillard's thesis, of course, is not that "nothing happened," but rather that the television war and the event itself so diverged that one cannot claim that the former represented the latter. As a simulacrum, the television war not only *mis*represented but *out*represented the real thing, pushing the event into the realms of the screen and the hyperreal.[52] The most striking indication of this inversion of meaning is the fact that this high-tech, one-sided atrocity even registered as a "war." In step with the spirit of Baudrillard's critique, Noam Chomsky also questioned the use of this most fundamental representation: "As I understand the concept of 'war,' it involves two sides in combat, say, shooting at each other. That did not happen in the Gulf."[53] Media scholar George Gerbner recognized the Persian Gulf War as a critical point in history where the new screen power in a sense caught up to the power of material violence. "A boiling point is reached when the ability to wage war merges with the ability to direct a movie about it."[54] Gerbner named this sublimation the "Gulf War Movie" to signal that the enterprise of war had shifted its center of gravity in a decidedly mercurial direction and into the logics of the spectacle.

If the careful choreographing and filtering of Desert Storm did not itself constitute a "war movie," the Pentagon and NBC collaborated immediately following the Persian Gulf War on a made-for-TV film called *The Heroes of Desert Storm* (1991). Disregarding reality altogether, the film intercut news footage with scripted material read by both professional actors and actual Gulf War veterans. *Heroes* thus worked to annihilate the viewer's capacity to distinguish between fact and fiction, which appeared to have been the intended consequence. A disclaimer noted up front that, in the interest of something called realism, "no distinction is made among these elements."[55] The film most directly addressed the trajectory of the spectacular war where "deceit deceives itself" by piling on multiple layers of simulation. Simply put, the decision to air a made-for-TV movie was a natural one given that the Gulf War had already aired in made-for-TV form. The brains behind *Heroes*, director Lionel Chetwynd, made a career of bringing official administration narratives to the big screen, working closely with the Reagan, Bush I, and Bush II presidencies. For example, Chetwynd was one of the main authors of the support-the-troops fervor that threatened to eclipse public debate leading up to the Persian Gulf War. Chetwynd penned the high profile film *The Hanoi Hilton* (1987), which helped burn the POW permanently into the public memory as the prime motive for the destruction of Vietnam. Chetwynd also wrote and produced a 1988 television series for the A&E Network called *To Heal a Nation*, another Vietnam tale of the trials of US soldiers, this time on the home front. This series meshed with Reagan administration attempts to reverse the Vietnam Syndrome by appealing to the stabbed-in-the-back narrative.[56] Chetwynd was well familiar with this appeal having served on Reagan's campaign team in 1980. Naturally, he was the man best positioned to later direct *The Heroes of Desert Storm* in cooperation with the George H.W. Bush administration, which opens with a special address from the president. Here, in classic support-the-troops redirection, Bush urges us to think not of the generals who make history, but of the average soldiers who are the real heroes of Desert Storm. Chetwynd's corpus, which extends further into the Bush II administration, captures two distinct trajectories of the spectacular war: a collapse of screen power into military power and a refocusing of public attention from policy to the military apparatus itself.[57]

The Persian Gulf War of 1991 thus appeared at the point where, freed from the burdens of representation, a more plastic war could comfortably settle into the logics of its new televised home. From one direction, the interests of television demanded constant, real-time access to the free stream of "news" issuing from Pentagon and State Department public relations organs. This demand allowed the executive branch a high degree of control over imagery, language, and framing of events. From the other direction, television as a medium exerted its own set of conventions on these public relations practices, forcing conformity to the demands of flow, advertising, and ratings. The military-media coupling during this war, in other words, increasingly cast official public relations organs into the position of programmers and producers. The adaptation of the consummate unconsumable to the commercial screen was also in part facilitated by the unchallengeability of American military power following the collapse of the Soviet Union. The extreme asymmetry between the US and Iraqi militaries, for example, allowed for the precise programming of the conflict. The executive openly scheduled the first bombings to commence on January 16, 1991, during evening prime time. Moreover, the administration decided that the conflict would be known in the history books as the "hundred-hour war" to distinguish it from the sluggish and dissent-inducing "quagmire" of Vietnam, adjusting the length of fighting accordingly.[58] Military action could thus be packaged as a miniseries in what Tom Engelhardt called "war as total television."[59]

Settling into its appropriate time slot, Desert Storm took on the features of

Sit in front of a warm fire.

Staying warm is no problem at the Indiana Jones Epic Stunt Spectacular, where Indy's stunt-double outruns a fiery explosion! Relive the days of big studios, and even bigger stars. And experience the glitz and glamour that truly made Hollywood a "tinsel town."

Figure 1.1 Advertisement for Disney's Indiana Jones Epic Stunt Spectacular in *News-week*, February 4, 1991, during the height of the Persian Gulf War bombing. Appeals such as these were entirely at home amidst the spectacular coverage of the war.

other spectacular events. Journalists showed a tendency to reduce war to a spectator sport, borrowing such metaphors and adjusting episodes for easy digestion.[60] War took on the catharsis, glory, and identification common to the dramatics of sports. Anchors assumed an uncharacteristic machismo while the coverage resembled play-by-play announcing complete with instant replays.[61]

Conflict became a celebratory event, a habitual exercise in "recreational violence" within a larger sea of fictitious violent entertainment. Consistent with the alienation of the spectacle, according to Busah Ebo, these habits created a "shock-absorption cushion, a no-surprise buffer zone in public consciousness." If the veneer of the clean war were to fail, that is, the violence might seem as unreal as everything else on TV.[62] By melding into the scene of illusory entertainment, war became a festival of fireworks and machinery, asking no more of the citizen than a ball game or an action movie. The war also powered an array of ancillary markets like any respectable entertainment franchise—from memoirs to special edition video box sets to T-shirts to model toys—practices that Kenon Brezeale argues translated the act of consumption itself into an act of "support."[63] Indeed, the consumable war, in the idiom of feature film and its merchandising, had arrived.

The consumable war eventually came to wear two faces, however. While the spectacle retained a place as a part of post-industrial war and its reception, in the years following Desert Storm a new set of discourses and practices began to take shape that again restructured the interfaces between citizen and soldier, home front and battlefield. Rather than simply presenting war as a spectacular event, this new militarism increasingly invited the citizen into the drama. Still working within practices consumption, these discourses began to provide opportunities for the citizen to step into the screen and dabble as a virtual soldier on a battlefield playground. This shift accelerated the familiar tropes of the spectacular war—clean war, technofetishism, and support-the-troops rhetoric—in new ways of encountering war. If the spectacle had worked to deactivate the citizen through the opiate of distraction, the new war worked to channel civic energy through the amphetamine of interactivity.

Interactive War and the Virtual Citizen-Soldier

New War, New Military

To understand the nature of the interactive war, one must first consider the landscape from which it grew, which includes certain changes in the profile and philosophy of the US military at the end of the twenty-first century. Chief among these changes was rise of "informational warfare," which hailed an erasure of distinctions between home front and battlefield. This version of "war" had been anticipated in 1993 by John Arquilla and David Ronfeldt, fellows of the RAND Institute, in an influential defense planning brief entitled "Cyberwar is Coming!" This document asserted that war in the post-industrial age challenges modern centralized military institutions and eventually replaces them with diffuse and decentralized networks. Moreover, deception outpaces destruction as a means of dominance and information replaces emphasis on manpower. According to Arquilla and Ronfeldt, the methods by which these strategies are deployed are not necessarily "military" in the traditional sense. Instead, they increasingly work within economies of trade and information exchange, including a particular focus on psychological operations and media management. And the thesis holds that information-based warfare tends to dissolve conceptual boundaries between civil and military spheres.[64] Here "war" occurs on a spectrum between "cyberwar" on one end (traditional high-intensity conflict using command-control-communication systems) and "netwar" on the other (the information war that bleeds into societal and cultural realms). This latter variety includes low-intensity conflict, so-called "operations other than war," psychological operations, and public relations.[65] In this sense, netwar is even more "total" than total war, since it involves controlling disparate populations at home and abroad while turning the "balance of information" in one's favor. Netwar, in other words, decompartmentalizes war. In May of 2000, the Defense Department reconceptualized this philosophy in the term "Full Spectrum Dominance," a phrase that implied total control over land, sea, air, space, time, and information.[66] As Michael Hardt and Antonio Negri have suggested, "War seems to have seeped back and flooded the entire social field," a presumption that has become something of an axiom of social theory in addition to military theory.[67]

A simultaneous "turning inward" of the martial gaze accompanied the militarization of the civic field. Writing in Foreign Affairs in 2002, Secretary of State Donald Rumsfeld described this as a transformation of the US global military profile from a "threat-based" model, which dominated Cold War thinking, to a "capabilities-based" model appropriate for the post-9/11 world. Instead of concentrating power on external, adversarial nations, the capabilities model sought to turn attention inward to examine points of weakness in the military apparatus itself. His ideal consisted of a lightweight, highly mobile, high-tech force that could strike anywhere in the world with instantaneity and precision, capitalizing on the so-called Revolution in Military Affairs (RMA).[68] Later the Pentagon proposed a dramatic restructuring of the global military posture largely in line with Rumsfeld's vision that featured the diffusion of large permanent military bases into a multiplicity of "lily pads" or impermanent jumping-off points.[69] This ongoing transformation signaled the evolution of the military to an ever-present, mobile, global police force that made no distinction between domestic and foreign operations. Coincidentally, this "capabilities-based" military entered the scene precisely at the point when the military apparatus had crossed an important threshold of expansion. Beginning with the invasion of Afghanistan, the US military for the first time outspent all other nations on Earth combined.[70] Nietzsche once wrote that "under peaceful

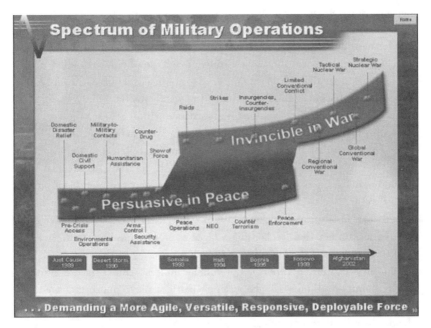

Figure 1.2 A visual rendering of the idea of Full Spectrum Operations from an Army report.

Source: Fontenot et al. (2003), 8.

conditions a warlike man sets upon himself."[71] Having reached a level of unchallengeability, the US military machine set upon the task of what Paul Virilio recognized early as "endo-colonization" or the internal translation of the population—even the body—into an appendage of the military machine.[72]

The preferred metaphor for understanding this new kind of conflict was "home security." In his pseudo-folksy way, Rumsfeld illustrated the new military strategy with the image of a house fortified with deadbolts, alarms, guard dogs, and the police.[73] This xenophobic metaphor was made literal in early 2003 when hardware stores experienced a massive rush on duct tape and plastic sheeting, items that Tom Ridge of the Department of Homeland Security suggested might protect homes in the case of a chemical or biological attack.[74] Rumsfeld's vision of post-9/11 warfare and the new public perception of the battlefield thus met one another on the front doorstep of the American home. The vision of a battlefield self-identical with the home front, moreover, had been reinforced after 9/11 by the new Department of Homeland security, which released among other missives a pamphlet entitled "Homeland Security Begins at Home." This rhetoric not only revived the Cold War project of renovating the home-as-bunker, but intensified trends toward the encapsulation of the individual as the "front line" of a networked geo-political conflict.[75] James Hay argues that such rhetoric was symptomatic of broader neo-liberal shifts toward a state of self-managed security that "recruits citizens where they live" thereby creating a new type of citizen-soldier.[76]

This is all to say that, in terms of everyday political discourse, the citizen had come into an unprecedented proximity to "war," situated amidst an internal intensification of the security state in accordance with the "war on terror." In a sense, this made the citizen by default an interactive participant, hailed by the permanent threat of threat-level-orange terrorism, billeted in the American home, and recruited into a war. It is not enough, however, to say that these developments once again called the citizen to take on the mantle of citizen-soldier, reinvested as an actor in the military apparatus after a long hiatus. Indeed, the institutional chasm between the citizen and soldier had never been wider. Rather than reclaiming a place as an active *subject* of the military as in the days of the citizen-soldier, all indicators suggest that the citizen had become an even more potent *object* of military interest. Under these conditions, citizen identity itself increasingly became a battle space to micro-managed. The interactive war represented just such a process, the endo-colonization of civic identity by a military-corporate-media complex.

The 9/11 Rupture and Beyond

The logics of the spectacle thus gave way to those of interactivity as war flooded the social field. In many ways, September 11, 2001, represented this transitional moment. As a zenith in the evolution of the spectacle, the events occupied virtually all eyeballs simultaneously, pushing the screen closer to the center of "war." In Jean Baudrillard's words, 9/11 represented the "absolute event, the 'mother' of events, the pure event which is the essence of all the events that never happened."[77] September 11 vibrated violently between the absolute reality of death and an uncanny cinematographic quality, as if the previous century of cinema had fatefully led up to the moment of impact. The 1990s had seen a concentration of such disaster films that featured scenes of urban destruction, especially involving the iconic New York City skyline. Films that seemed to foreshadow 9/11 included the *Die Hard* franchise (1988, 1990, 1995), *Independence Day* (1996), *Armageddon* (1998), *Godzilla* (1998), *Deep Impact* (1998), *The Matrix* (1999) and others. On September 26, 2001, the satirical newspaper, *The Onion*, issued an apt story titled "American Life Turns into Bad Jerry Bruckheimer Movie." The repeated appraisal of 9/11 as "just like a movie" meant that the screen value of the event posed a serious threat to its reality value. Ultimately, the towers fell decisively in the direction of the screen such that the horrible reality of the event could not be separated from its televised reception. Even if the event exceeded the boundaries of the screen for a time, it would later be disciplined to fall in line with film's visual conventions. Geoff King notes that documentaries such as CBS's *9/11* (2002) spliced together multiple reels of amateur footage to achieve the kind of temporal continuity effect expected in feature film. HBO's *New York City: In Memorium* (2002) went further to use an overlap cutting technique commonly used in Hollywood blockbusters to temporally stretch and magnify pyrotechnic explosions.[78] Later films such as *World Trade Center* (2006) and *United 93* (2006) proved the inevitability of cinematic adaptation. Certainly, the spectacular potential of the event was a major consideration for the murderous architects of the event. Rather than "creating a spectacle," however, one might say that the attacks entered the machinery of the spectacle at the optimal angle of inci-dence, the momentum of the planes setting the logics of the spectacle into high gear. A consolidation of executive power predictably pooled in the shadow of the event, making good on Debord's thesis that "the dominion of the spectacle in its concentrated form means the dominion, too, of the police."[79] On the one hand, then, 9/11 represented the final maturation and triumph of the spectacle, consummating the love affair between war and the screen.

On the other hand, the event represented a rupture in the spectacle, a bursting and diffusing into a new order of power. It was at this moment that the logics of the spectacle—alienation and inactivity—gave way to the logics of interactivity. "War," the discourse in which the Bush administration would eventually characterize 9/11, had "hit home." The event traumatized the alien-ated citizen-spectator that had been so carefully cultivated since Vietnam. The new War on Terror thrust the citizen through the safety glass of the television screen into the new war zone. The pieces of this shattered screen rained into the crevices of everyday life, each serving as a portal to a new, more participa-tory version of war. The moment tacitly hailed the return of the citizen-soldier ideal. Ordinary citizens aired their war stories, near misses, triumphs, and travails. Police officers, firefighters, and civilian volunteers became characters in powerful performances of civic heroism, one of which was captured iconi-cally in a photo of three firefighters raising a flag in the rubble in the style of the famous Iwo Jima photograph. The armed forces experienced a meaningful spike in voluntary enlistment.[80] Masses of people joined long-distance relief efforts, and donors turned out in high numbers to give blood. In his subsequent speech to the joint sessions of Congress, President Bush opened by introducing Todd Beamer, a passenger on United Flight 93, who had tried to wrest control away from the hijackers before the plane barreled into a Pennsylvania field.[81] In May of the next year, Pat Tillman, star safety for the Arizona Cardinals, gave up a $3 million football contract to join the Army Rangers and fight in Afghanistan.[82] Lauded for their personal sacrifice, both Beamer and Tillman stood as metonymic symbols of the new American citizen-soldier. Though the interest in Tillman suggested a symbolic environment that tied spectator sports to war, the new heroes appeared to challenge the core logics of the spectacle as it invited a shift toward responsibility and investment in the military, a symbolic shift from "support for" to "service with."

This seeming revival of the citizen-soldier, however, occurred largely in accordance with the logics of a highly evolved military-media complex. The direction of post-industrial war had increasingly opened up a vast capillary network of military-media channels—from Vietnam's television war through the real-time war of Desert Storm and on into the new century. When the new participatory urge gripped the polity, this complex of channels stepped in to offer an array of prescribed modes through which this urge could be exercised. Rather than civilizing the military, which is the ultimate aim of the citizen-soldier ideal, power flooded in the opposite direction, from high to low ground and toward the militarizing of the civic field. The most visible instance of this new model was the relationship between the military and journalism, which was soon characterized through "embedded reporting," a discourse explored in depth in Chapter 3. From one standpoint, embedded reporting appeared to represent greater penetration of the civilian journalism into military operations, and indeed it was through this democratic discourse that executive and the corporate media sold the embedded system to the American public. More accurately, however, embedding represented the assimilation and absorption of the civic field into the military apparatus.[83] The metonym of the embedded reporter served as a kind of seed crystal that provoked interactive couplings that replicated themselves to the far reaches of popular culture. Rather than increasing accountability of the military to its citizenry, the new participatory war represented a military colonization of civic space.

Though reaching its full expression in the new century, the interactive idiom was not entirely novel to the post-9/11 environment. Traces of interactivity can be found in the civic experience of the Persian Gulf War in 1991, which contained an element of immersion that drew oblique but fairly consistent scholarly attention. In 1992, for example, the journal *Public Culture* featured a special section entitled "Engulfment," where scholars weighed in on the war's unprecedented saturation of civic space. Here Victor Caldarola argued that the novelty of real-time CNN coverage created a phenomenology for the viewer not unlike a video game, "compress[ing] ordinary time into the hyperactive realm of imaged experience."[84] Robert Stam also references the video-game visuals cultivated by the Pentagon's release of crosshairs video, which imbued the viewer with a bomb's-eye view of the world. For Stam, this point of view bore a structural resemblance to the iconic final scene of the Cold War satire

Dr. Strangelove, where Slim Pickens rides a falling atomic bomb, gleefully yelping and whipping his cowboy hat in the air rodeo-style.[85] Even while hinting at a more interactive aesthetic, however, scholars of this period cleaved to the spectacle as the guiding critical lens. Stam notes, for example, that such a war "recruits," but it specifically "recruits spectators" and "armchair imperialists," delivering not a projection into the screen but rather the libidinous pleasures of an alienated, godlike voyeurism.[86] Perhaps this tendency is best represented by Douglas Kellner's touchstone *The Persian Gulf TV War*, which references the game aesthetic while couching its analysis solidly in the critique of the spectacle.[87]

These glimmers of the interactive war gave way to noticeable changes with regard to the 2003 invasion of Iraq. The debut of the term "militainment" in scholarly discourse marked the sense that something had qualitatively shifted. A number of scholars associated the word with the more obvious innovations: the explosion of war-themed reality television and the embedded reporting system.[88] The exact nature of the qualitative change remained murky, however. Among commentators on the "militainment" phenomenon, Robin Andersen offered the most sophisticated take. In her formidable book *A Century of Media, a Century of War*, Andersen advances three relevant observations. She first suggests that the new war film—represented by the likes of *Black Hawk Down* (2001) and *Saving Private Ryan* (1998)—defined itself by sacrificing all else to deliver a virtual experience of combat, which created a scene strangely lacking in any reference to war's political justification.[89] Second, Andersen likens the embedded reporting system to reality television, a choreographed extravaganza where journalists lost their independent spirit in a "war as adrenaline rush."[90] Finally, and perhaps most pointedly, Andersen describes the increased appearance of a video-game sensibility on the news, particularly transferring varied aspects of the Pentagon's cyberwar onto the civilian screen, an aesthetic that she argues moved viewers into a "participatory mode" that is "fundamental to the new visual rhetoric of war."[91] This appraisal is unique in that it delivers the first real recognition of the emerging interactive war aesthetic across a variety of media.

Andersen's analysis does leave open some questions, however. Her description of the pleasure economy of the new war film, for example, falls back on the thematic of the voyeur, where extreme violence is normalized to "sit comfortably next to all other forms of pointless violence so prevalent on television."[92] Andersen's account does not venture far beyond the critique of the spectacle, concluding that such phenomena imply a cool, detached receptor. As such, it is unclear whether these rhetorics and practices represent an intensification of the spectacle or function in a novel way. This is not to say that her analysis is inconsistent; rather, it signals an opportunity to explore what might be a crucial transition point in the critical language of war. Andersen's thematic of "war as adrenaline rush," for example, captures the vital mood of embedded reporting. What is not as clear are the symbolic mechanics that produce these pleasures, which she and others have connected to the genre of reality television. Finally, Andersen's analysis of the video game war limits itself mainly to an account of how military technologies—the cockpit, the gun sight, and the simulator—have come to typify the news aesthetic. How does this "digital spectacular," as she notably calls it, mesh with the rising tide of war-themed commercial and military games? Moreover, what role does the game-centered war have in producing the player? These questions, which the current book addresses, are not raised as a counterpoint to Andersen *per se*, but rather an attempt to complement, amplify, and strengthen her provocations. Her insights provide a valuable reference point for understanding those symbolic practices that broke through the proscenium of the television war to envelope the viewer in a decidedly first-person regime of signs.

We can begin to define the features of the interactive war. Like the spectacle, the interactive war is a discourse that operates through consumption and the production of pleasure. Each features distinct pleasures, however. The spectacle offers those of distraction, bedazzlement, and voyeurism, pleasures driven by a kind of alienated looking. In contrast, the pleasures of the interactive war are predicated on participatory play, not simply watching the machine in motion but wiring oneself into a fantasy of a first-person, authorial kinetics of war. These two experiences interpellate two different characters: a citizen-spectator who sits in fascinated immobility and what might be called a "virtual citizen-soldier" who mobilizes to surf the detailed intricacies of the military machine. Perhaps most importantly, the two represent distinct modes of control. The spectacle operates negatively, figuring as a type of coercion designed to suppress the political impulse by other means. Instead of deactivating the political subject, the interactive war works positively, seducing the virtual citizen-soldier to expend energies through prescribed activation. If it can be said that the pleasures of the spectacle clear the way for a corresponding police state, the pleasures of the interactive war sublimates power into a symbolic immersion that contains, modulates, and produces the citizen-subject.

Retrofitting for the Interactive War

The production of the virtual citizen-soldier has involved the translation, and often acceleration, of discourses already in circulation. Support-the-troops rhetoric, following its long trajectory of development since Vietnam, approaches its logical end point in the virtual citizen-soldier. As noted, this rhetoric has acted within the idiom of the spectacle to sever the legislative connection between citizen and soldier, replacing civic responsibility with a distant, personal sympathy. The interactive war intensifies these logics by increasingly bringing the citizen into proximity to a vision of the soldier and battlefield. In doing so the interactive war draws the subject further away from its point of deliberation and toward the point of policy's execution. War films like *Saving Private Ryan* and *Black Hawk Down* exemplify the interactive acceleration of support-the-troops rhetoric. In essence, these films place the viewer in the midst of an excruciatingly bloody battle scenes intended to show, in hyperreal detail, "what it was like." *Saving Private Ryan*, for example, penetrates the fourth wall by splashing the lens with blood and mud. In doing so, the film demotes the camera/eye from its objective status, implies a subjective body in its place, and invites the viewer into that body. Here, identification as and sympathy for the soldier combine with exhilarating alchemy in a kind of death simulator, while pushing questions of political context and justification further off the screen. If the spectacular war supports the troops at a depersonalized distance, the interactive war translates such rhetorics into the virtual occupation of the soldier's body. The tone of the Omaha Beach landing scene in *Saving Private Ryan* is thus contradictory. The experience is couched in revulsion to the horrors of battle, but it is also a fantastic thrill ride, an exercise in "playing soldier" under the most exotic of circumstances. In the age of militainment, this experiential template has been replicated through a variety of media.

The interactive war both accelerates and complicates the trope of the clean war. In terms of war news coverage since Vietnam, death has been virtually eliminated from the screen. This feature has facilitated the easy consumption of war. While this fiction may function well with a distant, abstract war, when media purport to project one onto the battlefield, the contradictions of the clean war become even more absurd. Consider, for example, the schizophrenic extremes in the presentation of war—between the hyper-violence of *Black Hawk Down* and the hyper-hygiene of the real-time embedded war, both of which were authorized and materially supported by the Pentagon. Both represent a vision of interactivity. In the case of *Black Hawk Down*, the subject matter rested beyond the citizen's political influence and thus was less beholden to the mandates of the clean war.[93] Embedded reporting, by contrast, sought to deliver a clean conflict close-up and in real time. This interactive war therefore had to work more desperately to obscure its own violence even as it purported to bring the war consumer in contact with that violence. Embedded journalists, for example, struggled with news directors back home over the airing of gruesome realities. News agencies did not care to risk losing a valuable embedding slot to air photos that, in the climate set by the Bush administration, might well be considered an "anti-war statement." As such, self-censorship and the clean war ultimately triumphed on screen.[94] This inherent instability will persist so long as the presence of death is anathema to popular support for war. Social mores regarding the visibility of death are subject to change, however. Tolerance for the death of soldiers may grow, for example, with the outsourcing of the military to the private sector, which may further code the military as "them" instead of "us." Such developments may embolden the common response to soldier deaths engendered by the move to the all-volunteer military, the dismissive sentiment that "It's sad, but they knew what they were getting into when they joined up." The interactive war has showed signs of becoming more tolerant of the presence of death in dealing with foreign populations. For example, since the invasion of Afghanistan in 2002, the Pentagon released a number of gun sight videos that featured the killing of persons on the ground rendered in ghostly infrared. These persons were abstracted to the extreme, but the very presence of dying human beings suggests that the viewership at large had begun to overcome a long-standing aversion. This may be a byproduct of the thinning membrane between realism and reality, a separation that cannot always be maintained. Developments like these may point to a future where the pleasures of playing war assume a more sadistic posture in order to make sense of death in the interactive mode.

The "technofetishism" trope too has made the transition from spectacular to interactive wars. It soon became clear that the urge to push buttons could be taken to the bank. As part of its new "Cross into the Blue" campaign, for example, the Air Force likened flying the Predator unmanned aerial vehicle to the childhood thrill of flying a model airplane. CNN contrived a segment where a reporter blew up a truck with a remote control detonator to "see what the troops are experiencing in Iraq." The centerpiece of the performance was the reporter's thrill in pushing the button. The interactive war also intensifies trends toward the weaponization of the civic gaze. Integrating the citizen subject into the machinery of sighting has been a motif since Desert Storm in 1991. The most visible icon of Desert Storm was a video released by the Pentagon from the point of view of a smart bomb going "down the chimney" of a supposed Iraqi ammunition warehouse, a construction typical of war discourses that symbolically sodomize the enemy. In this famous video sequence, the camera approaches the building, the image grows larger and larger, and a blank screen signifies the moment of impact. The bomb-mounted camera footage, H. Bruce Franklin argues, captured the "virtual reality" ethos of the techno-war: perfect visual identification with the weapon, perfect precision, and a perfectly clean and invisible result.[95] If this image was singularly iconic during Desert Storm, the weaponizing of the civic gaze became an institutionalized feature of Operation Iraqi Freedom in 2003. The television war progressively favored first-person relationships with weapons, fanning the

Figure 1.3 Glimpses of the interactive war. (column one) The display of a weapons sight during a 1991 Gulf War press conference; cockpit footage from Fox News in 2003; a CNN correspondent blows up a truck to simulate a roadside bomb in 2005. (column two) Air Force ad sequence from 2002 likening the Predator drone to a model airplane.

gaze out through an array of machines. Night-vision goggles fitted to news cameras tinged the home front screen a grainy green. Having gone mobile in *cinéma vérité* fashion, cameras showed a marked preference for riding in the cockpit in view of a control panel, gazing out from inside F-18s, and skimming across the desert in Abrams tanks. Weapons-view footage supplied by the Pentagon deputized the citizen as a vicarious warrior during Operation Iraqi Freedom. If one's identity as a virtual foot soldier prompted one to "fall in line" behind executive orders, identifying with smart weapons implied an even more restricted politics: the inevitable carrying out of predetermined programming. The interactive transaction, rather than representing a civic recapturing of an estranged military, signaled the colonization of civic identity and its disciplining in accordance with the logics of the war machine.

If the technofetish template for the Persian Gulf War was *Top Gun*, by 2008 the fantasy had morphed into the shape of *Iron Man*. Like its predecessor, *Iron Man* received generous assistance from the Pentagon's Hollywood Liaison Office, which provided Edwards Air Force Base and a squadron of aircraft. Air Force Capt. Christian Hodge, who served as liaison officer for *Iron Man* (and *Transformers* the year before) expressed his satisfaction with the deal: "This movie is going to be fantastic. The Air Force is going to come off looking like rock stars."[96] Naturally, the arrangement encrusted *Iron Man* from head to toe with military hardware, seamlessly melding visions of hot rods, fighter planes, and the armored suit that the main character, genius designer Tony Stark, develops in his spare time. Stark represented the big-screen debut of the celebrity weapons contractor, a character that manufacturer Raytheon Sarcos leveraged to publicize its prototype "exoskeleton," a wearable robot foot-soldier system. The company issued a press release on the film's US release date that drew specific parallels between its exoskeleton and the *Iron Man* suit.[97] Both Raytheon and the film capitalized on the same pleasure: the fantasy of embedding the body in the military machine. In *Iron Man*, Stark became the vessel through which the viewer could "try on the weapon."

Indeed, trying on the weapon has been a stock theme of science fiction for some time. Orson Scott Card's novel *Ender's Game* (1985) as well as films like *The Last Starfighter* (1984), *War Games* (1983), and *Toys* (1992) all feature civilians making the short leap from interactive games to actual battle. Theorist Paul Virilio, writing about Operation Desert Storm in 1991, posits a similar

Figure 1.4 (left) Raytheon Sarcos' XOS exoskeleton suit; (right) Stark Industry's suit in *Iron Man* (2008).

trajectory in what he identifies as the "tele-audition" of WWII, the "tele-vision" of Vietnam, and the nascent "tele-action" of Desert Storm.[98] Virilio's vision of a "tele-active" war blurs the lines between the pilot punching in coordinates for a satellite-guided bomb and the civilian home gamer doing the same thing on a commercially-released military flight simulator. Perhaps, the narrative goes, we all might become button pushers in the push-button war. Taking into account certain trends, one might be able to envision a version of this sci-fi dystopia. In the past two decades there has been much cross-over between military simulation and civilian gaming technologies. This cross-over is in part a product of the military's need to generate technology savvy recruits. One can speculate on a future where military gaming cultures, adept at playing real military simulators, could circulate gaming experts in and out of the push-button, long-distance war. The Army already sponsors gaming tournaments using sophisticated war simulators. The next logical step might be awarding champion players the prize of carrying out a real remote-controlled military mission. Such a mission would have obvious "entertainment value." The rising private security industry might be a logical sphere for such a transaction, and the increased use of unmanned drones has made such an *Ender's Game* economy technologically feasible.

We ought to cautiously follow this narrative to its conclusion, however. The metaphors of "interface" and "tele-action" imply a re-arming of the user, a high-tech reintroduction of the citizen-soldier. Dominant trends in post-industrial war suggest the opposite to be the case, however. The citizen has been progressively disarmed and dissociated from playing an active role in the actual military institution. Rather than reversing these trends, the interactive war intensifies them, encouraging the citizen to engage in a closed, constructed system that channels the civic urge through fantasies of military participation. That is, instead of positioning the citizen as *subject* of war, this interactive war further cements the citizen's role as *object* of the military apparatus. The "interface" between citizen and military is therefore not one where the citizen has any real role in "playing the war," but rather should be thought of as a sophisticated means through which the military-entertainment complex "plays the citizen."

The politically charged "gun-camera" provides a useful illustration of the difference. Beginning in the Persian Gulf War of 1991, the civic field became increasingly familiar with the view through the weapon's crosshairs camera. On the surface, this point of view might seem to have been a reintroduction of the citizen-soldier ideal, a reconnection to the basic, morbid transaction of war. The Pentagon, of course, managed gun-camera imagery through a filter that limited citizen exposure to the simulacrum of the clean war. As a thought experiment, Margot Norris suggested that the filter be removed, thus making the gun-camera widely available to the civic gaze. This, she argued, would reintroduce the citizen-witness into the equation. The viewer would then be drawn into the position of having to identify as agent of the military machine, as operator of the gun, and one who authorizes the pulling of the trigger on a visible, concrete, living individual.[99] Norris's updated version of the citizen-soldier ideal is perhaps a realistic picture of what tele-action might entail. In violating a central tenet of the clean war, however, it is precisely the opposite of how the military has chosen to deploy the gun-camera. As such, the notion of tele-action is only useful in conceptualizing some of the thematic pleasures that the interactive war offers. This battlefield playground—like the clean cross-hairs camera footage released by the Pentagon—goes to great lengths to divorce rather than connect the citizen to war.

In this environment, the discourse of recruitment functions in complex ways. Indeed, "recruitment" in the interactive war has expanded beyond its normal boundaries to become a generalized cultural condition. While the appeal to actually join the military is one aspect of this condition, the interactive war consistently offers the civic sphere a standing invitation to become a "virtual recruit." As discussed, this virtual recruit is a product of the demilitarization of the citizen as *subject* of the military on the one hand, and the remilitarization of the citizen as the *object* of the military on the other. That is, while the citizen became surrounded with opportunities to engage in a first-person relationship with war, these channels of engagement have been increasingly programmed to redirect civic energy away from actual participation in war policy or its deliberation. The following chapter examines how the transition to the interactive war has been mediated through the changing discourse of sport, which has been thoroughly integrated with the larger rhetorics of recruitment.

Chapter 2

Sports and the Militarized Body Politic

The Big Game

The halftime show at Super Bowl XXV was an inaugural moment in the marriage of spectator sport and warfare. The 1991 contest between the Buffalo Bills and the New York Giants got underway twelve days into Operation Desert Storm. Fans underwent extensive searches, sat among anti-terrorist squadrons, and found small American flags distributed on each seat at Tampa Stadium. An F-14 Tomcat fighter plane fly-over and shots of soldiers in uniform holding flags from various coalition countries accompanied a heart-stopping rendition of the national anthem by Whitney Houston. For the home audience, the halftime show began with an ABC report on Iraq consisting of four segments hosted by Peter Jennings. The last of these, entitled "Gulf War: The Super Bowl," tied spectatorship to "support" by explaining that the game was a morale booster for those American soldiers watching in the Middle East. ABC returned to the on-field halftime show in time for a version of "Wind Beneath My Wings" dedicated to the troops and sung by 2,000 children in front of a Disney World-style castle. During an instrumental break, a pre-recorded message from George H.W. Bush and Barbara Bush lit the Jumbo-Tron urging viewers to remember the men and women who "protect our freedom in the Persian Gulf and around the world." Yellow ribbons, flags, and a rendition of "America the Beautiful" filled out the performance, ending with a wistful transition from announcer Brent Musberger: "Dawn is now breaking over the Persian Gulf and some of our fighting men and women have been watching this Super Bowl throughout the night, and our hearts go out to them. Now for the second half . . ."[1] Later in the year, the Phoenix Cardinals' inaugural preseason game boasted a halftime show with 750 servicepersons, Humvees, Apache helicopters, a Patriot missile, M-60 machine gun emplacements set behind sandbags, an ejection seat demonstration, and more. A former POW from the Gulf War presided over the coin flip, a ritual that the New York Giants later repeated.[2]

Such tendencies intensified in the subsequent decade. On October 7, 2001, President George W. Bush appeared on the television screen to announce a US incursion into Afghanistan. The speech read like a playbook with "strikes" against "installations" and terrorists who "burrow deeper in caves and entrenched hiding places," food drops, the disrupting of communications, and other strategies.[3] The next day *The New York Times* noted that the address came on "a perfect day for football . . . just as many people were sitting down in front of their television sets for their weekly dose of gridiron glory."[4] Veterans Stadium broadcast Bush's speech to cheering fans waiting for the Philadelphia Eagles to play the Arizona Cardinals.[5] Later, in December, the president showed up at the Army-Navy game to conduct the opening coin toss and announce to the players that in the new war, "we will prevail." Navy coach Ed Malinowski explained how Bush's presence and indeed the game itself represented acts of heroism: "There's no better terrorist target in America. A full stadium."[6]

The real reprise of the 1991 Super Bowl, however, came in 2003 as Americans geared up for another invasion of Iraq. ABC broadcast much of its Super Bowl XXXVII coverage from the deck of the *USS Preble*, a destroyer furnished for the event by the Navy. Fighter jet flyovers and fireworks festooned both Celine Dion's rendition of "God Bless America" and the Dixie Chicks' "Star-Spangled Banner." On the ground, the VFW color guard flanked soldiers standing in formation and re-enactors dressed in Revolutionary War waistcoats and tricorn hats. Throughout the game, the scoreboard in San Diego's Qualcomm Stadium intermittently flashed electronic postcards from soldiers going through frontline readiness exercises.[7] The signs of the "War on Terror" filled any remaining spaces. An array of surveillance cameras searched every corner; private vehicles were disallowed in the stadium's parking lot; the airspace above was declared a "no-fly zone" that excluded even the Goodyear blimp; game-goers encountered numerous checkpoints and searches; the nearby Coast Guard and Navy stood on "high alert."[8]

Pregame programming also took on martial themes, making way for some notable synergies among industry, military, and media. In 2003, the yearly special *Howie Long's Tough Guys* teamed up with the Department of Defense. In addition to the former linebacker's usual role of profiling players, the show visited each branch of the military so that Long could ride alongside soldiers in tanks, planes, and helicopters. The show ended with Long awarding a chosen football player—the "tough guy"—with the prize of a new Ford truck, another one of the show's sponsors. All metaphors firmly in place, the military walked away from the venture with a festive recruitment ad, Ford with its truck brand "toughened," and ABC with a block of cheap programming. The trend toward such complexes gathered momentum when military contractor Bell Helicopter-Textron struck a deal with ESPN in 2006, agreeing to change the name of the college football Fort Worth Bowl to the Bell Helicopter Armed Forces Bowl. Alongside a fighter jet flyover and a military skydiving performance, Bell Helicopter—makers of the Cobra and Kiowa helicopters among other aircraft—constructed an exhibition that one commentator called "the largest display of military hardware ever seen at a football game" where fans of such equipment could try their hand at simulators and browse an array of recruiting booths.[9]

While the signs of war bled into the world of spectator sports during this period, television war coverage also absorbed the signs of spectator sports. This kind of coverage had been thoroughly tested in 1991. Christine Scodari notes that during the first Gulf War, television war coverage volleyed between anchor commentary and "highlights." Select scenes were chosen for slow motion instant replay. Anchors narrated play-by-play, while military experts provided color commentary.[10] Sue Curry Jansen and Don Sabo observed that generals like "Stormin' " Norman Schwarzkopf took on the visage of celebrity coach in the tradition of Knute Rockne or Vince Lombardi, drawing "game plans" on screenwriters overlaying maps of Iraq.[11] Journalists dropped pretense to objectivity, instead taking on the role of cheerleaders with "us" versus "them" language schemes. The argot of the football announcer infused the language of journalism as well with Hail Marys, end runs, blockers, kickoffs, touchdowns, sudden deaths, and Super Bowls.[12] Anchors discussed ongoing sporting matches during war coverage itself such that the war and sports programming combined in the smooth televised flow. Such language maintained as strong a place in the second Gulf War as it had in the first.

Having naturalized the spectator-sport war in 1991, television coverage in 2003 capitalized on the anticipation of the new "war by appointment" by appropriating the genre of the pregame show.[13] On March 17, President Bush announced the administration's intentions to invade Iraq if Saddam Hussein refused to leave the country within 48 hours.[14] Coupled with promises of a pyrotechnic "Shock and Awe" bombing of Baghdad, the countdown took a prominent place in the language of news anchors and on the screen. As part of their "Countdown Iraq" coverage, for example, MSNBC attached a countdown clock to the corner of the screen that did not significantly differ from countdown-to-kickoff clock in the corner of the screen during the Super Bowl pregame show. MSNBC took the pregame aesthetic further by airing a special called *Waging War: General Schwarzkopf's Diary*, which chronicled the 1991 Gulf War through the eyes of US military officers. The program provided meaning and historical context to the upcoming conflict, detailing the longstanding rivalry between the US and Hussein in the genre of the "coach's retrospective."

Such anticipatory programming introduced other accoutrements of spectator sports to the television war experience. In early 2003, a new industry of booking agents emerged that allowed gamblers to wager on the exact time of the war's commencement as well as when the US would kill Saddam Hussein. Just four days after the invasion of Iraq, the online betting site *Tradesports.com* reported that the amount of money wagered on Hussein's life ran second only to the amount sitting on the outcome of "March Madness," the yearly college basketball championship.[15] The competition for attention between the spectator war and spectator sports clearly roused ire in the world of college basketball. NCAA president Myles Brand directly tied the tournament to the impending war at a press conference. Announcing that the tournament would proceed as planned, Brand struck a pugilistic pose: "We were not going to let a tyrant [Saddam Hussein] determine how we were going to lead our lives."[16] The choice to cast the decision as a patriotic act might well have been an attempt to harness the swell of nationalism in the service of ratings. If so, it was an uphill battle. Viewership for the tournament fell about 16 percent as television war coverage commenced, suggesting that the audience had migrated to the main event. The larger world of sports widely reflected this trend. ESPN's senior vice president for research, Artie Bulgrin, noted that the Iraq war had a way of siphoning off the 18–35-year-old male demographic, "forcing sports to take a back seat."[17]

In many ways, the hybrid of war and sports should not be surprising. The two have always been connected in intimate ways, existing for much of human history on a continuum of gradations. Dario Del Corno notes that the ancient Greek masculine form *aethlos* means both the fight of warriors and the contest of athletes; the neuter *aethlon* means both the prize of the athletic contest and the spoils of battle.[18] Johan Huizinga goes further in his classic treatise on play: "Ever since words existed for fighting and playing, men have been wont to call war a game."[19] Sports have long served to commemorate war and, in the case of the "judicious game" of the Middle Ages or arguably even the modern Olympics, functioned as a substitute for war. Sports have functioned also as a forum for military training. WWII-era newsreels of young men doing calisthenics in formation attest to this practice as do the athlete-warrior bodies displayed by the Germans in *Triumph of the Will* (1935) and *Olympia* (1938). Dwight Eisenhower reportedly pronounced that "the true mission of American sports is to prepare young men for war."[20] Ronald Reagan remarked in 1981 that "sport is the human activity closest to war that isn't lethal," suggesting that sport is something of an ideal training laboratory.[21] The idea that sports and war are two sides of the same coin provides a certain measure of resolution.

From another angle, the athlete-warrior strikes twenty-first-century sensibilities as antiquated, and the consumption of war as a sporting event perverse. In today's world, with our multiple sports channels and Mega-Bowls, we have trouble conjuring the same positive connections between the body and body politic imagined by the Greeks or even by Eisenhower. The critiques have become familiar, extending back to Thorstein Veblen and his suggestion that sports institutionally fosters chauvinism, nationalism, and "predatory" values more conducive to the authorization of state violence.[22] George Orwell voiced a similar objection in his essay entitled "The Sporting Spirit," where he called sports "war minus the shooting."[23] In the classic critique of the spectacle, others suggest that sports distract the citizen with "bread and circuses." Noam Chomsky, for example, argues that spectator sports serve a depoliticizing function, molding a submissive, opiated populace by channeling enormous stores of attention and intelligence away from matters of real importance, such as US foreign policy.[24] Still others critique the pervasive crossover of military language in sports and sports language in war. Matthew Nadelhaft argues that sports metaphors used to describe military action do not justify the reasons for war, but rather justify war itself as a legitimate means for resolving conflict. The sports metaphor casts war as a clean, two-sided affair conducted under egalitarian rules-based strictures that eventually determine a winner based on merit.[25] In the case of the Persian Gulf War, the sports metaphor deflected attention from certain aspects, such as the fact that the war resembled less a fair competition than a high-tech, illegal, one-sided slaughter.[26] Arguably, the number of such mismatches has increasingly called forth the sports metaphor in the interest of maintaining a veneer of the "just war."

Such critiques, though enlightening on their own terms, do not generally take into account the changing quality of the sport–war coupling. The significance of this relationship is not just that these two worlds combine in an ongoing ebb and flow. Sport and war continue to co-evolve in a persistent partnership of meaning production. Sport represents a vital broker between civil and martial spheres, condensing larger power relations into ritualized reenactments. Functioning between body and body politic, sports provide a symbolic microcosm for playing out the prevailing vectors of force that imbue war and international relations with meaning. As a cultural interface through which war discourse enters civilian life, sports play a vital part in structuring the civic relationship to war. This relationship is dynamic. In the athlete-warrior of the Greeks or described by Eisenhower lies a vision consonant with the *citizen-soldier* ideal. In the rituals that dominate the experience of war at the end of the twentieth century, the relationship moved beyond generating fit bodies for fighting and into the sphere of televised consumption and the *citizen-spectator*, especially with regard to many the rituals surrounding the two interventions in Iraq.

The predominance of traditional spectator sports in American culture continues to condition the "spectator sport war" described above. In the 1990s, however, a new sports paradigm began to emerge that refigured the meaning of competition, the participant body, and audience. What came to be known as "extreme sports" (or, interchangeably, the "X-game") not only surfaced as a new mode of amusement, but also as a new understanding of the global environment. If traditional competition had re-enacted the dialectics of the Cold War, the X-game increasingly linked up with the logics of the post-Cold War world and the emerging discourse of terrorism. Like traditional sports before it, extreme sports present an entire set of pleasures and anxieties that have come to thoroughly saturate the citizen's mediated consumption of war. The metaphor of the X-game interpellates the citizen into an intimate relationship with war different from spectator sports, however. This new discourse takes its primary pleasures not from watching but rather being in virtual proximity to pain and danger. In colonizing discourses of recruiting, war journalism, terrorism, and others, the metaphor has given birth to the rhetoric of the "battlefield playground." Such a relationship to war is a vital aspect of the virtual citizen-soldier. Put simply, extreme sports discourse has been put to use as an entry point through which the citizen has been invited to play soldier.

Empire Xtreme

> Disciplinary man produced energy in discrete amounts, while control man undulates, moving among a continuous range of different orbits. Surfing has taken over from all the old sports.
>
> (Gilles Deleuze)[27]

In their seminal work, *Empire*, Michael Hardt and Antonio Negri provide a theoretical apparatus to think about the changing nature of the global body politic: "What used to be conflict or competition among several imperialist powers has in important respects been replaced by the idea of a single power that overdetermines them all ... that is decidedly postcolonial and postimperialist."[28] Power, in Empire, does not function in terms of a center/periphery, internal/external, or First World/Third World. Rather, Empire describes an evolving matrix of nation-states, trans-national private corporations, international political bodies (NATO or UN), and non-governmental organizations. Here, Hardt and Negri argue, the colonial urge feels its limits and begins to turn back upon itself, setting upon the task of self-legitimation. This process utterly transforms the idea of "war." Notably, the metaphor of international security displaces sovereign defense as war's primary signifier. War thus appears more as a police action for regulating Empire's internal dynamics and less in terms of states in conflict. Here, the notion of a just war is increasingly associated with expedience and effectiveness rather than ethics or the rule of law. The moment when the politics of Empire were in full view was the first major world conflict following the crumbling of the Soviet Bloc, the Persian Gulf War of 1991. This conflict featured an aggressive tyrant who became "the Enemy, an absolute threat to the ethical order."[29] The idea of the "rogue state" is a product of this rhetoric, while "terrorism" has become its *sine qua non*, signifying instabilities within the dominant order: the "cell," the enemy within the security apparatus, or the evil lurking within a totalizing cosmos. War thus becomes a kind of ongoing self-transformation. As Secretary of Defense Donald Rumsfeld advised the public after 9/11, "Forget about 'exit strategies'."[30]

In the logics of the War on Terror, civilians displace armies as the target of choice, and it is this everyday body that signifies the "front line." As imperial power turns inward, it thus begins the process of intensifying its institutions as they imply the body. Technological advances have played no small part in this intensification. Military global surveillance mechanisms like C4ISR (advanced command, control, communications, computers and intelligence, surveillance, and reconnaissance processing), innovations in military theory (Rapid Deployment, Netwar, and the Revolution in Military Affairs), non-lethal weapons, surveillance and identification technologies, the World Wide Web, and other advances in the global information infrastructure have been integral in hastening this political landscape. Hardt and Negri call this intensification the move from disciplinarity to the control society, borrowing from Gilles Deleuze. The control society is that in which "mechanisms of command become ever more 'democratic,' ever more immanent to the social field, distributed throughout the brains and bodies of the citizens."[31] Whereas disciplinarity was a process of colonization and individual atomization, the control society produces a network, weaving a global matrix of power that fully implicates the micropolitics of the cyborg body.[32]

It is within this political and corporeal milieu that extreme sports appears as a meaningful phenomenon. Just as traditional sports have been a microcosm of imperial politics, extreme sports represent a microcosm of the post-imperial politics of Empire. Paul Virilio touches on the relationship between extreme sports and the vanishing horizons of globalism: "Oddly, since the expanse of the world is progressively being reduced to nothing [via communication technologies] ... the individual becomes his own training ground."[33] If the "new world order" announced on September 11, 1990 refigured the playing field, the "new kind of war" announced after September 11, 2001 described the rules of the game.[34] The new global politics mapped themselves onto the surfaces of the body, transforming the individual into a site for acting out the dramas of security and terror in the post-Cold War period.

The term "extreme sports" coincidentally arrived in the 1990s, providing recognizable shape and form to a constellation of existent cultural practices.

This family of sports can be traced back to the rising popularity of surfing in the 1950s and 1960s from which skateboarding was born. Peter Donnelly notes that high-risk sports or so-called "vertigo sports" (borrowing the term from Roger Caillois) increased dramatically in the 1970s when activities like rock climbing, scuba diving, parachuting, hang gliding, and kayaking entered the cultural scene. Such sports, he argues, bear the mark of 1960s-inspired individualism, primitivism, and rebellion.[35] The 1980s further saw the growth of mountain biking, BMX biking and windsurfing, and the 1990s snowboarding and inline skating. Though the term had been in quiet circulation in the early 1990s, it took a corporate entity—ESPN with its 1995 Extreme Games—to bestow a singular body to these disparate activities. This occurred mainly in the interest of exerting some commercial control over a range of phenomena.[36] With the commercialization of extreme sports in the 1990s some of the more spectacular sports like bungee jumping, skydiving, and free climbing achieved the level of iconicity.[37] Less common high-tech sports such as NASCAR, powerboat racing, and motorcross have found their way under the umbrella, suggesting a high-tech element. In the late 1990s, activities labeled "extreme" enjoyed exponential gains in popularity. Participation in individual "lifestyle" thrill-seeking sports rose and team sports fell.[38] In 2001, skateboarder Tony Hawk beat out Shaquille O'Neal and Tiger Woods for most popular athlete among American youth.[39] After several years of sponsoring and airing its bi-annual X-games and Gravity Games, ESPN launched the first major cable network devoted to the genre in 2003, spin-off channel EXPN, and a host of other channels followed.[40]

Extreme sports represent a pronounced shift in the philosophy of athletics. Traditional sports are generally linear, goal-oriented, and dependent on the possibility of domination. Sports like pole vaulting and Olympic swimming, for example, enter competition through measurements and a currency of record-keeping, a practice that Allen Guttmann argues distinguishes modern sport from premodern sport.[41] Extreme sports, though not devoid of these elements, are more circular and process-oriented, positioning the self as the terrain for exploration and conflict.[42] While traditional sports anchor their identities in place through the colonial metaphor and the taking of "territory," extreme sports tend toward the nomadic, organizing themselves around mimicry rather than record.[43] The body invoked in extreme sports operates on a different order as well, distinguishing it from the discrete individual competitor or the team. The X-game implies a prosthetic body, an organic combination of flesh, machine, terrain, affect, and cultural discourse. Donna Haraway's cyborg ontology perhaps describes the scene best. Extreme sports represent a field of being immanent to itself, finding its occurrence and transformation as "stress in the machine," always in the process of negotiating its own stability.[44]

Extreme sports are situational, making their way in wizardly fashion through an array of constraints, blurring boundaries between "sport" and "art." Cultural critic Jeff Howe, for example, finds skateboarding at the fringes of the athletic and the aesthetic, suggesting that we "account for skating as a subculture, a cultural response, as a dance and a political act and a religion."[45]

Because the body has become the terrain for playing out the geopolitical drama, it has an intimate relationship to violence, working ecstasy and death into a curious amalgam.[46] Anthropologist David Le Breton describes the particular ethic to be

> [a] symbolic deal with Death, with the body as the currency, nature as the site of the event and Death respected only remotely, metaphorically solicited rather than approached for real, even through sometimes it arrives on the scene with a reminder that it is the one limit that can never be exceeded.[47]

Here, the pleasures of extreme sports reveal themselves as more akin to ecstatic practices: stress, pain, and panic coupled with an adrenaline high, bliss, and an intense fusion of actor with action. In fact, the X of extreme sports and the X used to refer to the popular hallucinogenic stimulant ecstasy gained mass exposure in the same cultural moment. Ecstasy (ek stasis: literally "outside of the normal state") can be understood either as the transcendence of the body or as an existential collapse of the self-reflective capacity into animality. Georges Bataille describes this latter state as the animal existence of "water in water."[48] Psychologist Mihaly Csikszentmihalyi, using another liquid metaphor, calls it the "flow experience."[49] The ecstatic pleasures are described quite elegantly by the bungee jump, a sport revived from its ancient South Pacific origins in the early 1980s to become wildly popular in the West. This revival involved the New Zealand system of binding the ankles for a head-first freefall. In the common bridge jump, the point is to reach the end of the cord, dip one's head in the rushing current or touch the ground with a hand before snapping back up again, thus experiencing a taste of oblivion.

The prevalence of this suicidal play has a particular resonance with the new logics of war as they imply the everyday body. Following Georges Bataille, one might describe the phenomenon as a new sacrificial ritual, a symbolic distribution of violence throughout the social field to accompany the fact that the military order has done likewise.[50] Pronouncements of the "end of history," the "new world order," or even the simple idea that war after 9/11 will be "everywhere and always," signal this new state of affairs. The new narrative stations the front lines of the new war throughout mundane life: the bus stop, the office high rise, and the matrix of media. Michael Hardt and Antonio Negri suggest that this militarization has become so pervasive, so intimate with the body and the biopolitical production of life, that is should perhaps be called the "military-vital complex."[51] If war is essentially biopolitical, Stuart J. Murray suggests that Empire also contains a built-in "thanatopolitics" that pervades the symbolic order.[52] The suicide bomber is perhaps the primary example, embodying a response to the biopolitical production of life by denying access to body itself. In contrast to the run-of-the-mill bomber, the suicide bomber creates destruction, media spectacle, and other reverberations for which no body can be held accountable. The particular symbolic threat is that this character produces while refusing to be produced. Moreover, the suicide bomber is a sign that war increasingly plays itself out on the surfaces of the body and everyday life. As Jeremy Packer puts it, "the war is on, and we are all becoming bombs."[53] That is, violence has invaded the micropolitics of the citizen body just as it has come home in the macropolitics of Empire. This internalization of violence is apparent in the affective dimension of the new war, where the twin terrors of potential disaster and surveillance haunt one's everyday existence. As an analogue, extreme sports represents a new set of practices and discourses which stage the drama of war on the corporeal level. Just as modern competitive sports reigned in and re-enacted industrial age war, the X-game engages post-industrial war with a new death ritual to replace the old—one that skirts, scours, and surfs the contours of the city, the landscape, the machine, and the self.[54] This may explain why it has become such a useful discourse for turning war into a consumable event.

The Battlefield Playground

> I can't wait to hop in my Jeep Liberty, drink some Mountain Dew, and go waterboarding.
> (Jon Stewart on *The Daily Show*, speaking on the subject of torture)[55]

By the late 1990s, the extreme sports ethos had fully work its way into the pleasure economy of mainstream consumer capitalism. Highly rated reality TV game shows like CBS's *Survivor*, NBC's *Fear Factor*, and their many copy cats played out the body politics of the X-game. *Survivor*, in its global tour of exotic locations—the Australian outback, Africa, Thailand, the Amazon—staged the drama of wilderness survival and excommunication. *Fear Factor* dared contestants to eat disgusting foods, appear naked in public, and to confront fearful animals, claustrophobia, and heights. Such programs gave witness to the body under duress—flinching, shivering, vomiting, and generally confronting its limits. The popular phenomenon of MTV's *Jackass*, which ran in television form from 2000–2002 before spinning off two major feature films, went a step further in turning acts of self-torture and self-humiliation into hot commodities. The show's concept can be traced back to skateboarding culture. In the late 1990s, soon-to-be star of the show, Johnny Knoxville, offered a prominent skating magazine video footage of himself testing out non-lethal weapons (weapons of the security state, it should be noted) on his own body. The magazine included this and subsequent footage in their video mail-outs before MTV picked up the act.[56] The show thus grew directly out of the genre of the "slam section" popular in homemade skateboarding videos, which features painful bloopers, wipeouts, and tricks gone wrong. *Jackass* essentially worked to reproduce the kernel of extreme sports culture for mass consumption, the money shot reel of self-directed pain with minimal plot.

Compelling television like this eventually found its way into television news. In late 2006 and early 2007, a number of television news reporters—Rick Sanchez of *CNN*, Mike Straka of *Fox News*, and Amanda Congdon of *ABC.com*—each submitted their own bodies to on-screen taser tests, a fact lampooned by *The Daily Show*.[57] *Fox News*'s Steve Harrigan opted to undergo the controversial interrogation technique of simulated drowning for the benefit of home viewers, a technique euphemized in the more sporting language of "waterboarding." Harrigan found the experience to be "scary," but ultimately "not that bad."[58] In March, 2008, *60 Minutes* correspondent David Martin, in an investigative piece about the Pentagon's new non-lethal microwave gun, volunteered to be shot a number of times.[59] Such programming might be said to represent a soft version of the public execution or "snuff film." These metaphors, though convenient, do not capture the gratifications of the drama. The consumption of violence here is not the spectacular variety of the Roman coliseum, where pain is inflicted upon an other, a criminal or scapegoat. Instead, a stand-in for the viewer undergoes the trauma. As such, the primary metaphor is more akin to a human sacrifice than a public execution in that one is encouraged to identify with the victim.[60]

"Lifestyle sports," as extreme sports are often called, went mainstream just as "lifestyle marketing" took its place at the center of advertising.[61] Rather than sell a sneaker or even an activity, lifestyle marketing sought to colonize life with a totalizing symbolic universe signified by the brand. This did not come easily as resistance, rebellion, and mutation prefigured into the equation, generally going by the names of "anti-corporatism" or "advertising cynicism."[62] In order to combat these resistances, advertising largely assimilated the rebel ethic in what Thomas Frank calls the language of "hip consumerism," which, through advertisement, relentlessly admonished the populace to rebel through prescribed consumption.[63] The discourse of extreme sports thus proved to be a mother lode for advertisers, who mined the discourse for signs of insurrection

Figure 2.1 The biopolitics of pain. (clockwise from top left) Steve Harrigan of *Fox News* undergoing waterboarding; Mike Straka of *Fox News* submitting to a taser test; CBS's David Martin being shot with a microwave gun or Active Denial System on *60 Minutes*; Rick Sanchez of CNN submitting to the taser.

that could be put to the task of building brands.[64] Among other things, this meant integrating the "X" into consumer capitalism as a marker of variability, rebellion, negation, and the unknown.[65] Companies strove to speak to this character presumably in all of us, what Colin Grimshaw of the marketing magazine *Campaign* painted as a "disaffected, thrill-seeking young male with [a] goatee beard and a penchant for Eminem and substance abuse."[66] Perhaps the most visible of these campaigns was PepsiCo's "Do the Dew," a slogan that itself rang of substance abuse.[67] Pepsi advertisers urged Americans that the best way to parachute off a cliff on a mountain bike was to also "slam" a special wide-mouth can of Dew. The marketing and presentation of sport utility vehicles (SUVs) provided a similar example of the commercial appropriation of extreme sports, a discourse that might be characterized as "safe danger" or "suicide chic."[68] Nissan's Xterra, for example, came self-consciously equipped with a first-aid medical kit. Advertisements for the company's X-Trail featured the unlikely image of a broken arm X-ray, reflecting the danger and adventurism of extreme sports. (This was not, apparently, a reference to the SUV's high rollover rates.) Already coded into the SUV were the pleasures of cruising the home-front battlefield in an armored capsule, a theme most succinctly captured by the Hummer, a civilian version of the distinctly American military vehicle. Writing in the *New York Times*, James G. Cobb called the Hummer— with its logo suspended over a horizon shot of planet Earth—a symbol of unilateralism, exceptionalism, "preemptive driving," and the "Army of One."[69] With its rebel yell and search for new ways to tempt death, the discourse of extreme sports found a comfortable home in post-9/11 symbolic landscape. Indeed, the War on Terror appeared as a veritable war of rebels, presided over by a "rebel in chief" who battled the rebel at large.[70] The satirical newspaper, *The Onion*, picked up on the rhetoric of "extremism" common to both the new war and sport in their February 14, 2007, article entitled "Radical Islamic Extremists Snowboard into U.S. Embassy."

A number of films set out to capture the seemingly natural confluence of war, rebellious consumerism, and extreme sports. The 2002 hit spy film *xXx* (pronounced "triple X") self-consciously melded the discourse of extreme sports into a post-Cold War terrorism motif. *The Boston Globe* described the film's main character, Xander Cage—played by Vin Diesel—as a "brutish and inarticulate" James Bond.[71] Instead of an Aston Martin, Cage drives a Pontiac GTO. Instead of a tuxedo, Cage dons massive sheepskin coats, thermal undershirts, and a host of tattoos: 3 Xs on the back of his neck, two guns crossed to form an X on the small of his back, and on his arms a tribal band, a bull charging out of flames, the words "dis," "order," and "chaos." In the film, Cage is the star of "The Xander Zone," a website that features his own extreme sports exploits, and he lives in what looks to be an abandoned industrial underground lair filled with half-pipes, street urchins, and slinky women. After his arrest performing an illegal stunt, he is given the chance to either run missions for the National Security Agency or go to jail. Cage chooses to be sent into Prague to infiltrate of group of expatriated Chechnyan terrorists named Anarchy 99, whose goal it is to poison all of Western Europe with biological weapons of mass destruction. He eventually saves the day by infiltrating the group, stopping the doomsday device, and getting the girl. Given the resonances with the War on Terror, it might not be surprising that in an interview with Larry King, *New York Times* columnist Maureen Dowd referred to Secretary of State Donald Rumsfeld's new vision of the military as a "Vin Diesel kind of light force that would speed through, and you could intervene in more countries."[72] Dowd's shorthand revealed the intimate interplay between the extreme sports and popular understandings of the changing geo-political landscape.

For Xander Cage, the military does not offer a chance to serve his country. Rather, the dramatic core of the film centers on the fantasy of a civilian utilizing the battlefield as a gigantic extreme sports playground. As one critic pointed observed of the film, "Neither words of ideology nor dialectic pass the lips of these spies good or bad—they just want to have fun and cause a little trouble, not unlike the teenagers that are considered to be the film's primary audience."[73] Indeed, Cage is much less concerned with being a hero for a righteous cause than getting his thrills in this new amped-up and militarized version of his extreme life. As he parachutes from a plane on a mission, Cage spits into the camera, "I live for this sh*t!" While being hunted by a helicopter gunship at a cocaine production compound in Colombia, Cage executes some of his more spectacular feats, striking poses all within the idiom of motorcross dirt biking. On snowboard, he successfully smothers a group of Anarchy 99 terrorists in an avalanche while evading their snowmobiled pursuits. At the climax of the film, while chasing down a remote-control hydrofoil containing the deadly biological weapon, he launches into the air by means of an American flag-emblazoned parasail. Just before leaving the ground, he aptly frames the drama not in terms of any kind of moral imperative, but rather barks, "I wish I had a camera!"

Gazing into the Abyss

With these words, Mr. Cage identifies one of the notable features of the extreme sports aesthetic, the first-person camera. In contrast to spectator sports, where the gaze moves through a variety of audience positions, the rationale for the camera in extreme sports discourse is to project the viewer into the endangered body itself. This aesthetic owes itself to the increasingly small and inexpensive hand-held video camera, which entered into skateboarding, BMX and other sports as a vital tool. The world of skydiving and its more experimental half-sister sky surfing further integrated the camera with the

Figure 2.2 (left) Slim Pickens riding an atom bomb in the satire *Dr. Strangelove* (1964); (right) Vin Diesel riding a weapon of mass destruction with extreme chic in *xXx* (2002).

helmet cam.[74] This technology became instrumental in the commercialization of extreme sports. Televised events like the X-Games, for example, featured a mixture of traditional stationary shooting techniques (mostly for establishing scene) and heavy doses of wobbly, hand-held, and helmet-cam shots. The heart of the extreme visual aesthetic thus became the radical identification with the body at its limits, swinging from a bungee line or hanging onto a cliff face, with the viewer positioned as virtual subject in the death drama.

These camera relations played a key role in the 2002 film *Extreme Ops*, a film that, as its name suggests, performed at the intersection of war and extreme sports. At the center of the story is a team of athletes, adventure-seekers, and television producers out to shoot an advertisement for a hand-held video camera. The producers of this advertisement want footage of snowboarders and skiers racing in front of an avalanche, so the team heads up to the Austrian Alps to shoot both the avalanche and the downhill stunts. Along the way, the team accidentally captures film of an international Serb terrorist group in hiding. The team later discovers that the terrorists plan to "blow up the court in Holland in 48 hours." Mistaken for CIA agents, the advertising team is then drawn into an extreme stunts-riddled battle to the death, which eventually ends well for the team but not for the terrorists. The battle royal triggers an avalanche that the team successfully evades, the footage of which the team later uses in their ad campaign. In this way, *Extreme Ops* self-consciously positions the discourse of war and terrorism as the ultimate backdrop for an extreme adventure.

The most immediately striking visual feature of the film is centrality of hand-held cameras and the aesthetic of the first-person virtual player. The sequence for the opening credits sets up this aesthetic. The film leads the viewer through a variety of hand-held camera point-of-view positions. We see, for example, a skydiver in freefall before we zoom out to realize we are witnessing the scene on the mini-cam viewfinder of another diver. We see a river full of kayakers, some of whom have cameras themselves, before we are transported again out of a camera viewfinder into the body of one dangled above the river shooting the action. The scene presents the activity as a tunnel of screens and subjectivities, the gaze passing through one falling camera-body after another. The ubiquity of the hand-held camera reaches absurd levels at many points in the film. In the logic of the X-game, the more life-threatening the situation, the more necessary the camera. When this credo is taken past the point of utility, it provides a glimpse into some important visual and thematic relationships. A particularly poignant example of this occurs at the dramatic apex of the film when one of our heroes is stranded on a cliff face and hunted by terrorists circling in a helicopter. Finding himself dangling from a rope in a vulnerable spot, the character decides the best course of action is to film his own imminent death. Instinctively he points the camera up the barrel of his attacker's shotgun. Here, in the idiom of the helmet cam, the viewer's gaze switches to the camera's perspective and assumes the victim's point of view. As viewers, we are then asked to make substitutions. The death limit staring into our cam is not the ground rising up to meet us but rather a "terrorist" with a bead on our foreheads. As counterpart to the terrorist, this X-gamer/soldier/ viewer is intent on witnessing his own death through the viewfinder. Importing the discourse of extreme sports into the context of terrorism demands that we read the encounter as a ritual of pleasure, perhaps the ultimate extreme sport, one whose brush with death is so intimate that it demands to be filmed—not *even* at the risk of one's life, but *especially* at the risk of one's life.

The 2008 film *Cloverfield* featured a similar economy of the extreme war gaze. As a kind of *Blair Witch Project*-does-9/11, the film relied entirely on a hand-held camera as plot device, which begins with some young professionals having a party in a Manhattan loft. During the party, an enormous, unseen monster—presumably a space alien—attacks and begins to level the city. One character, who has been documenting the party, captures all of the ensuing action on hand-held video. The video tape comprises the entirety of *Cloverfield*, which, we are told, the military eventually recovered from the rubble of "the area previously known as Central Park." The references to 9/11 in the film are too many to list, including the vertical collapse of the Empire State Building.

Figure 2.3 The ultimate extreme sport: the death ritual of player and terrorist in *Extreme Ops* (2002).

Cloverfield thus becomes an exercise in transporting the viewer onto the streets of lower Manhattan on such a day to experience the terror first-hand. Indeed, the cause of the destruction runs a distant second place to the immediacy of the first-person experience within the destruction. More than once on this harrowing journey, the viewer experiences a first-person style death as the camera falls from one victim's hands to the next. The 9/11-as-theme-park-ride metaphor is not so subtle. One of the film's gimmicks is that the destructive action has been recorded over the characters' previous trip to Coney Island. The Coney Island trip tape occasionally bleeds through into the apocalyptic scenes of Manhattan's demise, thus forming a parallel running joke. The end of the film reads as a punch line. When burning rubble engulfs the camera along with the two remaining characters, the scene cuts to the end of the amusement park adventure where the same two characters admit they had a pretty fun day. The opportunity to be visually transported into the danger zone has come to be a primary pleasure of contemporary culture. The discourse of extreme sports serves as a model for the relationships among consumer, camera, and battlefield that increasingly informs the virtual citizen-soldier's relationship to state violence.

These logics translated into the more proper war film genre during this period as well. Films like *Black Hawk Down* and *Saving Private Ryan* were in part or whole predicated on experientially delivering the viewer, through *cinéma vérité* aesthetics, into this environment. The most explicit positioning of war as

Figure 2.4 The embattled gang with camera intact in *Cloverfield* (2008).

extreme playground can be found in the first major war film released following 9/11, *Behind Enemy Lines* (2001). The film depicts the story of Navy pilot Lieutenant Chris Burnett (Owen Wilson) who is bored with the routine of life on an aircraft carrier during the American-NATO intervention in Bosnia. Unless he gets to see some action, Burnett tells his father-figure, Admiral Reigart (Gene Hackman), he intends to resign. Reigart scolds this petulance and sends Burnett off on a Christmas Day reconnaissance flight near a no-fly zone. Ever the rebel, Burnett decides that he and his co-pilot ought to break code and take some photos in the no-fly zone. Immediately a group of Serb militants on the ground shoots them down. Burnett parachutes into the countryside where the militants relentlessly pursue him because they suspect he has taken pictures of fresh mass graves. Back on the aircraft carrier, Admiral Reigart attempts to send in a rescue team, but a distinctly French NATO commander thwarts his plan because doing so would "destabilize the peace process." With no help, Burnett must make his way several miles through the wilderness to a legal pick-up point, all the while dodging Serbian bullets. Near the end of the film, Admiral Reigart has clearly had enough of this red tape. He disobeys orders with a bellicose "Let's get our boy back!" that echoes through the corridors of the ship and into the movie trailers. The film ends with the helicopter pick-up of Burnett and a wholesale slaughter of dozens of angry Serbian militia men.[75]

Behind Enemy Lines clearly follows a number of predecessors, continuing in the tradition of the soldier rescue story thoroughly revived from *Rambo: First Blood Part II* (1985) and *Saving Private Ryan* (1998). The film is thus relieved of engaging any issues larger than the immediate crisis of a soldier and the support-the-troops response that has increasingly worked to depoliticize the question of war. The film also borrows the go-pilled technofetishism that made *Top Gun* such a popular hit and recruiting success, with music video speed cuts, freeze and flash frames, and high-speed tracking shots all riding a soundtrack of power chords and electronica. As Burnett's F/A-18 Superhornet slingshots off the carrier deck, the soundtrack lyrics chant: "He's got a brand new car/Looks like a Jaguar/It's got leather seats/It's got a CD player." Indeed, many of the bookend and transition shots aboard the aircraft carrier deck hearken back to *Top Gun*, with their slow-motion, flight-suited, helmet-carrying heroes. The emphasis on cool weaponry was evident in the decision to hold the film's premier gala for the critics at the San Diego naval base aboard the *USS Nimitz*, the same aircraft carrier generously supplied by the Navy for use in the film's production.

Beyond these themes, *Behind Enemy Lines* offers viewers a story of the battlefield playground. The entire film revolves around the issue of whether Burnett will find the Navy exciting enough to stay on board. When he is not allowed to fly one day, Burnett remarks to his co-pilot, "[We're] wound up tight today—guess that's the price of peace," and the two go off to toss around a football on deck. Frustrated, Burnett offers a letter of resignation to Admiral Reigart saying, "If we're at war, why don't we act like it?" Reigart resolves to keep the letter "in his back pocket." Later, just before Burnett's plane is shot down, his co-pilot asks about his possible resignation: "Aren't you going to miss all this excitement?" he facetiously asks. Burnett replies in kind, "Oh, absolutely," just before the first missile signals the alarm on their radar. The scene could be read with a be-careful-what-you-wish-for moral, except that we learn that Burnett got what he wanted, a near-death experience. The film answers Burnett's complaint of "Are we having fun yet?" by shooting down his plane.

As Burnett parachutes down, he travels from the polished world of *Top Gun* to a washed out landscape rendered in grainy blues and grays. The Serbian countryside is foggy, devoid of sunlight, and the towns are bullet-riddled husks strewn with rubble and twisted, corrugated metal. The effect is essential to the idea that Burnett has indeed crossed a line from the clean, safe orderliness of the aircraft carrier to the chaos and filth of a war-torn land full of chain-smoking militia men and wizened civilians. Here Burnett undergoes series of terrible trials. He is hunted, shot at, and blown up. His close friend is executed in front of him. He survives a tank blast so close it deprives him of his hearing. (Here, in experiential mode, the film's soundtrack goes dead for a few moments apart from the sound of a heartbeat.) At one point, Burnett buries himself in a stack of dead bodies while his hunters bayonet the earth around him. Such events would normally be points of trauma, but the logic of the film defines them as points of pleasure. They are reasons for him to reconsider his previous desire to get out of the Navy. Upon Burnett's eventual rescue following the final climactic blood-bath, Reigart hands him the letter (from his back pocket, of course) as if to ask "Do you still want to resign?" With a smirk, Burnett crumples the letter and tosses it out of the helicopter as it lifts into the sky. The film finishes with a few biographical still photos overlaid with whatever-happened-to blurbs. We learn that Burnett "stayed in the Navy," and we logically infer that he did so not because he had the opportunity to do something good, but because he got to taste the adrenaline of a near-death experience.

Extreme Branding and the Millennial Military

The US Navy had a heavy hand in producing *Behind Enemy Lines*. As per the usual transaction of this kind, in exchange for military equipment and personnel (the *USS Carl Vinson*, Apache helicopters, fighter planes, uniforms, gear, etc.), Twentieth Century Fox gave the military script-doctoring rights.[76] It is thus no surprise that the film mimicked a recruiting poster. In this case, however, the Navy went further to make explicit use of the film in their new "Navy: Accelerate Your Life" recruitment campaign ads. Flashing scenes from the film on a bed of guitar-textured electronica, the ad asked, "Wish they would make a movie about your job?"—another way of asking, "Want to step through the screen?" The Navy ran the spot in theatres during the entire run of *Behind Enemy Lines* and also included it in the preview section of the film's video release. Naturally, the ad featured heroic shots on the deck of the aircraft carrier and the glamorization of gadgetry. As John Davis, the film's producer, stated, "The movie should do for [the Navy] what they thought it would: to show a brand-new generation that being a pilot is really fantastic, unless you get shot down."[77] The curious thing is that, unlike the main character in *Top Gun*, Burnett's plane does get shot down. Moreover, this feature of the film is prominently portrayed in the ad, which shows Burnett in mortal danger, running through a hail of bullets, slithering through mass graves, and dodging explosions. Rather than appeal to career advancement, job skills, or patriotism, the ad offers to the prospect of being shot at, a strange enticement to join any organization. Here the Navy gives an official stamp of authenticity to what would normally be an absurd Hollywood fantasy, a vision of war where the soldier dodges danger as if he were wearing "magic underwear," in the words of one movie critic.[78] More importantly, the Navy's choice to appeal to the battlefield playground speaks to the virtual citizen-soldier who is not only accustomed to consuming the clean war but also compelled to experience its safe danger first-hand.

The *Behind Enemy Lines* spot was a continuation of the Navy's $40 million "Accelerate Your Life" campaign, whose first ad aired in March 2001 on CBS's *Survivor*.[79] *Adweek* described the campaign as "in your face" and relying upon "extreme sports-type training" footage. A print ad for the campaign captured

Figure 2.5 Two ads from the Navy "Accelerate Your Life" campaign featuring war as extreme sport. (left) A television ad featuring *Behind Enemy Lines* (2001) with the main character running through enemy gunfire; (right) a print ad equating war with a leisure activity.

the dominant flavor, featuring two images of a young man, on the left in a wetsuit holding a surfboard and on the right in uniform holding a rifle. A caption unites the two images: "When the weekend is over, say hello to Monday morning." Implying that the weekend never ends, the ad portrays military affairs as an extension of playtime. Other branches followed up on these extreme themes. Just weeks following 9/11, the Colorado Army National Guard unveiled a recruiting campaign called "Escape from reality." The website read, "Get your thrills from the originators of Extreme Sports—the U.S. Army! We were skydiving, parachuting, mountain climbing, rappelling and 4-wheeling before it was considered cool."[80] A number of military branches found the demographic of those who watch or attend "adrenaline sports," from NASCAR to BMX, to be a "gold mine" for recruiting efforts.[81] (The fantasy of combining stock car and armed vehicle was later replayed in the 2008 action film *Death Race*.) The Marines began using a no-ropes rock-climbing motif in their ads. The Air Force aired an ad where a young man jumps off a 50-foot waterfall to save his sister's backpack. As he rises to the surface, the scene has changed to helicopter airlift. The words "We've been waiting for you" appear at the bottom of the screen. This ad, which began airing in 2002 as part of the Air Force's new $30 million "Cross into the Blue" campaign, followed a similar logic to the Navy's "When the weekend is over . . ." that position the military as a way to "accelerate" or "cross into" the next level of extreme. Army recruiting also took the extreme sports motif and ran, and this was not just limited to the decision to build the Philadelphia's Franklin Mills Mall "Army Experience Center" purposefully near a popular indoor skate park.[82] Since 1981, Army recruiting had been waged under the industrious and career-oriented "Be All You Can Be," which became the flagship slogan of the all-volunteer force.[83] The "Army of One" campaign, christened in 2001, cast the military as an ultimate field on which to play out the pleasures of risk and survival. One of the first and most visible ads, "Ice Soldiers," features a lone figure in climbing gear making his way up a snowy mountain peak. The sound-track is punctuated with heavy breathing, snowy footsteps, and computerized blips as the character checks his high-tech watch and global positioning device. Unlike previous recruitment ads, there is no visual indication that this person is in the army. "I am a soldier, an army of one," he tells us. "Even though I am a part of the strongest army in the world, I am my own force." Another ad entitled "Desert Run" repeats these themes point-for-point as the camera closes in on a lone runner lit by lens flares in another hostile environment.

The new "Army of One" motif provoked bewilderment. Kevin Baker wrote in *Harper's* magazine, "Surely this has to be one of the most disingenuous recruiting slogans that have ever been devised, for no army has ever been about promoting individualism but rather its exact opposite."[84] Indeed, the first

Figure 2.6 Extreme recruiting. (top) "Army of One" television ads; (bottom) Army NASCAR print ad and National Guard BMX 2008 campus tour at the University of Georgia (photo by the author).

significant appearance of the phrase appeared a decade earlier with the film *Army of One* (1994) featuring small-time action star Dolph Lundgren. In this film Lundgren plays an embattled bank robber on the run from the police and other thieves. The "rogue element" sense of the phrase was invoked in 2003 by the mayor of Murphy, North Carolina, when at a press conference he described a terrorist—an abortion clinic bomber—as an "army of one."[85] The "Army of One" campaign may have been at odds with traditional military sensibilities, but its underlying rhetorics conformed to the dominant dramas of consumer culture with its hyper-individualism and rebel ethic. Secretary of the Army Louis Caldera, a Harvard Business School graduate, described the strategy with respect to the target demographic: "It's the me-now group . . . They are going to get the ethic of selfless service, duty, honor and country in basic training and in every unit they are assigned to. But you've got to get them in the door to try selfless service."[86] The slogan also suggested unity, as in the "one army," a double meaning that allowed ad makers to evade the charge that such a campaign promoted values contrary to military service.[87] As a motif, the campaign resonated with the geopolitics of Empire, an imminent military field where the one army meets the army of one, the very structure of asymmetrical warfare.

Because the pleasures of the battlefield playground have become so widely available, the notion of "recruitment" cannot be contained as it once was, separated from propaganda and other forms of public relations. Rather, it is continuous with the larger rhetorics of the interactive war. The recruitment metaphor that has come to animate the virtual citizen-soldier functions, more-over, according to the logics of the brand. Rather than sell a specific career path, the military is increasingly presented to the entire social spectrum as an identity to be vicariously consumed. As such, an "Army of One" and "Acceler-ate Your Life" have joined the likes of "Tommy Boy" and "Just Do It." In 2001, all four major military branches self-consciously renovated their recruiting strategies to stake their new brand identities.[88] In the case of the Army, this included a new logo—a white star with gold and black edging—that eventually made its way into the Army's product line of sports gear. In 2008, the Army formalized this practice with a new "All American Army" branded fashion line marketed through Sears.[89] The Army also began sponsoring rodeo teams and, followed by all of the other major branches, a NASCAR team.[90] The new strategy also included the seamless melding of a series of television spots with the newly-launched website, GoArmy.com, the suffix of which indicated a new marketing philosophy.

This broad invitation to participate in the Army brand extended in other directions, too. As part of the Army of One campaign, the Army aired ads urging one to visit the GoArmy.com website and view a set of "webisodes" featuring recruits going through the rigors of basic training. Produced by the Leo Burnett ad agency with a $200 million contract, the online series gave the campaign a highly personal touch, featuring both grueling obstacle course challenges and sit-down interviews in the confessional style pioneered by *The Real World*. The series exchanged the standard themes of patriotic service, career training, and world travel for personal thrills and the satisfaction of having met a fearful challenge. One television ad for the series, for example, features Richard, a young man who must cross a gauntlet called "Victory Tower," a three-story wooden structure that must be scaled after climbing a rope ladder and braving a rope monkey bridge. The drill sergeant barks, "Your duty today is personal courage." Richard tells us that his "biggest fear is climb-ing down." We see several shots of his anguished face and hear cheers from an invisible audience above the sound of his heavy breathing. "The tower is going to be a rope and me, and I'm going to have to come down on my own," he says. A voiceover narrates, "Today, Richard will climb victory tower. It's forty-five feet high. Once you get to the top, the view [is] . . . breathtaking. Especially if you're afraid of heights." The drill sergeant sums up the message: "This is the only place you can do this, in basic training, so enjoy the ride." In the final scene, the fish-eyed camera plummets headlong down the rope toward the ground in the idiom of the helmet-cammed bungee jump. These motifs were prevalent in the campaign, where the admakers made liberal use of rope ladders and parachutes.

What does this merging of extreme sports and war discourse mean? On one level, this chapter has argued that extreme sports culture provides a way of negotiating the new narratives of the global body politic through the body. More significantly, however, the discourse of extreme sports has been central in integrating war into consumerist practices. In contrast to spectacular consumption, extreme sports provides a set of pleasures that translate war into an interactive event, a battlefield playground that invites the entry of the virtual citizen-soldier. That is, extreme sports provide a storyline and purpose that enables the interactive consumption of state violence. The problem inherent to the discourse is that it steers the citizen away from deliberative questions like "Is this war just?" and toward an anti-democratic enclosure in a universe where there are no such questions or responsibilities, only the pleasures of vicariously dealing out or experiencing violence. The extreme sports ethos perhaps played itself out most vividly in the realm of reality television, of which the Army-produced extreme sports reality show was only the tip of the iceberg. Indeed, the Army show floated in a veritable sea of war-themed reality television let loose through cooperation between television studios and the Pentagon. The so-called "embedded reporting" system devised for the press coverage of the 2003 invasion of Iraq was perhaps the purest form of this new genre, marshalling all of the pleasures of the first-person, battlefield playground.

Chapter 3

Reality War

Boot Camp for Everyone

Early in 2003, during the US invasion and occupation of Iraq, the extent to which war coverage took on the hues of so-called "reality television" started to draw attention. Matthew Gilbert of the *Boston Globe* introduced the metaphor by noting that reporters who had once hosted reality programs—CNN's Anderson Cooper (*The Mole*) and CBS's Julie Chen (*Big Brother*)—now hosted the embedded war. Moreover, Gilbert observed, field correspondents looked like *Survivor* hosts.

> The direct-to-camera confessions of "Married by America" contestants are cousins to the crying-war-widow spots, and the I-almost-drowned "Fear Factor" interviews are in the same family as the comments by soldiers in Iraq. Indeed, reality shows that revolve around physical challenges may be the most awkward right now, as they mirror the risks of soldiers whose lives truly are at stake.[1]

By the time Gilbert voiced this realization, however, reality television had thoroughly been transformed into a robust arm of the military-entertainment complex. Beginning at the turn of the twenty-first century, the Pentagon had colonized the field, extending its public relations assistance to a variety of programs. The networks made out well on these deals too. When the televised 2003 invasion of Iraq arrived, all of the necessary templates for the "reality TV war" were in place ready to be mobilized by the new embedded reporting system, which was itself inspired by a reality show. As the *Washington Post* put it, "If 'reality' television programming is, as some TV execs have suggested, crack cocaine, their biggest dealer these days is the Pentagon."[2]

As an offshoot of its new "Accelerate Your Life" recruitment campaign in March of 2001, the Navy made a deal with MTV and its show *Real World/Road*

Rules Extreme Challenge. Here, the cast of *The Real World* competed for points against the cast of *Road Rules* in emergency submarine drills similar to those undergone by new enlistees. The Navy provided the contestants with mono-grammed uniforms, "fine Navy chow," training, and beds in the barracks. According to the Navy publication *All Hands*, "From the moment they arrived at the submarine school, the competitors were treated as submarine students fresh out of boot camp."[3] The drills carried the death-defying flavor of extreme sports, one of which featured teams attempting to manage a crisis of a sub-marine cabin filling with cold saltwater at 1,200 gallons per minute. "It was so cool, like being in a movie," said Julie of *The Real World*. "It was so *Hunt for Red October*," an apt observation indeed as *The Hunt for Red October* (1990) also received extensive cooperation from the Navy in its production of the submarine mystique.[4] This episode of *Extreme Challenge*, however, featured an altogether different fantasy designed for MTV's coveted 16–25-year-old age bracket, a fantasy not of marveling at the might of military technology, but rather one that walked the viewer through the pleasures of the civilian-playing-soldier.

The Air Force took heed of the Navy's successes in reality television. While the submarine episode aired, the Air Force joined MTV to begin shooting the first two-episode finale in the ten-year history of *Road Rules*. According to Master Sergeant Mark Haviland of Air Force public affairs, the hour of airtime "represented months of behind-the-scenes coordination and effort throughout the Air Force."[5] In all, 30 million "recruitment-age viewers" watched the road rulers train with the 421st Ground Combat Readiness Squadron in a humanitarian medical relief scenario, which included simulated enemy fire and casualties. The finale reached a climax when the *Road Rules* team was taken up in a KC-10 Extender aircraft to witness the airborne refueling of the B-2 Stealth Bomber, showcased as the most expensive plane in the fleet.

As the *Road Rules* team did their drills, TBS Superstation piloted a two-hour special called *War Games*, a "pseudo-documentary" produced with heavy involvement from the Pentagon. The show featured readiness exercises per-formed by actual members of the Air Force, Navy, and Marines. Apparently unaware of the Pentagon's concurrent projects, one reviewer writing for *Variety* magazine noted that the show was "easily digestible," portraying military life "like a 'Real World vs. Road Rules' challenge show, absent the confessionals and seething sexual tensions."[6] In addition to the guitar-driven soundtrack, the hosts of the show undoubtedly set the tone. Football icon Howie Long offered his persona as a long-time Fox NFL football announcer. Anne Powell, daughter of Secretary of State Colin Powell and brother of FCC Chairman Michael Powell, accompanied him and provided a certain institutional gravitas. *War Games* also promoted itself with a video game designed by the company

WildTangent, which specialized in the use of games to promote offline brands. The "War Games" online game appeared on the superstation.com website two weeks before the show giving players the chance to participate in some of the same readiness exercises featured on the show. The game put players in command of military vehicles such as the M2 Bradley Fighting Vehicle, the M1-A2 Abrams Tank, and the Apache Helicopter. According to Richard Turner, director of TBS's online marketing, the game allowed further penetration into the "Regular Guy" audience, "push[ing] our enhanced television efforts to a new level by putting our viewers directly into the action of a combat scenario."[7] The central role of the video game illustrates the general thrust of this new genre of militarized reality television, which encouraged viewers not only to watch but to actively and seamlessly project themselves into the military fantasy.

War Games was not the only game in town, however. On the same day— March 28, 2001—Fox network inaugurated its new reality series, *Boot Camp*, whose debut performed so well in the ratings that Fox contemplated adding an extra episode to the season.[8] The show put teams of civilians through a version of Marine boot camp training (excluding weapons training and academics) at a specially designed set in southern Florida. While the show's *Survivor*-style elimination plotline was an obvious retread of an established genre, this was new territory for the military.[9] The entertainment liaison officer for the Marines, Captain Shawn Haney, expressed her enthusiasm for the cooperative project with Fox: "Right now, reality TV is the big thing. We are the first service to step into the survival reality shows."[10] Though the reality TV genre offered a sure-fire way to reach the hearts and minds of younger viewers, the show's relationship to "reality" was less clear. Haney told the *New York Times* that the show "is not Marine boot camp, and we never pretend that it is." In the same breath, Haney also noted that her office "looked at [*Boot Camp*] as an opportunity to give the public a glimpse into the Marine Corps."[11] The confusion over the show's representational value did not end there. Executive producer Eric Schotz noted that the show's success stemmed from a certain familiarity: "From movies, books, and TV shows, everybody knows what [the military is like] and everybody understands it."[12] Indeed, from its conception, *Boot Camp* relied less on actual boot camp than on the Hollywood version implanted firmly in the American imagination by films like *Full Metal Jacket* (1987), *Forrest Gump* (1994), and others.[13] The show flickered in this twilight zone between waking and dreaming life, providing yet another entry point for civilians to play out military fantasies. *Boot Camp* thus served as the Marine Corps equivalent to the Army's web-based boot camp reality show that aired during the same period. If Army of One series represented the military's embrace of the commercial aesthetic, *Boot Camp* extended the reach of commercial reality TV into the military sphere. Meeting in the middle, the two imbued one another with new meanings. Commercial endeavors like *Boot Camp* suddenly resonated with official legitimacy. Likewise, depoliticized values of entertainment and play struck deep into the public meaning of the military.

Boot Camp's resemblance to *Survivor* may have been what eventually prompted *Survivor* creator Mark Burnett to get into the war-themed reality game. Burnett had ideal training for this kind of venture, having served as an advisor to the British Special Air Service in Central America in the 1980s as it was ravaged by guerilla and counterinsurgency warfare. Burnett went on to launch his television career as the creator of extreme sports special *Eco-Challenge* in the mid-1990s. After establishing himself, Burnett conceived *Survivor* for CBS, whose first season ran in 2000. Francine Prose mused in *Harper's Magazine*:

> Reading Mark Burnett's resume cannot help but make *Survivor* seem even more like a weekly dispatch from the Central American terrorist training camp to which he may have been headed when he was lured off course by the siren song of Hollywood.[14]

In December of 2001, Burnett assembled contestants from all four military branches to compete in the USA Network's *Eco-Challenge: U.S. Armed Forces Championship*, a dangerous, cross-country race across Alaska, narrated by Charlton Heston. For the 2002 spring season, Burnett devised *Combat Missions* for the USA Network, where two dozen ex-military officers competed in a variety of war games for cash prizes. The show was shot on an Air Force base in California with the assistance of Pentagon advisors.[15] Burnett brought with him a stable of workhorses from previous ventures, too, including one of the final four contestants on the previous year's *Survivor*, a former Navy SEAL by the name of Rudy Boesch. Boesch had already lent his fame to Blue Box Toys, who marketed a Navy SEAL action figure with his visage, so he was already somewhat of a celebrity reality soldier.[16] Burnett's first pick for a contestant on the show was another former Navy SEAL named Scott Helvenston, whom Burnett had met on *Raid Gauloises*, an international adventure race that served as the precursor to *Eco-Challenge*.

Amidst the pyrotechnics of *Combat Missions*, the story of Scott Helvenston offers a sobering lesson in the reality of war. After finishing his term with the show, two friends he had met on the set, John and Kathy Potter, offered Helvenston a position with largest private mercenary firm on the government payroll, Blackwater USA. Helvenston was assigned to guard the architect of the occupation, Paul Bremer, in Baghdad's "green zone." At the last minute, Blackwater moved Helvenston to a subcontractor who provided security for army supply convoys, an infinitely more dangerous job. Moreover, the sub-contractor had cut corners on essentials like vehicle armor.[17] On March 31,

2004, in the middle of Fallujah, Sunni rebels ambushed Helvenston's convoy dragging his and four other contractors' charred bodies through the streets before hanging them from a bridge. The insurgents taped and distributed the footage of the gruesome incident, which immediately seized international headlines and played on a rolling television loop. The juxtaposition of reality television and the realities of war spoke volumes. Burnett responded that, "It makes it all seem so much closer." Blending realities, he then added, "It reminds me of *Black Hawk Down*." [18]

On the heels of *Combat Missions*, the Air Force followed with *American Fighter Pilot*, a cooperative venture with CBS. The Air Force entertainment liaison office signed on two longtime associates to co-produce the reality show. Tony Scott had directed *Top Gun* (1986), which was perhaps the purest and most successful example of Hollywood film pressed into the service of military recruitment. His brother, Ridley Scott, brought with him his signature techno-noir style of *Black Hawk Down* (2001). Both films had given the military the right to steer the script in exchange for military hardware and consultation. *American Fighter Pilot* followed suit. The reality show shadowed three prospective pilots at Florida's Tyndall Air Force Base. *AFP* director

Figure 3.1 (top) *Combat Missions* on the USA Network and contestant Scott Helvenston; (bottom) broadcast of the 2004 insurgent ambush of Helvenston's motorcade in Fallujah, Iraq.

Jesse Negron described the show's hook as how an "everyday guy" becomes a "trained killer."[19] Aesthetically, one critic noted that the show "makes *Moulin Rouge* look static" with the effect of "MTV pilots" in "flying race cars."[20] This was precisely what the show's benefactors had wished for, and according to Negron, representatives from the Air Force "loved it."[21] A major part of the *AFP* aesthetic included a point of view from the cockpit, consummating the viewer's interactive identification with the "everyday guy" trainee. This particular aspect of the technofetish aesthetic began to appear regularly during the 1991 Gulf War, usually in the form of Pentagon-issued footage. *AFP* provided it in quantity and concentration beginning in March of 2002, a preface to the saturation of television war journalism with the cockpit cam during coverage of the 2003 invasion of Iraq. The show also effortlessly absorbed 9/11 into its plot. Though CBS shot the show before 9/11, the network took advantage of the attacks by lengthening *AFP*'s concept to include the pilots' deployments overseas. Moreover, the producers included 9/11 as a major motif in the show's opening teaser, which rapidly intercut frames of *Top Gun*-style aerial training with actual footage of airliners plunging into the Twin Towers. Grainy images of President Bush seated in the oval office attend his voice crackling through a lo-fi voice filter ("our country is strong . . .") as if he were issuing orders to a militarized populace through a gritty transceiver.

If Viacom—owner of CBS, MTV, and VH1—could produce the "MTV pilot," perhaps it could also produce the "VH1 soldier." In June of 2002, VH1 began airing *Military Diaries*, a show that put cameras in the hands of soldiers in Afghanistan. While a more measured documentary approach to war-themed reality television, the show satisfied the post-9/11 fever to virtually enter the body of the soldier through a first-person aesthetic. With cooperation and censoring oversight by the Pentagon, the show purported to show "what it's like to be a young man or woman in the armed forces right now," according to director R.J. Cutler, who had previously directed *The War Room* (1993). As a VH1 production, a primary theme of *Military Diaries* was music, specifically the kind of music soldiers consumed while on the job. According to Cutler, "we are hoping to uncover the soundtrack to the war on terrorism."[22] This metaphor, of course, positions the "war on terrorism" as a production for the screen, perhaps a reality television show itself.

Getting Personal, Depoliticizing War

This bumper crop of war-themed reality television was a culmination of wider cultural trends initiated during Vietnam and extending through the end of the century. Across this period, discourse focusing on the protection or celebration of the war machine displaced arguments regarding the objectives for which the war machine should be used. This gradual "zooming in" on the experience of the soldier paved the way for the eruption of war-themed reality TV at the turn of the twenty-first century. The seeds for this up-close and personal war were planted near the end of the Vietnam War. Chief among them was the use of the POW/MIA by the Nixon administration to justify the continuance of a war whose original justification (i.e. the containment of communism) had lost traction. This rhetorical strategy worked by redefining the purpose of war to a fight to save our own soldiers.[23]

Post-Vietnam war films amplified this new orientation. Here the memory of war has been progressively cleansed of references to political purpose. The period produced a series of existential dramas like *The Deer Hunter* (1978), *Apocalypse Now* (1979), *Platoon* (1986), and *Full Metal Jacket* (1987). These films, Karen Rasmussen and Sharon Downey suggest, can be considered "anti-war" in that they portrayed a pitched battle between militarism and moralism, terms that had previously kept close company in Hollywood's image of the warrior.[24] The serious war film could no longer rely on the Western triumphalism of John Wayne's *The Green Berets* (1968). A striking feature of these nominally "anti-war" films, however, is the lack of a critique of war policy. Indeed, policy, justification, and even the enemy are for the most part absent from the screen. Instead, these films are defined by the ghastly purposelessness of war, from the Russian roulette metaphor in *The Deer Hunter* to the blood sacrifice in *Apocalypse Now*. This emerging class of war films portrayed war as an internal crisis located neither in the field of politics nor between combatants but within the soldier himself.[25]

At the same time, another class of films approached the memory of Vietnam from the opposite direction. These included the *Rambo: First Blood Part II* (1985), the *Missing in Action* franchise (1984, 1985, 1988), and *Uncommon Valor* (1983). Taking Nixon's POW/MIA rhetoric as a central plotline, these films featured hypermasculine characters performing inhuman feats of rescue. Whereas *Apocalypse Now* journeyed into the heart of insanity, *Rambo* sought to re-establish an ordered agon of battle by retrieving American soldiers who had supposedly been left behind. As the projected fantasies of the POW/MIA justification, these films also largely ignored the larger reasons for a war that resulted in the death and imprisonment of American soldiers. Instead the films miniaturize the Vietnam conflict to the immediate crisis of the imprisoned soldier and the intrepid savior.

If the 1980s were a dialectical period between "anti-war" stories of existential crisis and "pro-war" stories of individual rescue, the 1990s began to resolve this stark division by combining "the horror" of an *Apocalypse Now* with a duty-bound *Rambo*. The result was a class of war films characterized by what Frank

Wetta and Martin Novelli call the "new patriotism."[26] These films conspicuously avoided even superficial references to reasons for fighting, but instead reduced the scope of the drama to an immediate crisis of a small group or individual.[27] Most frequently the crisis involves a rescue mission to save an endangered soldier as in *Saving Private Ryan* (1998), *Behind Enemy Lines* (2001), and *Black Hawk Down* (2001). The rescue motif is the staple drama of the "new patriotism" where immediate loyalty to one's comrades in arms fully eclipses any sense of duty to ideal or policy. This new standard answered the WWII question of "why we fight" with "for the soldiers themselves." *Forrest Gump* (1994) portrayed Vietnam from the standpoint of the new patriotism's ideal witness: a blissfully ignorant soul who, upon finding himself quite accidentally in the midst of a firefight with a literally invisible enemy, acts bravely to save his friend. This shift in perspective allowed for the mainstreaming of what Stephen Klein calls the anti-war/pro-soldier war film, a genre of which he takes *Black Hawk Down* to be a prime example.[28] Klein's formulation helps us understand why such films like *Black Hawk Down* or *Saving Private Ryan*—which displayed an ostensibly anti-war gory realism—received full production support from the Pentagon's Hollywood Liaison Office.[29] To be sure, these films speak to post-Vietnam sensibilities, such as the disillusioned aversion to the brutality of war. The new patriotism narrative, however, refigures the purpose of war as the rescue of one's own soldiers. The narrative is thus able to reverse the usual role of violence by selectively harnessing the cruelties of war to justify the soldier's salvation. That is, the crueler the war, the more necessary it is. Most importantly, the narrative takes war out of the realm of public debate by justifying it with the soldier-in-crisis, whose rescue is not up for debate. This is the essential plotline that has come to constitute the "new patriotism": the magnification of the military apparatus, the containment of the drama within the ranks, and the ultimate extraction of war from the sphere of public debate.

These shifts on the big screen encouraged subsequent shifts in perspective on the small screen. A central dramatic spectacle of the 2003 invasion of Iraq was a soldier rescue story. The April 1, 2003, televised rescue of Private First Class Jessica Lynch "from behind enemy lines" illustrated the depoliticized war with remarkable economy. The official Pentagon account of Lynch's rescue appeared to borrow its storyline directly from Spielberg's *Saving Private Ryan*. In fact, NBC aired a made-for-TV movie produced in cooperation with the Pentagon entitled *Saving Jessica Lynch* (2003), which was the highest rated venture of its kind for NBC in twelve years.[30] This official story suggested that Lynch's supply convoy had been ambushed, and though she fought valiantly, she had been captured, brutalized, and held at a hospital controlled by armed insurgents. The story continued that a squad of US commandos stormed the hospital and heroically rescued Lynch from her captors. To illustrate, the

Pentagon released night vision footage of the rescue filmed by cameras fitted to her rescuers' helmets. Though dramatic, Lynch and others quickly revealed it to be a gross falsification of events. The rescue had even been staged to a degree.[31] Beyond its blatant exaggerations, the public relations choice to feature Lynch in the US campaign signals the increased centrality of the rescue narrative in the larger official rhetoric of the war. The heroic story might have been the capture of an enemy commander or an act of self-sacrifice to protect an Iraqi family. Instead the representative anecdote was the rescue of one of our own soldiers: a small, blonde, "damsel in distress." Lynch served as an ideal victim, "one of ours" ostensibly caught in an unprovoked ambush doing her duty on a non-aggressive supply convoy. The drama of victimization was met with a nationally enacted rescue. With cameras literally embedded in the soldiers' helmets, viewers at home assumed the point of view of the rescuers. The drama was simple, unquestionably noble, successful, and freed from the cumbersome need to explain the rightness of the Iraq invasion.

The Lynch episode represented a point where the logics of the new patriotism meshed with the logics of reality television. The narrative of the new patriotism involved stripping off layers of political context until all that

Figure 3.2 Picturing the salvation motif of the new patriotism. (top) *Forrest Gump* (1994) and the televised rescue of Jessica Lynch in 2003; (bottom) *Saving Private Ryan* (1998) and *Saving Jessica Lynch* (2004) posters.

remained was a scene contained within the military itself. The Lynch drama accelerated the trend by "zooming in" to a personalized and experiential war. Moreover, this ostensibly "unscripted" and authenticated representation of a quasi real-time drama provided multiple points of entry into the scene. Mark Andrejevic notes that such an invitation is a defining feature of the reality TV genre, what he calls the "promise of interactivity," the sense that "it really could be you up there on that screen" accompanied by the pretense of the collective, democratic production of the event.[32] In the same vein, Su Holmes argues that reality television tends to flatten the hierarchy of celebrity, which has traversed media from movie "star" to television "personality" to reality television's "ordinary person."[33] Lynch's marked status as "ordinary" provided one point of projection, the equivalent of a randomly chosen contestant. In addition to identifying as captive, the Lynch production's use of helmet-cam technology allowed the viewer to enter the body of the rescuer. Finally, one could participate in the community of viewers who hoped and prayed for Lynch's safe return. The drama thus strove for a sense of live action and unscripted authenticity even while the producers worked backstage to construct the narrative structure. Though her subsequent "confessional" scene (in the form of memoirs and interviews) effectively threw a wrench of reality into the administration's well-oiled PR machine, the Lynch episode functioned in the short run to deliver the reality TV war's most essential element: the chance to step through the screen and experience the TV war in first person.

This opportunity, of course, came at a cost. Andrejevic argues in his insightful treatment of reality television that the "payoff" of the genre—taking over the means of production and the personal opportunity for celebrity—is balanced by an extraction from the individual that he calls "the work of being watched," which is a kind of information-age labor based on willing submission to surveillance.[34] The reality TV war contains its own version of this economy. The labor extracted for the opportunity to experience the safe danger of the battlefield comes in the willingness to abandon a political disposition toward war and instead be immersed in a militarized virtual space. That is, one pays by shedding citizen identity and submitting as a virtual recruit. By the time the Lynch spectacle aired, however, these features had already saturated the public mind in the form of embedded reporting, a Pentagon-press formation that took its cues directly from reality television.

Embedding as Reality TV

The Pentagon's plan to "embed" 500 journalists with individual units during the 2003 invasion of Iraq required that they not only don helmets and flak jackets but also endure a one-week training session.[35] Here reporters learned the usual safety rules as well as techniques for dealing with chemical or biological attacks. This transformative process by which reporters exchanged their civvies for fatigues was a key dramatic moment in the televised war. When the Pentagon initially announced the embedding scheme, mainstream journalism naturally turned self-reflective, excitedly wringing its hands about the dangers and travails that awaited the intrepid reporter. The television war was to be unfiltered, live, and unpredictable; reporters would be in mortal danger and might witness horrific violence; perhaps the viewer too might also witness the true face of war. It was as if the romantic mythos of the "war photographer" had been fermenting an entire century for this moment. Embedding thus positioned itself as a main event with news outlets previewing the coming attractions. While such a viewing economy depended upon the implied promise that the television war could deliver the dubious prize of "live death," the real seduction lie in promising the viewer a vicarious adventure within the ranks. Such was the tone in an *NBC Nightly News* broadcast on the training session at a Ft. Benning, Georgia "boot camp," as it was widely called. Embedded reporter Martha Brandt of *Newsweek* clearly summed up the dramatic kernel, which did not significantly differ from the concept driving Fox's *Boot Camp*: "I mean, there's a comedic element to this because obviously we're, most of us, middle-aged and out of shape. I am in serious pain right now after doing physical readiness training the other day." She added, "And you know, this is the trick, how do you cover these guys up close and personal in order to really tell the story and not get killed?"[36] By raising the stakes, embedding took on the reality TV mantle, placing ordinary people in extraordinary situations to see "what it's like."

The similarities between reality television and the embedded war were not coincidental. Embedding directly followed from an experiment in reality television called *Profiles from the Front Line*, a cooperative venture between ABC and the Pentagon publicly announced in February of 2002. Here ABC assembled two talents destined for the job. The first was action film producer *par excellence*, Jerry Bruckheimer, whose resumé included *Top Gun* (1986), *Black Hawk Down* (2001), *Behind Enemy Lines* (2001), *Armageddon* (1998), and *Pearl Harbor* (2001). Bruckheimer's status as the most commercially successful producer in the world was due in no small part to his uniquely symbiotic relationship with the Pentagon, which assisted many of his major ventures.[37] ABC also enlisted the help of Bertram van Munster, creator of the show that defined the reality TV "crimetime" genre, *COPS*. Having worked together on another reality show, *The Amazing Race*, Bruckheimer and van Munster were already well acquainted. Not surprisingly, this combination of talent produced a show that read very much like a cross between *COPS* and *Black Hawk Down*. *Profiles from the Front Line* featured cameras that followed soldiers in Afghanistan, mixing police raids with compelling character sketches of soldiers.[38] According to van Munster, Vice President Dick Cheney and Secretary of Defense Donald Rumsfeld personally signed off on the project. Phil Strub, who had brokered many such deals between Hollywood and the military as head of the Pentagon's entertainment liaison office, set out to manage the endeavor.[39]

Profiles was the brainchild of Victoria Clarke, who served as an advisor to Defense Secretary Donald Rumsfeld. Clarke was an expert in wartime public relations, having been a key figure in the campaign to convince Congress and the public to authorize the Gulf War in 1991. At that time, she was General Manager of the Washington, DC office of Hill and Knowlton, the largest public relations firm in the world. As the cornerstone of a massive PR campaign, the firm successfully disseminated a fabricated story about Iraqi troops stealing incubators from a Kuwaiti hospital and leaving premature babies to die on the floor. The faked atrocity story became a mainstay in the administration's case for war and arguably played a central role in pushing public favor for the intervention past the point of authorization. The entire episode later achieved some ignominy as the "Nayirah affair."[40] Having endeared herself to the Bush political apparatus with such successes, Clarke gained her position as Assistant Secretary of Defense for Public Affairs in 2001, a position she held until she resigned in June of 2003, likely due to mounting criticism regarding the veracity of the Pentagon's version of the Private Lynch rescue. Predictably, neither Nayirah nor Lynch appear in Clarke's memoirs, omissions reflected in the tome's refreshingly candid title, *Lipstick on a Pig: Winning in the No-Spin Era by Someone Who Knows the Game*.[41] Of all of Clarke's ambitious public relations stunts, the concept of embedded reporting would become her lasting legacy. The trade magazine *PR Week* noted that the embedding scheme not only made Clarke a "household name," but also inspired the corporate world to look into embedding journalists as a public relations strategy for controlling news flow.[42]

The producers of *Profiles* made no bones about the political role of the series. Bertram van Munster admitted, "This is going to be a very visual reality show with a strong patriotic message" and "Obviously, we're going to have a pro-military, pro-American stance. We're not going to criticize."[43] Bruckheimer, too, made it clear that he had no responsibility to impartiality and that the Pentagon rightfully held all the cards. "Again," he told the press, "we aren't the news."[44] In another interview, Van Munster reiterated, "It's a reality show. It has to be entertaining."[45] The notion that the *Profiles* crew was not the news became especially clear in the case of the US adventure in Afghanistan. Here, the Pentagon had taken a very conservative approach to the press, severely restricting access to the troops in a manner reminiscent of the invasions of Grenada or Panama.[46] For the Pentagon, the *news* was a liability. An entertainment show like *Profiles*, on the other hand, existed in the twilight dimension of representation, having some claim on the truth but not bogged down with the potentially "disloyal" ethic of journalistic objectivity. *Profiles* had much simpler interests: access to the battlefield on one end and ratings on the other. With scruples out of the way, the love affair between the camera and war long represented through the romantic myth of the war photographer could finally be consummated in what ABC billed as the "ultimate reality TV show."[47] Indeed, the Pentagon preferred a press more akin to a mobile army of Bruckheimers and van Munsters. Commanding General Tommy Franks named this ideal media posture the "fourth front," which, as opposed to the power-checking "fourth estate," acts to extend military power into the realm of domestic public consciousness.[48] If the press could not be excluded from battle, perhaps it could be refashioned as a version of domestic psychological operations: a *Profiles* writ large.

The core logic of reality TV thus extended through the 2003 invasion of Iraq. According to Vince Ogilvie, the Pentagon's project officer for *Profiles*, the show provided "a prelude to the process of embedding."[49] The final episode aired on March 11, 2003, just eight days before the US military initiated the invasion with the "Shock and Awe" blitz of Baghdad. The cancellation of *Profiles* coincided precisely with the appearance of the embedded reporter on the news. Moreover, ratings for the top four reality TV programs dropped once the embedded war went live, suggesting the shifting of audiences from one reality show to another.[50] At Victoria Clarke's behest, the Pentagon continued to keep Van Munster and his camera crews on the government payroll for shooting in Iraq, a tacit acknowledgment of embedding as an heir to shows like *COPS*. The ethos of such a conjunction could be heard in Van Munster's Janus-faced appraisal of his position, a chronicler at once "comfortable" with the fact that "the word propaganda is being used all the time" while staunchly asserting the "independence" and disinterestedness of his company.[51]

Clarke's embedded reporting system fundamentally transformed war coverage in ways resonant with the reality TV genre. Many in the press criticized the system for lacking perspective—that it was a "view through a soda straw," what Thomas Rid notes was the most popular metaphor for describing the limitations of embedding.[52] Indeed, Andrew Hoskins suggests that the real time war has gradually shifted toward "experiential" news. Between 1991 and 2003, war coverage both "sped up" and multiplied across increasing numbers of available simultaneous live feeds. The greater the insistence on "liveness," Hoskins argues, the greater the reliance on "down time" to feed the wide maw of the 24-hour news cycle. The demand of real-time liveness tends to yield reporters with little or nothing of substance to relate: "In this way, the significance of the content of news diminishes as the demand for immediacy increases."[53] This vacuum caused the reporter to increasingly fill the frame with experiential content. Talk of the immediate circumstances surrounding the reporter thus tended to displace perspective, analysis, context, and history. Put simply, the real-time war came to value experience over understanding as the primary objective of war coverage. Hoskins notes that such a shift in emphasis from the ends of war reporting (comprehension) to the means (the communications link) has much in common with reality television shows like *Big Brother* that are not "about" anything but the circumstances of living in strange conditions under the gaze of the camera.[54] Such orientations reduce thinking about war to contemplating the internal workings of the war machine. Empirical research bears out Hoskins' interpretation. The Project for Excellence in Journalism found that 94 percent of embedded stories were anecdotal or fact-based rather than analytical, suggesting highly detailed but conceptually fragmented coverage.[55] Embedding featured an overwhelming bias toward the immediate five senses and "being there," of riding in vehicles racing across the desert, smelling the gunpowder, or seeing the firefight through night vision goggles. The demands of battlefield secrecy compounded the problems of fitting "there" into the bigger picture of "where" or "why." On the screen, multiple satellite feeds each characterized by their own insularity resulted in "coverage" that appeared both schizophrenic and autistic.

The experiential reality TV war affected wider circles of war coverage. Scholars such as W. Lance Bennett and Kathleen Hall Jamieson have suggested that television harbors an inherent bias toward the personalization of politics.[56] The reality TV war exceeded the point of personalizing the story with its tendency to produce the reporter as the object of the story. Due to soda-straw limitations of the embedding structure, the dominant narrative told by reporters naturally revolved around the theme of "life in the field." Fox News' Oliver North described the mechanics of how to defecate in the desert using a standard-issue shovel. Reporters doted on the noise of machinery, the trials of sandstorms, and the risks of firefights. In a sense, this type of news had been pioneered by storm-chasing reporters doing live stand-ups in the middle of hurricanes, scenes where the stunt displaces the event supposedly covered. Embedding itself became the plot, and embedded reporters the main characters. While the first Gulf War in 1991 may have made celebrities out of the likes of CNN's Peter Arnett and Wolf Blitzer, the embedded reporting system in 2003 produced an array of stars, who afterward returned to show their war scars. Fox News' Greg Kelly received enormous media attention after he received a facial scratch in an explosion. CBS's Jim Axelrod said that he felt lucky to be alive. The major character at work here was less the romanticized "war correspondent" than a kind of "soldiered journalist." This popularity of this persona was reflected in NBC's decision to air a made-for-TV movie in 2004 called *War Stories*, which tracked the lives of photo journalists in

Uzbekistan amidst an Islamic uprising, a thinly veiled allegory for the ongoing action in Iraq. The title alone best describes the show's dramatic purchase, its ability to maximize fantasies of the civilian tempting the battlefield.

The case of NBC's David Bloom exemplifies the new cult of the soldiered journalist. Bloom was perhaps the most visible embedded reporter, having invented the "Bloom Mobile" camera configuration to broadcast pictures of himself riding on a tank while streaking across the desert. This scene became so iconic that later in the year, NBC's Carl Quintanilla would cover Hurricane Isabel using what he referred to as his own "Bloom Mobile," highlighting the resonance of embedded war coverage with depoliticized disaster coverage.[57] On April 6, 2003, during the height of the coalition ground offensive in Iraq, Bloom died of a blood clot in his lung, a condition usually caused by inactivity. Both MSNBC and Fox News broadcasted his funeral at St. Peter's Cathedral in New York. Mayor Rudolph Guiliani, Governor George Pataki, and White House Press Secretary Ari Fleischer were among the mourners. All that was missing, it seemed, was a soldier's funeral.

Six months later, Bloom received his soldier's funeral. On October 1, 2003, a cadre of Bush administration officials and media executives gathered in Burkittsville, Maryland at an obscure memorial for "war correspondents." The monument's last and only service had been in 1896 to honor chroniclers of the Civil War. The *Washington Post* described the ceremony:

> A lone cannon boomed across the green mountain ridge, and a bugle sounded taps, the melancholy melody traditionally played for fallen soldiers. But yesterday, the dirge honored a different set of war veterans: four correspondents who died covering the invasion of Iraq and the war on terror.[58]

Figure 3.3 Embedded superstars. (left) *Fox News*'s Greg Kelly receiving attention for a facial scratch and (right) NBC's David Bloom reporting from his "Bloom Mobile".

These included not only Bloom but also Daniel Pearl of the *Wall Street Journal*, Michael Kelly of the *Washington Post*, and Elizabeth Neuffer of the *Boston Globe*. Pearl was the only one "killed in battle" as he was brutally murdered by kidnappers in Afghanistan. Both Kelly and Neuffer had died in car accidents in Iraq. Regardless, language normally reserved for soldiers garnished the eulogies. Tom Brokaw described war correspondence as a "noble calling." Maryland Governor Robert Ehrlich, Jr. said the reporters had made the "ultimate sacrifice." Richard Gilman, publisher of the *Boston Globe*, said he was pleased that so many had attended a ceremony "to honor our fallen correspondents."[59] Deputy Secretary of Defense, Paul Wolfowitz, expressed his admiration for the reporters, and in doing so placed the reporter in the soldier's boots: "All of our freedoms are at stake when Americans go to war, but in a very special way, the lives of those we honor today testify to the preciousness of the freedoms we enjoy under the First Amendment."[60] In a twist on the notion that "soldiers protect freedom," Wolfowitz suggested that embedded reporters either uniquely championed or enjoyed freedom of the press, neither of which was the case.

The funeral might have honored all the journalists who had died covering the war, not just those "on our side" embedded with the US military. In fact, because Iraq was perhaps the most dangerous war since WWII, journalistically speaking, there were plenty of dead journalists to honor. This was particularly true for so-called "unilaterals," those journalists not embedded with coalition forces but who comprised the vast majority of journalist fatalities.[61] The numbers (including deadly American attacks on Al Jazeera offices and the Palestine Hotel, the latter of which housed a concentration of unilaterals) led organizations like Reporters Sans Frontières and others to contend that coalition forces deliberately intimidated those not embedded in order to better control the field of information.[62] In this light, the Maryland memorial to the war correspondent was highly selective, weaving reporters into a tableau of executive personnel, cannon salutes, bugle calls, and speeches evoking the heroic language of military remembrance. If the Burkittsville ceremony really sought to honor journalists who died so that we "might fully understand the grim realities of war," in Governor Ehrlich's eulogizing words, the memorial might have looked more like the one inaugurated on October 7, 2005, in the city of Bayeaux in France's Normandy province, which displayed the names of the 2000 journalists from around the world who had lost their lives in the course of their work since 1944.[63] Instead, nationalism and militarism were the order of the day, rhetorically positioning the embedded reporter less as a journalist than a celebrity-playing-soldier and spokesperson for executive power.

The emergence of reality television and journalism in the embedding scheme produced two distinct effects. First, it allowed the Pentagon to structurally assimilate war journalism and exert a high degree of control. The system limited the field of information by keeping the leash short, generating fragmented news copy that was high on immediacy but low on context. This shifted storytelling power to the $250,000 Central Command press briefing room in Qatar, whose backdrop had been built by a Hollywood set designer.[64] Military briefers gladly filled in the gaps in the soda-straw coverage for a contained, stenographic press corps. In transforming the media into an extension of military psychological operation, the embedded system challenged the role of the press as a check on power, an instrument of public deliberation, and a disinterested third party in the conflict. These values had to be negotiated, of course. When Assistant Secretary of Defense Bryan Whitman first met with media executives in January of 2003, critics naturally greeted him with questions about journalistic objectivity. Whitman attempted to answer these concerns:

> We know that Saddam Hussein is a practiced liar and skilled in the art of disinformation. What better way to deal with something like that than to have an objective press corps on the ground reporting on events as they occur?[65]

In spite of these reassurances by the administration, the question remained. Would the military censor? Would journalists self-sensor? The concerns usually echoed those expressed by the *Minneapolis Star Tribune*: "Because they will rely on those units for everything from the food they eat to protection from the enemy, [reporters will] lose their objectivity and become 'homers'."[66] That is, would the process of embedding taint the *information* relayed to the home front? This was a valid concern given the potential for embeds to take the role of "cheerleaders," a common metaphor used by critics. These concerns were short-lived, however. Whitman encountered almost universal approval for the plan from the mainstream press whose biggest concerns were not the loss of objectivity but instead reporter safety and the potential for accidentally revealing strategic information.[67] Indeed, a few years later, the trajectory of embedded reporting would become clear as the Pentagon assimilated civilian journalism altogether. By the Iraqi elections in January of 2005, the original figure of 800 embedded journalists had slipped to 150. In July of 2007, due to a stagnant story and elevated danger, this number stood at a paltry nine. In place of the embed, the Pentagon launched a multi-million dollar project, the Digital Video Distribution System (DVIDS), to distribute war images and footage to media outlets. Shot by "military journalists," the B-roll footage and soldier interviews served as free, pre-packaged news bites. This new economy of "journalism" was similar to the video news releases (VNRs) that became popular in the world of corporate public relations beginning in the 1980s.[68] Never before had the business interests of corporate media (inexpensive news) and the interests of the military apparatus (public relations) merged so seamlessly.

A second and perhaps more pervasive effect of embedded journalism was the fact that the face of war journalism had changed. The reporter literally traded in the trenchcoat for a standard-issue uniform. The figure that stood before the viewing public had assumed the position of a virtual soldier, riding in vehicles, eating MREs, responding to danger, and talking about life as a soldier. To be sure, this new character was born out of the consummation of corporate media's desire for access and the Pentagon's desire for positive public relations. But the embedded reporter was an entirely new performance of journalism, a militarized version overcoded with a novel but increasingly normative set of meanings and relationships. Television war coverage as a whole refashioned itself as an extension of this war superstar, a new primary signifier of journalism. The reporter in the tank had naturally come to use the identity language of "we" when speaking of the US military. Anchors at their desks back in the US followed suit. The performative structure of embedded journalism provided a distinct "trickle-down" model of wartime citizenship, or, as Robert Asen calls it, a performed "mode of public engagement."[69] In wartime, journalists are the most accessible and visible performers of citizenship. The embedded reporter filled the screen with a singular plotline: a civilian contestant relaying what it's like to be in a war zone under the gaze of real-time television. As such, embedding functioned to project the viewer onto the stage through this surrogate, refashioning the civic field into a fourth front infused with the interactive excitations and pleasures of reality television.

Chapter 4

War Games

In March of 2000, the release of Sony's new PlayStation 2 hit a minor snag. The Japanese government classified the game console as a "general purpose product related to conventional weapons" on the grounds that it was powerful enough to be used as an actual missile guidance system. Accordingly, the government applied export controls on the PlayStation requiring that a special license be obtained by distributors. This was the first time the Foreign Exchange and Foreign Trade Control law had been used to regulate a game console.[1] Meanwhile, the US military was in the process of designing the "Dragon Runner," a small, unmanned, remote control reconnaissance truck whose controller was modeled after the PlayStation 2. This design decision was reached under the practical assumption that incoming soldiers would already be partially trained to use it.[2] For its unmanned aerial drone, the Predator, weapons manufacturer Raytheon hired a team of video game designers to create a more ergonomic and intuitive control experience that resembled a souped-up PlayStation. The drone's control system, moreover, was based on an Xbox processor.[3]

The uneasy relationship between war and video games has been a perennial issue at least since the first Gulf War. At a press conference in February, 1991, General Norman Schwarzkopf felt compelled to remind Americans that war was "not a video game."[4] A decade later, however, the metaphor had been thoroughly naturalized. As Janice Kennedy of the *Ottawa Citizen* reflects:

> When we first saw those small crosshairs etched on to an eerie green nighttime sky—that would be 12 years ago now, in much the same sky— there was much bleating and wringing of hands about war, video games, and the convergence of the twain. War, they said wisely, is not a game. Except that it is, soldier. Get used to it.[5]

Indeed, strange technological marriages, the mediated presentation of war, and the language of describing the experience on the home front had all but proved Schwarzkopf wrong. After 9/11, real war and war games conspired to erase common boundaries. Television news coverage seemed to go beyond the video game metaphor in its broadcasting of pretty lights and smart bomb cameras. As if it were in competition with media more suited to the interactive war, television coverage began to gratuitously recreate events using digital animations with current game production values. Meanwhile, games attempted to re-create the television war in playable real time.

In addressing her reader as "soldier," Kennedy highlights a crucial aspect of the video game war: the invitation to cross over and try on a soldier identity. Twenty-first-century war games no longer project only a distant mock-up of military matters. Rather, games have become part and parcel of information-age warfare, merging the home front and the battlefield through multiple channels. As such, they represent a nexus of the militarization of cultural space, a medium perhaps best suited for the theme-parking of war into an interactive military thrill ride. The story here is perhaps a bit more complex as the military also finds video games internally useful for training purposes. This chapter begins by describing this economy, which has come to flow freely between military and commercial spheres, creating not only a complex in its own right but also cultivating a civilian thirst for authentic military simulators. The chapter then examines the merging of television news and video games in

Figure 4.1 Video game-style graphics on the news during the 2003 invasion of Iraq.

the real-time presentation of war. War-themed games have increasingly drawn from journalistic accounts for material and storylines, serving as platforms to play the television war. Finally, the chapter traces developments in military outreach and recruiting, particularly the way the Army has entered popular culture through its newly inaugurated recruiting game, *America's Army*. This game has done the most to formalize a larger culture of "virtual recruits" under the Army brand. The three—training, battle, and recruitment—triangulate trends in the screen logics of a war where games function as a primary conduit for the military assimilation of the civic mind.

Training

In October of 2001, shortly after the attacks on New York and the Pentagon, movie critic Michael Medved asked, "Will computer games win the war on terrorism?"[6] Medved seemed to be channelling sentiments expressed by Ronald Reagan in 1983 when he told a group of students at Disney's EPCOT Center, "The computerized radar screen in the cockpit is not unlike the computerized video screen. Watch a 12-year-old take evasive action and score multiple hits while playing 'Space Invaders', and you will appreciate the skills of tomorrow's pilot."[7] Advances in military training have born out these hopes. Since the Cold War, the military use of soldier training simulators has undergone a revolution.[8] Whereas computer training used to be limited to large and expensive shooting range, flight, or tank simulators (some costing up to a quarter of a million dollars), now simulators have penetrated almost every aspect of training with the help of PCs. *New York Times* reporter Amy Harmon notes, "What is new is both the way the games are filtering down through the ranks to the lowest level of infantry soldiers, and the broader vision that is being contemplated for them at the highest levels of the Pentagon."[9] Chris Morris, the technical manager for warfighting experimentation at Qinetiq, Britain's Ministry of Defence testing establishment, explained:

> We've been using flight and vehicle simulations for a long time now. However, it is far more difficult to create a realistic synthetic environment for foot soldiers. We decided to concentrate on the mental and procedural issues, so we started to look for a computer game we could modify.[10]

Back in the US, Michael Macedonia, director of the Army's simulation center in Orlando, was on the way to such a dream. Macedonia unveiled AWE (Asymmetric Warfare Environment) in 2004, a "virtual Afghanistan" that linked thousands of PCs for 24-hour training on a virtual battlefield. That same year, the US Joint Forces Command, a division of the Department of Defense, began testing of "Urban Resolve," a $195,000 effort that joined two mammoth supercomputers for training in urban combat situations. At the time the system was cutting edge, using complex artificial intelligence software to manufacture situations appropriate to urban battle strategy such as power outages.[11] Macedonia's hope was to recreate an economy similar to the 1985 sci-fi novel *Ender's Game*, which envisions a group of teenagers who battle aliens in a computer game only to find out they have in reality saved the earth. The novel, Macedonia confessed, had "a lot of influence" on the thinking at AWE.[12]

In the interim between Desert Storm and Iraqi Freedom, games and game technology regularly crossed the boundary from military to commercial applications. Due to the nature of the medium perhaps, relations between the military and the game industries was more interactive and wired than most. Indeed, both J.C. Herz's "military-entertainment complex" and James Der Derian's "military-industrial-media-entertainment network" were coined specifically to describe collaboration the realm of training simulators and other technologies.[13] In the 1990s, for example, Sega game systems developed simulator software for Lockheed Martin. Lockheed returned the favor by manufacturing essential chips for Sega game modules. During this period, too, Sega adapted Lockheed simulators such as *Desert Tank* (1994) for commercial release. The popular commercial helicopter simulator *Apache: Longbow* (1996) was first developed, according to Herz, "in the heart of North Carolina contractor country, right down the road from Fort Bragg" with the meticulous help of McDonnell Douglas.[14]

The trend continued through the decade. In 1997, defense contractor OC, Inc. developed a military strategy simulation game entitled *Joint Force Employment* for the Joint Chiefs of Staff designed to teach "joint doctrine" or the coordination of military branches. The simulator featured real-time strategy (RTS) control of military forces in the field from a god's-eye perspective. Designers naturally took the simulator's premise straight from US foreign policy, presupposing the hypothetical existence of the Independent Liberation Army (ILA), a terrorist group with access to a Russian-style arsenal. Taking on the role of the US or the ILA, players engage in conventional warfare as well as psychological operations (leaflet-dropping), propaganda, and media campaigns. Eventually, game designers realized it could be a hot home video game title and prophetically scheduled its commercial release for September 11, 2001, under the name *Real War*. When the fateful day arrived, distributor Simon and Schuster Interactive pulled the game, perhaps calculating its release to be in poor taste. By September 27, the company had reversed its position, and the game hit the shelves at the local Best Buy. A spokesperson for the company noted that *Real War* was received well after 9/11, "You get to blow terrorists up. Some people think it's a good release."[15]

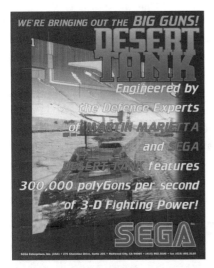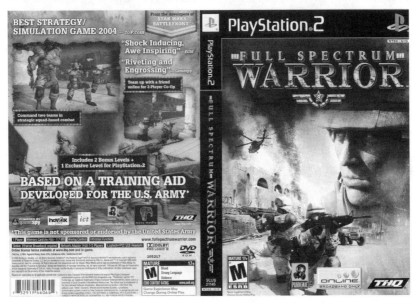

Figure 4.2 Promotions for military simulators gone commercial. *Desert Tank* (1994) advertisement, *Real War* (2001) advertisement, and *Full Spectrum Warrior* (2004) box cover.

Alongside *Real War*, the Pentagon commissioned design of another simulator to train foot soldiers. According to game director, Wil Stahl, "The Army's real goal was some sort of a party game. This was pre-September 11 and they wanted something that their recruits would choose to play on break, yet reinforce the things they were being taught."[16] The result was *Full Spectrum Warrior*, what turned out to be a full-fledged "tactical decision-making trainer," a foot-soldier first-person shooter with team capabilities. The game's storyline involved the fictitious Middle-Eastern nation of Zekistan and the overthrow of the character Mohammad Jabbour Al-Afad, a supposed former Mujahideen leader and current dictator and his band of "Taliban and Iraqi loyalists." In post-9/11 culture, such themes had potential mass appeal. Working with the Pentagon, private game designers THQ considered releasing the training simulator commercially.[17] In April of 2003 and the midst of the initial US invasion of Iraq, THQ investigated public sensitivities to a possible Gulf War-themed video game. The research seemed to support that such a game would be very popular, with only 8 percent responding that it would be "tacky and exploitative."[18] THQ released *Full Spectrum Warrior* in the Xbox commercial market in 2004, and one year later THQ released the game's sequel, *Full Spectrum Warrior: Ten Hammers*. Following the Army's lead, the Marines developed a Beirut-based ground training game called *Close Combat: First to Fight* with the assistance of the private software company Destineer. The game was commercially released on Xbox and PC in 2005 as an installment of the *Close Combat* series, which had been out since 1996.[19] The life cycle of these games illustrates the increasing institutional collusion between military and commercial gamemakers in the context of current events.

One might assume that cooperation between military and commercial entities would normally follow a path from cutting-edge military use to the home. This is the standard course for many technologies. Despite the fact that many games did travel this route, the opposite was the norm. The Atari game *BattleZone* (1980) provided one of the first realistic 3D environments, so advanced that the military commissioned the game makers to produce a tank training simulator.[20] As the commercial gaming market exploded, the military commissioned modified commercial games (mods) as quickly as could be developed. A more recent example is the Marines' use of the original first-person shooter, *Doom*. The mod, *Marine Doom*, was developed by Marine Lieutenant Scott Barnett and Sergeant Dan Snyder, who were asked to comb the civilian war game market for something that could be used for soldier training. Barnett recounts that after finishing technical school he was assigned a position in the Modeling and Simulation office at the Quantico, Virginia base. His superiors initially reprimanded him for having a copy of *Doom* on his office computer. Barnett recalls, "They read us the riot act. Now, I'm institutionalizing *Doom* in the Marine Corps."[21] Since the military found the game to be successful in teaching repetitive decision-making on the ground, its 1997 introduction served as a prototype for the further military use of commercial first-person shooters. In 1999, the Navy used the commercial release of *Fleet*

Command by Jane's Combat Simulations. In 2001, the Army commissioned Ubi Soft Entertainment's *Tom Clancy's Rogue Spear: Black Thorn* for help in training soldiers to fight terrorists on urban terrain.[22] Game maker Bohemian Interactive adapted its 2001 commercial tactical first-person shooter, *Operation Flashpoint*, for the Marine training simulator known as *Virtual Battlespace*. The company adapted its commercial update, *Armed Assualt*, for the Marines as *Virtual Battlespace 2* in 2007.[23] The British Ministry of Defence used a mod of the sci-fi shooter *Half-Life* in a project known as DIVE (Dismounted Infantry Virtual Environment).[24] The Secret Service, CIA, FBI, and other law enforcement agencies have expressed interest in similar ventures.[25]

In order to facilitate such collaborations, in 2000 the Defense Department devised the University of Southern California's Institute for Creative Technologies (ICT). Founded with a $45 million Defense Department grant, ICT amassed a motley collection of Hollywood talent, academics, toymakers, and game industry insiders to assist the military. Here, toy manufacturers help in generating ideas for futuristic weapons; Hollywood screenwriters brainstorm about potential terrorist plots; academics suggest strategies for urban combat and psychological operations; game makers devise new methods for soldier training; and set designers help build virtual environments. ICT's Entertainment Technology Center is the locus for much of the collaboration required for military simulation. The partnership does not just benefit the military. Giants such as Sony and others have donated to the center in the hopes that participation in the center will aid software development.[26] Such partnerships allow commercial game developers access to up-to-the-minute details of new weapons systems that the public is hungry to test drive. ICT thus represents a condensation of the much broader trend of military-commercial collaboration mobilized across an entire spectrum. Such institutions are a permanent and growing part of the military apparatus. In 2007, for example, the military established a center specifically devoted to game design called the Training and Doctrine Command's Project Office for Gaming, which is part of the Army's National Center for Simulation.[27]

Debates about these activities are manifold. Within the military, many question the relevance and efficacy of simulators, even as their use has been instituted on a mass scale. When such games spill into civilian life, they often activate "Columbine" debates about the psychological effects of games specifically designed to teach players how to kill. Though these questions are important, the primary question here is how the economy of war-themed games restructures the civic field. There are ways of killing that do not necessarily involve pulling a trigger oneself, of course, such as collectively condoning state violence. These are the rarest questions: In the "how" of killing, what do video games communicate regarding the "why" of killing? This is an especially urgent question given the manner in which war games are increasingly aligning with reality TV-style news coverage of war.

Battle

The attacks of 9/11 and the ensuing wars in Afghanistan and Iraq ushered in a boom in sales of war-themed video games for the commercial market. *Wired* magazine noted that the popularity of these and other war games reached new heights during the Christmas 2003 season.[28] Among these were titles like *Prisoner of War* and the highly successful sequel *Medal of Honor: Frontline*, both of which feature action in WWII.[29] Others played with more recent military interventions. *Delta Force: Black Hawk Down*, inspired by the game-feel of the Jerry Bruckheimer film, took players on a tour of Mogadishu, Somalia, in search of warlords. *Conflict: Desert Storm* gave players the chance to reenact the first Gulf War, a scene not so different from the contemporaneous occupation of Iraq that no doubt boosted the game's popularity. Games that focused on special operations, police forces, and insurgent hunting did particularly well. Examples included the *Tom Clancy* series (*Splinter Cell, Rainbow Six, Ghost Recon, Raven Shield*) where players become part of covert operations teams. *SOCOM: Navy Seals* earned its popularity by implementing voice recognition software for use with the player's headset so that team members could communicate in much the same manner as real soldiers.

The post-9/11 war game environment tended to avoid narratives that could possibly interfere with the ability to freely consume the pure experience of battle. Games tended to avoid legal, ethical, moral, or ideological consider-ations, including any other criteria used to measure the wisdom of war. Indeed, if there is a dominant "ideology" expressed in these game narratives, it is a marked disdain for diplomacy and preference for force consistent with the rhetoric of the war on terror (as in President Bush's mantra, "We will not negotiate with terrorists"). Game promotions and advertisements tell a similar tale. The subtitle to *Conflict: Desert Storm* in both ads and on game boxes is "No Diplomats. No Negotiation. No Surrender." A print advertisement for Deus Ex's *Invisible War* displays the obsolescence of citizenship in a "future war on terror" that is "Unseen, Unauthorized, Unstoppable." Promotions for *Tom Clancy's Rainbow Six* series offer a more complex version of this theme. A series of magazine ads for *Rainbow Six 3: Raven Shield* begins at the top with faux newspaper clippings whose headlines read "Foreign Ambassadors Report Peaceful Face-to-Face Negotiations with Terrorists in Venezuela" and "Diplomacy is Primary Weapon in America's Quest to End Indonesian Crisis." The clippings are torn away to reveal the real situation under the press veneer: troops of armed special operations soldiers doing business by force. While this may have been the reality of many of the covert US military interventions since WWII (including, incidentally, both Indonesia and Venezuela), such games naturalize and even celebrate the fact. Television ads for *Tom Clancy's Rainbow Six* feature black-clad soldiers, both live-action and computer-generated, sneaking around and blowing things up to a soundtrack where a young child sings "America, My Country 'Tis of Thee" or recites the Pledge of Allegiance. The juxtaposition plays on the theme of innocence lost, positioning the game as a pleasurable transgression. The narrator in an ad for *Tom Clancy's Splinter Cell* recites these lines: "I alone have the fifth freedom—the right to spy, steal, destroy, and assassinate to insure that American freedoms are protected." The bumper-sticker slogan "Freedom Isn't Free" frames these ads. Normally, this slogan suggests that freedom requires sacrifice. In the context of the game, its meaning is somewhat mysterious. Perhaps it is just another way of saying "this is a great game, but it will cost you money"; perhaps it acknowledges the sacrifice of certain values in order to play the game; or perhaps it carries through the larger themes of the ads, which cynically imply that freedom is just a meaningless buzzword.[30]

Beyond these themes, the real significance of the video game war lies in its temporal proximity to war. After 9/11, gamemakers seemed sensitive to the convergence of games and the political realities of war. Jeff Brown, spokesman for Electronic Arts, which publishes titles like *Medal of Honor* and *Command and Conquer*, went out of his way to remind the public that "[T]here's considerable physical and psychological distance between our games and the reality of current events."[31] The company soon dropped this pretense. In 2008, for example, EA published *Army of Two*. The game's plot revolves around two private military contractors who work for the fictional "Security and Strategy Corporation," a loose analogue for one of the largest real-life contractors, Blackwater USA.[32] In the game, two soldiers-for-hire wander the earth doing odd jobs in the war on terror. Reid Schneider, producer at EA Montreal noted the attraction to the idea: "These guys operate in a gray area. They're mercenaries. They're all about getting paid in cash. It's fun to play because this is obviously something people are thinking about, not only in the US but in many countries around the world."[33] This was true. People were thinking about mercenaries, especially because Blackwater had been under investigation for the unprovoked massacre of seventeen Iraqi civilians. Rather than depress game sales, Schneider concluded that the coverage was "pretty cool," perhaps lending that transgressive aura that game makers so actively pursued during this period.[34]

Army of Two is symptomatic of a larger temporal convergence of war games and war. Patrick Crogan provides an initial way to approach this question, first recognizing that such games have a role in militarizing social life through their "expansion into the domestic sphere."[35] Crogan argues that war games also tend to refigure time, driven as they are by an "anticipatory impulse." Games foster a mode of habituating history that he calls "gametime," a temporal aesthetic that favors a discourse of constant action and the suppression of ethical reflection. He notes, for example, that this aesthetic informs the "historical" film *Pearl Harbor* (2001) and explains why it reads much like a video game. Crogan's notion of gametime can be extended to explain the anticipatory impulse to close the history gap itself. That is, the logics of gametime also tend to collapse the temporal space between real-world events and the ability to recreate and "play" them in real time. This explains why the television war began to look like a video game in concordance with changes in its tempo, which included the initiation of a "war by appointment," public countdowns and deadlines, real-time broadcasting, and other prominent signs of time.[36] During the Persian Gulf War in 1991, scholars such as George Gerbner referred to the propagandistic manufacture of "instant history" by way of televised media spectacle.[37] A decade later, the interactive mode of Operation Iraqi Freedom was less about manufacturing history than annihilating it, leaving no trace of ethical reflection—only a live, interactive, ever-present present.

Indeed, war games have caught up with the wars themselves.[38] The lag time between the conflict as it plays out on the news and the mobilization of the game has gradually disappeared. Operation Desert Storm in 1991 taught game makers a lesson about the consumer demand created by a well-orchestrated television war. Gulf War-themed games appeared in its wake, including *LHX Attack Chopper* in which Libya was the last unconquered state; EA's *Desert Strike: Return to the Gulf*, which offered players the chance to fly Apache helicopter to defeat the Saddamesque "General Kilbaba" (kill baby?); *F-15 Strike Eagle III*, which featured missions in Iraq; and *Super Battletank: War in the Gulf*, a first-person tank simulator. Sequels like *Super Battletank 2* (1994) followed. Recognizing the strong demand for realism, game producers began doing business with the Pentagon and military contractors to commercially release training simulators, most of which appeared in the mid-1990s.

Having identified the market, game makers were well prepared for the March, 20, 2003, kickoff of Operation Iraqi Freedom. Take, for example, one of the most popular desert war games to hit the market, *Conflict: Desert Storm*, which was released in late 2002 as the US made clear its intentions to invade and overthrow Iraq. Flipping through the TV dial, one could see sandwiched between deadline clocks and stories of troop mobilization an ad for the game that featured what looked to be the mustached face of Saddam Hussein in the crosshairs. (In the game, this character is called Gen. Aziz, an apparent reference to Tariq Aziz, Deputy Prime Minister under Hussein.) The game makers released the sequel, *Conflict Desert Storm II: Back to Baghdad*, in October

Figure 4.3 Screenshots of two generations of military simulators gone commercial. (left) *Apache: Longbow* (1996) and (right) *Close Combat: First to Fight* (2005).

2003, during the beginnings of the long occupation. The slogan for the sequel, "Freedom Will Endure," acknowledged that the game was intended to appear in the midst of the conflict. In December, 2002, the software company Rtzen modified the popular WWII game *Battlefield 1942* in anticipation of Operation Iraqi Freedom. The result was *Desert Combat*, which was downloaded 250,000 times by April of 2003.[39] 3DO's *Gulf War: Operation Desert Hammer*, a tank-based game that allows players to storm Baghdad to "finish the job," tripled their sales during the build-up to and invasion of 2003.[40] In another attempt to capitalize on the war, PlayStation manufacturer Sony attempted to trademark the phrase "Shock and Awe" on March 21, 2003, the day the US military's so-called Shock and Awe strategy was unleashed over Baghdad. Sony, by far the largest of the thirty-odd companies that attempted such trademarks, had planned to use the slogan to market video games. The company dropped the rights a month later, presumably to avoid public criticism that the company was "turning the war into a video game."[41]

One of the biggest game franchises, *Call of Duty*, released a fourth version called *Modern Warfare* in 2007, which became the number-one selling game worldwide.[42] Breaking from its history of producing WWII scenarios, this installment features conflicts in the Middle East and, noting a growing rivalry, Russia. The game includes a level called "Death from Above," where the player controls an AC-130 Spectre gunship, a plane armed with a large caliber machine gun and mounted cannon. With a sophisticated infrared tracking sight, the AC-130—called Azrael by pilots after the angel of death in the Qur'an—can engage ground targets, particularly personnel. The AC-130 had received significant public exposure during the Afghan and Iraq invasions as the Pentagon periodically released infrared gunsight footage to the networks. The black-and-white video of small, ghostly figures fleeing and succumbing to explosions was perhaps the closest the clean television war came to referencing

Figure 4.4 (top) Two frames from *Desert Strike: Return to the Gulf* (1992); (bottom) advertisements for *Conflict: Desert Storm* (2002) and *Conflict Desert Storm II: Back to Baghdad* (2003), both of which were heavily marketed amidst the invasion of Iraq.

death. *Modern Warfare*'s "Death from Above" game sequence accurately repro-
duces the gunship's targeting sight, all to the sound of a transceiver voice that
tells the player "You got a runner here," "Light 'em up," and, apparently
oblivious to Vietnam's infamous free-fire zones, "Take out everything in that
village." The voices instruct the player how to feel about the game, celebrating
with the macabre "Good kill, see lots of little pieces down there"; the exuber-
ant "Hot damn!"; or a blithe and coolly detached "Kaboom." As such, the game
allows one to play the videos that had become so popular on network television news and YouTube. In fact, it was difficult to tell the difference between
the real thing and the game. On YouTube, a player posted captured scenes from
the game and fooled a number of people. One viewer commented: "I would
not want to be on the receiving end, what a display of firepower!" When the
video was discovered as a video captured from the game, another user chided:

> Stop putting videos of your gameplay of COD4 like its real life. damn.
> when i want to look up a real AC-130 bombing the crap out of towel heads
> i don't want to see some kid play a game that 2 million people have already
> beat. ok!

Elsewhere on YouTube, one real AC-130 video carried the description: "Note:
This is not Call of Duty 4!"[43]

Games like *Kuma\War* will likely become more prevalent as the trend to
approximate war in real time continues. *Kuma\War* is the name for a first-
person shooter and a website (www.kumawar.com) managed by Kuma, LLC,
an independent New York-based commercial company begun in 2004 by a
group of retired military officers. The game's target demographic is the tech-

Figure 4.5 The two video game wars. (left) *Fox News* airing video of an AC-130 gunship
operation in Afghanistan, and (right) the "Death from Above" AC-130 gunship level on the game *Call of Duty 4*, which allows users to play the familiar
footage. The light-colored hotspots in each infrared image signify personnel
on the ground.

and media-savvy adult with an average age of 26.[44] For a few dollars a month (later for free with ad support) *Kuma\War* gives players a chance to re-enact dramatic military scenes just weeks after they play out on television news. The game has also teamed up with the History Channel and Spike TV for cross-promotion. *Kuma\War* "[lives] between being the news and being a game," CEO Keith Halper explained. "We wanted to put people in the middle of situations they read about or see on TV so as to better understand them."[45] In his bolder moments, Halper has claimed, "What we are trying to do is be a news organization."[46] To that end, the game's designers research and painstakingly re-create each mission down to 3-D topography, important characters, hardware, and military intelligence. For a given mission, the game briefs players with newswire articles, television clips, interviews, satellite imagery, and weapons specifications. One of the first missions, for example, features the US siege of the Iraqi city of Mosul, where Saddam Hussein's sons Uday and Qusay were eventually killed. Here designers simulated the neighborhood site of the confrontation down to the detail of staircases and balconies. The game invites one to play the part of airborne squad members whose job it was to flush the brothers from hiding while eliminating defending Ba'athist soldiers. Before going in, players view actual news video of the battle, an interview with a retired Marine Corps general, and tips for play from a pre-game analyst. Not all news battles make good gaming fodder, however. The 2004 US-assisted coup of Haitian president Jean Bertrand Aristide, for example, was deemed not game-able by the designers at *Kuma\War*. "It just didn't seem that there was anything going on of any tactical importance," explained Halper, revealing that for a game to work, it must already have been framed as a consumable event.[47]

As *Kuma\War* evolves through its ever-tightening "broadcast cycles," the pressure to keep up with current events is enormous. According to Halper, the company has "a team of researchers which does nothing but pore through information related to the war on terrorism." The goal is an elusive simultaneity that matches real-time network news. "We're starting to get a very specialized knowledge which helps us guess the next thing that's going to occur."[48] The game is thus a logical extension of the idiom of the embedded reporter, satisfying an embeddedness even the reporter cannot offer. In doing so, the game compounds the myopia of embedded journalism. According to Halper, "The idea is that we go very deep on just a few events, rather than shallow over the broad news agenda like other news sources."[49] In this case, "going deep" means the game relays logistics in depth, rather than history or context. As a result, the *Independent* aptly called *Kuma\War* "CNN with an itchier trigger finger."[50] *Kuma\War*'s itchy finger sometimes causes it to shoot first and ask questions later. In late 2005, for example, the game released a

Figure 4.6 Kuma\War newsgaming. (clockwise from top left) Homepage; introduction to mission to capture Saddam Hussein; news briefing by the game's own anchor, Jacki Schechner; gameplay still.

scenario where Special Forces infiltrate Iran to destroy uranium production facilities. At the time, the US was officially and publicly in the process of negotiating with Iran. Unofficially, as Seymour Hersh revealed in the *New Yorker*, the US had been secretly conducting reconnaissance missions inside Iran since the summer of 2004, though the bombs had yet to fall.[51] Here, *Kuma\War* betrays the "anticipatory impulse" of gametime, filling in possible future events, such as the bombing of Iran, before they occur. This differs from the so-called "CNN effect" during Desert Storm in 1991, where real time news representations preceded and thereby affected action on the ground. *Kuma\War* exceeds even "real time" by anticipating the event and pre-creating its execution, all while borrowing from journalism a rhetoric of authenticity. Like mainstream news, however, *Kuma\War* would compromise its own profit potential if it were to become "too authentic." That is, so long as the game is to be consumed, it must mask its own absurdity. As game critic Suneel Ratan notes, "[*Kuma\War*] will have to be a fun game too for people to use it, which may sound an odd thing to say about something dealing with war."[52]

Recruitment

In May of 2003, two weeks after George W. Bush triumphantly declared the invasion of Iraq had been a "mission accomplished" aboard the USS Abraham Lincoln aircraft carrier, the Army made a showing at the Los Angeles Electronic Entertainment Exposition, the E3. More than 30 soldiers were present. Members of a Stryker brigade manned an armored vehicle. National Guard soldiers rappelled down zip-ropes from a helicopter hovering outside the Staples Center and down from walls inside. Green Beret soldiers hung from a Humvee. This was not a raid on a possible terrorist sleeper cell but rather a massive $500,000 spectacle designed to draw attention to *America's Army*, a video game developed by the Army for purposes of recruiting. The game had enjoyed the limelight since its initial unveiling at the E3 in 2002.[53] At that time, the game featured two parts, one training simulation entitled *Soldiers*, which included boot camp, and another more traditional first-person shooter game called *Operations*, where players worked in online teams to carry out missions.

Officially released on Independence Day in 2002, *America's Army* represented a monumental step into twenty-first-century military-consumer culture. The game initially cost $7.5 million over three years to produce, about three times the average for games of its type, and is a permanent, albeit evolving, fixture in the Army's advertising arsenal. Monetarily, *America's Army* is a sliver of the Pentagon's ballooning $700 million advertising budget of which the Army spent $75 million in 2004.[54] As new "operations" are added to the initial platform, the Army anticipates a yearly maintenance cost of $4 million. The money goes to both game development ($2.5m), a nationwide server network that can host 5,000–6,000 online players at a time ($1.5m), and the websites GoArmy.com and AmericasArmy.com, from which the game could be downloaded for free. By 2005, several million freely distributed game CDs had left the desks of military recruiters, appeared in gaming magazines, and been included as extras in store-bought software packages. In that year, the Army began mass distributing the game for the Xbox home console.[55] "We're going to be pushing out new versions of the game as fast as we can build them," noted game director Lt. Col. Casey Wardynski.[56]

America's Army was an immediate and resounding success in terms of exposure. The July 4th debut saw 50,000 downloads alone, and in one year the game had 1.3 million registered players. As promised, the Army introduced a new version in 2003 called *Special Forces*, which had more than 200,000 people playing in its first week.[57] By December of 2003, the game had 2.4 million users, thus making the short list of popular games for the Christmas season.[58] Major Chris Chambers, deputy director of the game, was clearly enthusiastic:

Figure 4.7 Screenshot from *America's Army: Rise of a Soldier.*

"Experts told us before we started that a runaway hit in this space is 250,000 registered users in a year. We beat that in the first two months."[59] In 2003, *America's Army* was consistently in the top five action games played worldwide on the Internet.[60] By 2006, *America's Army* had 7.5 million registered users, and two years later that figure had topped 9 million.[61]

America's Army exists as a part of the larger military strategy to move from television ads to more cost-effective methods of recruiting, such as games and NASCAR sponsorship.[62] Because the Pentagon spends around $15,000 on average wooing each recruit, the game must only result in 300 enlistments per year to recuperate costs. The available data suggest that the game has more than met that objective. According to military research as of May 2003, the game ranked fourth among things creating "favorable awareness" of the Army, behind the war in Iraq, homeland security, and tensions with North Korea.[63] Some 40 percent of enlistees in 2005 had previously played the game.[64] Also there is a wealth of anecdotal evidence that the game puts recruiters in contact with prospective recruits through public gaming events and recruiting office walk-ins.[65] For example, in January 2003, while troops were running through readiness exercises on the Iraqi border, the Kansas City Recruiting Battalion hosted gatherings at a technical college. Some 120 high school students broke into teams to play one another at *America's Army*. According to the Army, programs like this have been some of the most successful experiments in recruiting history.[66]

One reason for the tremendous popularity of the game is its cutting-edge design. Dan Morris, a game reviewer for *PC Gamer* magazine, commented that the game is of "Triple-A quality," that it is "ahead of the technology curve," and that it would display a high-end price tag of $60–70 if sold in stores: "I wish more civilian development shops would display the kind of ambition realized in this game."[67] The *America's Army* section of the GoArmy.com site boasted that "No one gets the Army like the Army" and the game makers have gone to pains to deliver "realism." Some of the missions are hypothetical, such as defending (or capturing) prisoners of war or the Alaska Oil Pipeline. Other missions deal with current events such as one in the initial release of *Operations* modeled after a raid conducted in Afghanistan. Military scenarios of low strategic sensitivity are reproduced in detail. Grenade explosions vary by grenade type. Target ranges and obstacle courses at Ft. Benning, Georgia are meticulously recreated. When firing a weapon, one's breathing and rate of fire affect accuracy. If a soldier breaks the Rules of Engagement by firing on his own men, he is likely to wind up at Ft. Leavenworth for a 10-minute prison sentence, listening to the lonesome drone of his cellmate's harmonica. In the integrative spirit of *Kuma\War*, the Army has also embarked on a project called "Real Heroes" that makes game characters, as well as plastic action figures, out of nine medal-winning, real-life soldiers.[68]

The realism does not extend to include the gruesome realities of war, however. The game has earned a "T" rating, indicating it is suitable for players thirteen years of age and up. When humans are hit with gunfire, they crumple noiselessly to the ground. Sometimes a mist of blood escapes an invisible wound, but the victims neither flail nor cry. Bodies tend to disappear as if raptured up to heaven. On its face, the level of violence appears to be a positive attribute of the game, and it is predictably cited by its promoters as proof of legitimacy. The point is "not to promote violence," noted Army Major Bret Wilson, one of the game's developers, "it is to promote the jobs that are done by the Army."[69] In the same language used by the Pentagon to praise the virtues of precision-guided weapons, Major Chris Chambers, the game's deputy director, notes, "The game is about achieving objectives with the least loss of life. It doesn't reward abhorrent behavior."[70] Game promoters are also quick to point out the parental control feature that turns all gun fighting into laser tag. The Army is apparently responding to multiple concerns. A gory game where limbs are blown off would not only rouse the easiest kind of reactionary criticism, it would also limit the audience for the game by virtue of a stricter rating. Moreover, a game that seriously approached the horrors of battle would undermine the recruitment effort. The game can reference death in the way the news cannot because it occurs in hypothetical space. Even so, the game must find its equilibrium in a sanitized vision that approximates mainstream American news coverage, following the spirit of the clean war even as its "realism," like that of embedded news, is emphatically extolled.

Perhaps the game's stated goals are most interesting. *America's Army* is the brainchild of Lt. Col. Casey Wardynski, director of the Army's Office of Economic and Manpower Analysis, who hatched the idea in 1999, the year when recruitment hit a low mark. Wardynski recognized both the significance of video games in his own sons' lives and the need to tap the market for technologically savvy recruits. Despite this impetus, Wardynski insists that the game is "definitely not" a recruiting tool. "Essentially, *America's Army* is a communication tool designed to show players what the army is—a high-tech, exciting organization with lots to do."[71] In describing the game's function as "education" and "communication," Wardynski draws attention to the fact that the game differs from campaigns past in that it makes neither offers nor arguments. As such, the game is an extension of the larger Army strategy of "lifestyle marketing," the creation of an immersive cultural universe. The use of interactive technologies to craft and market this universe— the video game as advertisement or "adver-game"—can be counted among the military's many firsts. In fact, the success of *America's Army* has been noticed by diverse corporations such as Coca-Cola and Daimler-Chrysler, who hope to promote their brands in similar ways.[72] *America's Army* has transformed the rhetoric of "recruitment" as well, smoothing distinctions between player and recruit. Arguably, the Army game has had a hand in introducing the language of recruitment into the realm of commercial war games. A television ad for *Conflict: Desert Storm* tells us, "All Americans Pledge Allegiance. A Select Few Show It." A print advertisement for the WWII game *Medal of Honor: Rising Sun* features an enlistment card and the slogan, "You don't play. You volunteer." In this new war gaming environment, recruitment has taken on a logic that is entirely harmonious with the brand, a kind of brand loyalty. *America's Army*, far from being a cultural anomaly, has become one brand among many, where the rhetoric of recruitment has spilled into the broader consumer economy. Col. Wardynski perhaps said it better when he bragged that the game has "achieved the objective of putting the Army in pop culture."[73]

Playing War

In the new interactive war, genres once thought to be discrete have forged new and strange alliances. Wartime news looks like a video game; video games restage wartime news. Official military training simulators cross over into commercial entertainment markets; commercial video games are made useful for military training exercises. Advertisements sell video games with patriotic rhetorics; video games are mobilized to advertise patriotism. The business of play works closely with the military to replicate the tools of state

Figure 4.8 Recruitment as a theme in commercial games. (left) *Medal of Honor: Pearl Harbor*, which alongside the slogan "You don't play, you volunteer" ran this advertisement on card stock featuring a draft card. (right) *Freedom Fighters* advertisement extolling that one "recruit accordingly" for the war.

violence; the business of state violence in turn capitalizes on playtime for institutional ends.

More than any other cultural manifestation, video games represent the emerging politics of the virtual citizen-soldier, produced by the changing configurations of electronic media, social institutions, and world events. This new figure represents a reprogramming of the citizen subject in accordance with the logics of Netwar where citizen identity itself becomes a battle-ground. As the new security state "thickens," it tends to reproduce the social field in its image, resulting in a culture that progressively integrates the citizen into the momentum of the war machine. The new generation of war-themed games is central to this culture, inviting one to inhabit a political world conditioned through the aesthetic of "gametime." Gametime moves quickly, subordinating critical and ethical questions to movement and action. Historic-ally, the spectacle of war emerged to shift emphasis from the rational question of "why we fight" to the dazzling display of "that we fight." Gametime integrates the citizen, however virtually, into the mechanical pleasures of "how we fight."

Media effects scholar Arthur Asa Berger writes:

Games aren't models of reality and don't claim to be; what they do is represent an emotional reality that generates the desired fantasies in the minds of players. Thus, criticizing games for not being real or realistic misses the point.[74]

This is a wise suggestion on one level. The litmus test for what ought to be subjected to "the reality principle" should depend on what the art form "claims to be." When a war-themed commercial game begins to make claims about authenticity, or better yet, when a state institution like the Pentagon begins to make claims about authenticity (and what is *America's Army* without this claim?), then the culture has entered another reality altogether. War-themed video games, armed with this newfound legitimacy, gain a profound rhetorical force. What was once a fantastical and entertaining sidebar becomes the very presentation of war.

Presenting war in the guise of a game alone is not alone sufficient to play at war. The presentation must also be absent the horrors a high-tech military machine can effect. The virtual citizen-soldier, whether playing *Kuma\War* or following an embedded reporter on MSNBC, fights a war largely without human consequence. This player has intimate knowledge of the whir that the $3000 night vision goggles make when flipping the switch, as this was meticulously reproduced for *America's Army*, but he or she does not see through those goggles "little girls with smashed up faces," as one commentator from the *Ottawa Citizen* observes.[75] In terms of video games, Alexander R. Galloway notes the difference between the two, naming one "realisticness" (the ability to reproduce attributes of the physical world) and the other "realism" (the correspondence to realities of social life).[76] In a sense, the power of *America's Army* lies in its use of the former to make a claim on the latter. The problem, of course, is that integration into a sanitized fantasy of war is a seduction whose pleasures are felt at the expense of the capacity for critical engagement in matters of military power. One might say that the freedom to play war in the midst of war is not free.

The crossover between military and civic uses of war-themed video games has closed into a feedback loop consisting of the technological ability to produce an increasingly "realistic" war and the will to selectively reproduce political events in playable real time. This loop appears to be tightening and accelerating. In his investigation of high-tech military training, *Virtuous War*, James Der Derian argues that the apparent virtue of war is facilitated by, and is in large part inseparable from, its virtuality.[77] He admonishes us: "[L]ike reality's most intimate counterpart, the dream, virtuous war requires a critical awakening if we are not to sleepwalk through the manifold travesties of war, whether between states or tribes, classes or castes, genders or generations."[78]

Whether or not we will enjoy this critical awakening, the premise remains: video games are increasingly both the medium and the metaphor by which we understand war. Unless we confront their significance in crafting citizen identity, video games will march on, leading training exercises on military bases and taking up quarters in our hearts and minds.

Chapter 5

Toying with Militainment

Buying the War

On September 11, 2001, Wal-Mart reportedly sold 116,000 American flags. The numbers stayed strong thereafter. By May 2002, another 4.9 million had passed through the Wal-Mart checkout aisle and untold millions had sold elsewhere.[1] They showed up on porches and picture windows, as license plate frames, decals, bumper stickers, car magnets, and T-shirts.[2] The frenzy of purchasing of course drew its energy from a heightened sense of American solidarity and nationalism in the face of an attack. Those who feared being judged as "foreign" defensively hung flags on their homes and workplaces as well. Merchants quickly capitalized on these impulses, incorporating the flag into advertisements for everything from cars to pizza to long-distance service, admonishing consumers to "show their patriotism" through purchase decisions. Jennifer Scanlon notes that such an orgy of flag merchandising wove consumer goods, consumption, the bumper-stickered automobile, Wal-Mart, and geo-politics into a seamless symbolic fabric that swaddled and insulated the "citizen-consumer."[3] This vision of the good wartime citizen also drew meaning from the official Washington decrees. Speaking on September 27, 2001, President Bush exhorted a Chicago audience that the best way to deal with terrorism was to keep the consumer dollar moving. Rather than stop to think, the president suggested that Americans "Fly and enjoy America's great destination spots. Get down to Disney World in Florida. Take your families and enjoy life, the way we want it to be enjoyed."[4]

Coincidental with the invasions of Afghanistan and Iraq, this brand of patriotism turned its eye from memorabilia toward a new array of war-themed consumer goods that flooded the market. Some of the more bizarre merchandise appeared in the form of collectables for adults, namely teddy bears. An astonishing number of venders hawked Army, Air Force, Navy, and Marine-themed teddy bears. The Hamilton Collection issued a military bear complete

Figure 5.1 A selection of flag merchandising after 9/11 collected by the author: pizza box, plastic flag with "Made in China" imprimatur, and long-distance telephone service mail offer.

Source: Photos by the author.

with rifle and desert combat gear, striking that careful balance between unconditional love and unstoppable killing machine. An ad proclaimed the bear to be "On the Front Lines of Freedom!" and a "Salute to America's Military Heroes." Gemmy Industries of Irving, Texas, rush delivered its Chinese imports of military-garbed plush hamsters in anticipation of the Iraq invasion. A company spokesperson called the hamsters a "marketing home run."[5] One of the more popular items from the specialty stuffed bear dealer WeMakeBears4U.com—among The Tooth Beary, The Prayer Bear, and The I Love You Bear—was a duo entitled The Shock and Awe Bears, a reference to the US blitzkrieg-style opening bombardment of Baghdad, an attack whose "sheer size" had "never been seen before, never been contemplated before," according to one Pentagon official.[6] The company naturally embroidered one bear with the name "Shock" and the other with "Awe." The website advertised them as a means to cope with the unfathomable: "While the world seems to be engulfed in 'Shock and Awe,' this company tries to soften the effect."[7]

The collectable market paled in comparison to the boom in war-themed action figures, however. With 2002 sales up 21 percent over 2001 (in contrast to standards like Barbie, which lost ground by 14 percent), war toys became the prize of the traditional toy sector. "A whole new generation has discovered G.I. Joe," declared Hasbro's director of communications, noting a massive

Figure 5.2 Military bear offered by the Hamilton Collection in its line of "Faithful Fuzzies," from *Parade* magazine, March 30, 2003.

Source: Photo by the author.

46 percent profit increase in 2002.[8] The crop of post-9/11 war toys was more than an inflation of a long-standing market. The toys themselves changed in significant ways. Like video games, toys of this period gained a much closer thematic relationship to real-world events. In January of 2003, as the invasion of Iraq appeared imminent, Hasbro launched a "Desert Tactical Advisor" figure modeled on the Army's Delta Forces.[9] The top sellers of 2002 were a line of toys from the Hong Kong-based Dragon Models, Ltd. entitled "American Freedom Fighters: Live from Afghanistan's Frontline." One of these figures went by the name of "Tora Bora Ted," whose job, according to his makers, was "centered around Tora Bora, a mountainous stronghold, riddled with caves, where US soldiers battled Taliban fighters in their anti-terror campaign in Afghanistan." JC Penney offered the "World Peacekeepers Playset," which, despite its name, was entirely constituted by American military forces. Blue

Box Toys issued a line called "Freedom Force" action figures to accompany the US invasion of Afghanistan. Small Blue Planet, another large toy manufacturer, introduced a series entitled "Special Forces: Showdown with Iraq." The president of this company, Anthony Allen, described the marketing process: "We started work when the 'Showdown' buzzword hit the airwaves. There's fierce competition among manufacturers to get the new things out first."[10] Both toy makers and retailers recognized this dictum. Christian Borman, president of Plan-B Toys, related a piece of advice from a potential buyer: "He told us we should wait until the war starts, and whatever logos we saw on CNN, to put that on our toys."[11] Such market forces increasingly drew the world of consumer toys into the television war in much the same way that previous decades had discovered the merchandising of feature films.

Renditions of actual world leaders picked up in sales as well. Website retailer HeroBuilders.com made a name for itself with talking Vladmir Putin, Jacques Chirac, and Gerhardt Schroeder dolls, the leaders of the three largest and most vocal Western nations opposed to the Iraq invasion. Protect and Serve Toys of Indiana released the "head of Osama Bin Laden" to "allow enthusiasts to enact what it may be like when we finally catch" the number one bad guy.[12] HeroBuilders.com released popular dolls entitled "Osama in Drag" and "S&M Saddam" (dressed in whips and chains), an extreme take on wartime emasculation of the enemy. Hussein's reputation as a sadist, a certain pronunciation of his first name, and various news anchors' preference for calling members of his Ba'athist party "Saddamites" fed into the curious symbolism of this action figure.[13] For Independence Day, 2004, the Missouri-based company Crazy Debbie's Fireworks distributed a package entitled "Game Over" that featured "Exploding Head Terrorist" fireworks, all manufactured in China. The featured four are "Rag Hat Arafat," "Sadly Insane Hussein," "bin Laden Noggin," and "Cannibal Gadhafi." When lit, the effigies emitted screeches and blood-red fountains before their heads blew off. The set sold well. Keith Christensen, owner of the large Nebraska retailer Stars and Stripes Fireworks, said he had trouble keeping them stocked.[14]

The most popular of these collectables by far was the Blue Box Toys "Elite Force Aviator" figurine of George W. Bush. The figure portrayed the president as he had appeared on May 1, 2003, in a carefully constructed event. Landing in a fighter jet and dressed in flight suit, the president strolled around the deck of the aircraft carrier *USS Abraham Lincoln* before delivering a speech declaring an "end to major combat" under the infamous "Mission Accomplished" banner. On *Good Morning America*, former Clinton advisor George Stephanopoulos critiqued the event's choreography: "For those who grade Presidential photo ops, this was an A++. I mean, look at the pictures of the President on the flight deck. He looks like one of the pilots."[15] After the carrier landing, K·B Toy

Stores found their customer service lines overwhelmed by requests for an event-themed toy of some kind. They found a place for it in the Elite Force action figure line made by Blue Box Toys (makers of "Hello Kitty"). K·B Toys stocked the 12″ Aviator, the first ever presidential action figure of its kind, with a product description that carried Stephanopoulos' enthusiasm:

> On May 1, 2003, President Bush landed on the *USS Abraham Lincoln* in the Pacific Ocean, and officially declared the end to major combat in Iraq. While at the controls of an S-3B Viking aircraft from the "Blue Sea Wolves" of Sea Control Squadron Three Five, designated "Navy 1," he overflew the carrier before handing it over to the pilot for landing. Attired in full naval aviator flight equipment, the President then took the salute on the deck of the carrier.

While playing to the interactive war's fantasy of sitting in front of the controls, the presidential action figure did not please everyone. Upon receiving complaints from veterans groups that Bush was not a "war hero," Blue Box issued a

Figure 5.3 Merchandising the television war. Three CBS screenshots of George Bush's May 1, 2003 televised landing on the aircraft carrier *USS Abraham Lincoln* and action figure issued after the event.

Source: Action figure photo courtesy of Daniel Cota.

statement: "We don't condone or endorse the president, but he fit the criteria of our Elite Force collection. It would have to be somebody in a uniform, a military hero of some kind, or depicting a military uniform."[16]

The US military did not want to be left behind in the onslaught of commercial war toys. On November 15, 2007, the Army released its own line of action figures. The "Real Heroes" series consisted of four initial figures (with more on the way) each based on a live, medal-winning soldier. In the idiom of a *Star Wars* figurine, the plastic action figures came with trading cards detailing each soldier's rank, title, awards, and other stats. Jazwares, Inc., a company previously holding licenses to produce Mortal Kombat, Disney, Mega Man, and Street Fighter toys, worked closely with the Pentagon to perfect every detail of the "Real Heroes" set before deploying them to the shelves of Toys 'R' Us.[17] The series was an outgrowth of the *America's Army* video game, which had featured these same soldiers as playable characters. In both cases, the Army recognized the direction of the market—trends toward greater "realism" and fidelity with the television war—and used its official capacity to push beyond the inherent limits of its commercial counterparts. In doing so, the military gave its unique seal of approval to a culture increasingly accustomed to consuming the television war as a playtime activity.

The Army's decision to include trading cards with its action figures was likely inspired by the success of the Topps company, which launched a line of war-themed cards in November of 2001. Though widely known as a sports card company, Topps issued a set entitled "Enduring Freedom Picture Cards" that commemorated the events of 9/11 and cheered the Afghan invasion. Half of the series featured character cards: firefighters braving the wreckage of the Twin Towers, members of the president's Cabinet, world leaders, and Osama bin Laden. The other half of the 90-card set depicted weapons systems used in the invasion.[18] Topps' main rival, Upper Deck, released its own 9/11 series called "United We Stand," inserting individual cards into its "Legends of New York" baseball packs.[19] US Trading Cards, LLC, rolled out a similar but more bellicose set soon after, containing 42 "terrorist cards" featuring the likes of Saddam Hussein, Osama Bin Laden, Yassir Arafat, and Moammar Ghadafi. Other cards depicted the president's cabinet and weapons systems along with tag lines like "Kicking Some Serious Butt is the Only Thing these Terrorists Understand!"[20] On the board game front, in 2005 Jiggi Games released "Battle to Baghdad: The Fight for Freedom," where, according to the instructions, "You will take out airports, night bomb cities, hunt down Saddam Hussein, and take over Baghdad." Drawing cards, a player might gain troops via an airlift or lose troops in a car bomb attack. One card shows a female soldier holding a detainee on a leash and reads: "Disgrace: Some soldiers are found guilty of unlawful treatment and inhumane acts of violence toward Iraqi prisoners. You lose 100 troops!"[21]

Figure 5.4 One of the official action figures merchandised by the US Army. Sergeant First Class Gerald Wolford, a real-life soldier depicted in the *America's Army Real Heroes* collection.

Source: Copyright 2007 by Matthew Kessen and used with permission from Figures.com.

Figure 5.5 (top) Trading cards from *America's Army Real Heroes* collection; (bottom) cards from Topps' "Enduring Freedom" trading card set.

Source: Copyright 2007 by Matthew Kessen and used with permission from Figures.com.

This kind of merchandising was not entirely new. During the Persian Gulf War in 1991, the makers of the Dungeons and Dragons game, TSR, Inc., released a board game called "Line in the Sand," with scoring devices called "War Fever Gauge" and "Jihad Gauge." The game did a year's worth of sales in three months. The company updated the game twice to reflect the actual fighting. Toy model manufacturer International Hobby Corporation saw its overall sales triple during the war. The company could not keep its best-selling SCUD missile set on the shelf, nor, for that matter, its second best-selling model, the Abrams tank. Revell/Monograph models issued an "Aircraft of Desert Storm" series after their Stealth fighter kit sales soared to five times their pre-war levels.[22] Also during this period, Topps decided to get into the war trading card business with its three-part Desert Storm set. The Persian Gulf War was thus a pivotal moment in the development of war toys during which retailers worked to cultivate nascent markets of toy consumption tied directly the television war experience. The lesson of this period was that consumers desired souvenirs of the war spectacle. By the time the 2003 invasion rolled around, toy manufacturers were poised to exploit these trends by pushing the envelope of "realism" and providing venues by which consumers could act out more synergistic fantasies of war play.

These trends demanded much tighter integration between toy manufacturers and the military-industrial establishment. Part of the mission of Institute for Creative Technologies (ICT) at the University of Southern California was to institutionalize a symbiosis between the weapons manufacturers and commercial toys. Such cooperation allowed toy manufacturers access to precise specifications for military hardware for increasingly realistic war toys. In 2003, for example, ICT brokered the Army-to-Hasbro transfer of the design for the "Objective Force Warrior," a prototype of a futuristic wired cyber-soldier. "It's kind of cool to see this stuff being fielded by G.I. Joe," one defense contractor told the New York Times.[23] Zodiac of North America, the company that manufactures dinghies for the Marines, also licensed its name, logo, and design to Hasbro.[24] Toy manufacturers are not the only beneficiaries of this transaction. Weapons contractors receive free "advertising" for their products, which translates into enthusiasm from the civic sphere and ultimately legislative appropriations. Weapons manufacturers also benefit from this partnership as the military searches for ideas on smaller, lighter systems. For example, such collaborations resulted in the "Dragon Runner," a 15-inch remote-controlled truck. Model airplanes inspired the "Dragon Eye," a remote-controlled reconnaissance aircraft. As the Times notes, if any of these weapons are then released on the toy market, the process will have come full circle.[25]

Such collaboration eventually did come full circle. Beginning with the 2003 invasion of Iraq, viewers of the television war—especially the 24-hour

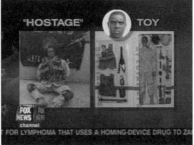

Figure 5.6 (left) Lester Holt on *MSNBC* with model fighter plane during the 2003 Iraq invasion; (right) the "Cody" action figure hoax on *Fox News*.

networks—became used to seeing war toys on the set. MSNBC, for example, lined its "Situation Room" with model aircraft to accompany the steady fare of video game-like animations. Realistic toys eventually made their way onto the battlefield in January of 2005, when an announcement appeared on an Iraqi insurgent website that an American soldier had been captured. The website posted a photo of the captive, who looked to be wearing standard issue gear. The Associated Press picked up the story but soon learned that the US military had recorded no missing American soldiers. A representative from the toy company Dragon Models, Inc. eventually revealed that the "captive" was really one of their realistic "Special Ops: Southern Iraq" action figures named "Cody" photographed close up with his own miniature M-4 rifle held to his head.[26] For many commentators, the story hook was one of an impotent insurgency resorting to hoaxes. Others speculated that the picture might have been posted by the US military as part of a "black propaganda" campaign to discredit insurgent groups.[27] The real news story, however, was the increasingly absurd relationship between toys and war, where an action figure, in its ultra-realism, could enter into the sphere of information warfare. A decade earlier, CNN's real-time broadcasting of war began to feed back into battlefield calculations, resulting in the so-called "CNN effect." The Cody incident revealed that a similar absorption might develop in other branches of the culture industry. That is, the cycle of weapons design and war consumption formed a rapidly collapsing feedback loop. This process of drawing the realities of state violence ever closer to fantasies of playtime is treacherous business, however, accompanied by a host of instabilities.

Full Circle: Points of Instability and Resistance

> Gentlemen, you can't fight in here! This is the War Room!
> (President Merkin Muffley in *Dr. Strangelove* (1964))

In September of 2002, White House Chief of Staff Andrew Card candidly explained to reporters why the administration waited to roll out its case for invading Iraq: "From a marketing point of view, you don't introduce new products in August."[28] The metaphor captured the tenor of the coming Christmas season in which both the administration and retailers pressed full steam ahead to "market the war." Card's comment struck its memorably sour note just as war toys too appeared to have crossed a line. At the center of one controversy was toy company Ever Sparkle's "Forward Command Post" playset, sold by such outlets as JC Penney, Toys 'R' Us, K·B Toys, and Amazon.com. The playset resembled a shell-shocked dollhouse complete not only with home furniture, but also bullet holes, torched walls, sandbags, and armed soldiers—a metonymic vision of contemporary war "coming home." Retailers soon found themselves swarmed with newspaper editorials and criticism from watchdog groups like the Lion and Lamb Project, which compile toy advisories for parents.[29] The playset garnered so much attention that the myth-debunking website snopes.com even devoted a fact-checking entry for the playhouse, confirming that it was indeed a real toy.[30] Another controversy surrounded the 2003 marketing of Easter baskets bristling with war toys at Walgreens, K-Mart, and Wal-Mart. The "Military Combat Set" featured toy fighter jets, action figures, and a camouflaged tanker truck, all tucked in a basket and wrapped in cellophane. The "Military Force" set came with miniature automatic weapons and a section of barbed wire fence.[31] Demonstrators collected outside a Grass Valley, California K-Mart and elsewhere, some carrying signs reading "Don't Candy Coat the War," and a woman in a bunny suit was arrested outside of a Manhattan K-Mart passing out leaflets.[32] Due to such press exposure and consumer complaints, Walgreens opted to pull the baskets from shelves. Wal-Mart and K-Mart declined to do so. Karen Burk, a Wal-Mart spokesperson, explained: "We share in the pride of Americans toward our service men and women." K-Mart expressed a different ideological position: "We wouldn't continue to sell action figures if they didn't sell well."[33]

The consumption of war toys has always been tacitly tied to the vicissitudes of public opinion and foreign policy. Empirically, Patrick Regan found a high correlation between economic militarization in twentieth-century US culture and the prevalence of war toys and movies.[34] This relationship can be traced back to the advent of modern war. In Europe, toy soldiers co-evolved alongside chess in the Middle Ages and later in tandem with the nineteenth-century

Figure 5.7 EverSparkle's Military Forward Command Post, a hit during Easter of 2003.
Source: Image from page 486 of JC Penney's 2002 Christmas catalog.

German *Kriegspiel*, a strategy game found mainly in the homes of military officers. By the mid-nineteenth century, economic conditions enabled the mass production of toy soldiers, usually solid lead figurines emanating from factories in Nuremberg, Germany. Late in the century French manufacturers became major players in the toy soldier market, finding a great number of consumers in Victorian Britain. In 1893, the British took the mass production of toy soldiers to another order of magnitude. By 1910, one British factory churned out 200,000 figurines a week, and the number of manufacturers multiplied. In this environment, certain nationalistic patterns of production and consumption developed. Reflecting larger developing trade conflicts, for example, British manufacturers eventually stopped producing renditions of German soldiers.[35] The same systems of mass production that enabled mechanized war thus also flooded the population with a new standard means of socialization into the building war economies. Though no causal claims can be made about the war fever that gripped Europe just prior to WWI, Kenneth D. Brown argues that the pervasiveness of the toy soldier cannot be ignored.[36]

The explosion of war toys just prior to WWI is perhaps why the toy soldier achieved a prominent place in the most enduring critique of militarism immediately following WWI, Ernst Friedrich's 1924 tract *Krieg dem Krieg!*

(*War Against War!*). The book amounted to a photographic tour through Friedrich's Anti-War Museum, which he established in Berlin in 1923. Like the museum, the book stands as a visual witness to the horrors of WWI, a time when mechanized warfare met the mature medium of photography. *Krieg dem Krieg!* went beyond displaying fields strewn with bodies. One of the more famous sections, for example, entitled "The Face of War," features page after page of recovering soldiers' horribly mangled and disfigured faces, many with enormous holes or missing jaws. The book does not simply overload the reader with images of destruction. Instead Friedrich consistently juxtaposes atrocity photos alongside idealized images of war, heroic poetry, and grandiloquent statements by military officers. The most obvious example of this strategy is Friedrich's decision to begin the book with a section entitled "How Children are Educated for War by Means of Toy Soldiers." Here, images of figurines, paper cut-outs, and war-themed children's books give way to images of enthusiastic young soldiers going off to war. The remainder of the book is a catalogue of war cemeteries, destroyed villages, and mutilated bodies. As Susan Sontag characterizes it in *Regarding the Pain of Others*, the book was "shock therapy" even for a Europe whose every home had been marred by World War I.[37] *Krieg dem Krieg!* worked its shock therapy by comparing the euphoric romanticism of war that swept through Europe—what in Germany became known as the "Spirit of 1914"—with the war's aftermath. Such attempts to de-aestheticize war soon encountered resistance, however. In *Mein Kampf*, published one year after the publication of *Krieg dem Krieg!*, Hitler reminisced about his time as a young man in 1914 amidst the powerful nationalistic exuberance that directly preceded WWI. Part of the goal of National Socialism, he wrote, was to reinvigorate that spirit and recreate it as a permanent condition. The party went so far as to explicitly pronounce the year 1933 as a rebirth of 1914.[38] Naturally, it was also in 1933 that the Nazis imprisoned Friedrich, destroyed the Anti-War Museum, and transformed it into a notorious site of torture. The museum, with its collection of turn-of-the-century toy soldiers, did not reopen its doors until 1981.[39]

The story of G.I. Joe is a more recent example of these tensions. Hasbro's quintessential war toy served as a barometer for fluctuations in public attitudes toward militarized play. The "action figure" had been introduced in 1964 as a rather generic toy soldier, a reflection of the established heroic war film and American confidence in its role in Vietnam. The next four years were a stunning commercial success for Hasbro. The rising tide of anti-war sentiment caught up with G.I. Joe, however, cresting after the 1968 Tet Offensive. Forced to respond to the growing mainstream aversion to war—what certain policy leaders would later call the "Vietnam Syndrome"—Hasbro gradually decommissioned the toy. In 1969, the company renamed the line "G.I. Joe

Adventurer" and in 1970, simply the "Adventure Team." In the process, the new toy shed much of his military garb for safari gear, a beard, and an array of not-so-threatening animal adversaries. The Action Team logo even bore an uncanny resemblance to a peace sign, superimposing an "A" over a "T" in a circle.[40] The arrival of *Star Wars* (1977) and the hyper-merchandising of the film prompted Hasbro to shift Joe's image again to "Super Joe" the space warrior, a visage that persisted two years before Joe fell out of production entirely. Between 1982 and 1995, the toy returned as "G.I. Joe: The Real American Hero," successfully mimicking *Star Wars*-style marketing techniques with its own animated television show. Accompanying the enemy set, C.O.B.R.A. Command, Joe reproduced the cold war drama of the Reagan era. In 1991, Joe took advantage of the fervor surrounding the Gulf War to experiment with a "desert arena" collection as well as reintroduce its pre-1969 twelve-inch models. Hasbro also lifted its long-standing prohibition against spring-loaded weaponry and depictions of G.I. Joe actually killing.[41] The post-9/11 toy environment precipitated a new wave of Joe products, all highly realistic forces equipped for arid and high desert terrain, and all modeled more or less on the television war. These included Strategic Operations Forces, Navy Seals, and Israeli soldier sets. As Hasbro CEO Alan Hassenfeld proclaimed in 2003, "G.I. Joe, obviously, is riding a crest of, you know, American patriotism, and we've tried to open on every front possible there."[42]

To be sure, the basic contradictions and tensions of war toys have persisted for over a century. Some things have changed, however. Chief among these is the development of a toy market that *Salon.com* called "custom-branded to current conflicts."[43] That is, the representational space between the war and the war toy has gradually waned. War toys have gained perilous proximity to war in their quest to satisfy the interactive urge. With increasing realism, however, the realities of war are more likely to intervene and interrupt the experience, to tear a hole in the thinning membrane that separates the two. The interactive war, moreover, comes with a range of authorship tools and thus a heightened potential for re-authorship, re-production, and the re-inscription of meaning. In other words, the more powerful and pervasive the interactive war in its subject-making potential, the more vulnerable it is. The tensions represented by war toys are those inherent to broader militainment culture. As such, they are a productive place to begin looking for ways to meaningfully engage this culture, and, yes, "toy" with it. The following investigates a few ways that artists and activists have done so, not only in the realm of toys but across the spectrum of militainment.

Some of these strategies involve getting inside and "jamming" certain kinds of entertainment practices. A provocative example of this inside job approach was a project initiated in 2002 called "Velvet Strike," a series of interventions performed on the multi-player, first-person shooter *Counter-Strike*. Large online games like *Counter-Strike* routinely deal with "hacks" or software modifications that allow players to cheat.[44] The Velvet Strike hack instead allowed players to alter the symbolic environment of the game to critically engage with war gaming culture. Anne-Marie Schleiner, a researcher and designer at San Jose Museum of Art in Silicon Valley and co-editor of the online journal *Switch*, devised the project. As a leading scholar of so-called "hacker art" in online environments, Schleiner described the projects "as a means of talking back to the industry and as well as amongst [programmers] themselves, and as an alternative gift economy flourishing in the crevices of the dominant consumerist system."[45] Using Velvet Strike, activists enter the *Counter-Strike* environment armed with tools to scrawl anti-war and nonviolent slogans on the virtual floors and walls. Demonstrations have been *de rigueur* in role playing games since the popularity of their text-based ancestors. After September 11, 2001, for example, players of *Everquest*, the most popular online game in the US at the time, called a ceasefire and held virtual candlelight vigils.[46] Velvet Strike, however, was perhaps the first to explicitly question the meaning of the game by working within it. Using a wide palette of "spray paint" patches, hackers tagged rooms with unlikely scenes, such as hearts on the wall or a child's hopscotch game on the floor. A team of activists also devised a series of "intervention recipes" or strategies that use the mechanics of the game to "hack" without hacks. The tactics range from "love and peace" sit-ins to group suicide missions, thus drawing comments on Schleiner's message board that folks who do this are "hippies with nothing better to do" or even bona fide terrorists.[47] One reporter noted that through the messages "fluctuate between painfully earnest and flat-out goofy" although "the payoff is in the idea, in infiltrating a game in order to subvert its subconscious message with a pro-peace agenda."[48]

Critical projects like Velvet Strike are often described as "culture jamming," a term Christine Harold defines as "an insurgent political movement" that "seeks to undermine the marketing rhetoric of multinational corporations, specifically through such practices as media hoaxing, corporate sabotage, billboard 'liberation,' and trademark infringement."[49] Harold describes two general approaches to jamming that she names "sabotage" and "appropriation." Whereas sabotage is the act of negation, of clogging the system of signs, appropriation is a more sophisticated approach that harnesses and channels the existing system of signs in some productive direction.[50] Much of the Velvet Strike strategy is the virtual equivalent of blocking traffic, an act of sabotage. Its strategy, however, cannot help but take on elements of appropriation too, doing its work from within the architectures of the game, creating new virtual spaces, and provoking public debate. For a number of reasons, the interactive

Figure 5.8 Scenes from Velvet Strike, a hack for the online game *Counter-Strike*. (left) Hopscotch; (right) "Hostages of Military Fantasy" spray-painted on a virtual wall.

Source: Screenshots courtesy of Anne-Marie Schleiner.

war in particular opens itself up to appropriation. As the interactive war threads itself into an ever closer-knit relationship with the citizen-consumer, it makes itself increasingly accessible. The strategies of engaging militainment culture generally assume one of three forms: collapse, acceleration, and reversal.

Collapse

This first strategy very simply seeks to collapse the alienation that allows for militainment in the first place. In a classic critique of ideology, this method seeks to pull back the curtain by injecting the unconsumable war back into practices of consumption. The vigilantes of Velvet Strike mobilize this strategy by introducing hopscotch into the scene, an incongruent reminder that war is not a battle between automatons on a space station. Other examples include a satirical bear sold in 2003 with a T-shirt that read "Give Us Your Oil or We Will Kill You" to offset the military bear market. In the same year, the website InfiniteJest.org offered a set of printable war-themed trading cards entitled "American Crusade" that rode the tail-end of the war trading card craze. The cards feature a rogue's gallery of corporate, media, and administration figures along with weapons systems juxtaposed against photos of civilian dead.[51]

During the US build-up to the invasion of Iraq, Mikel Reparaz sought to juxtapose the practices of prosecuting and playing at war. Reparaz, a 24-year-old copy editor and videogame reviewer for the *Marin Independent Journal* in Novato, California, embarked on a fundraising campaign to "Buy President George W. Bush a PlayStation 2." Along with the console, Reparaz proposed to send the White House *SOCOM: Navy Seals* and *Conflict: Desert Storm*, games both

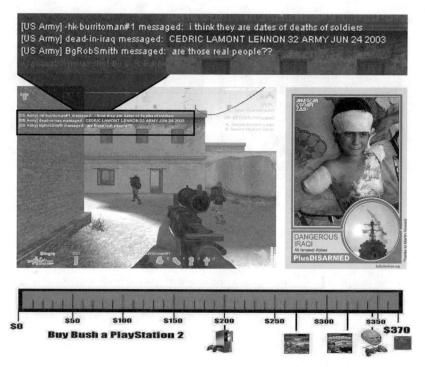

Figure 5.9 Militainment interventions. (top) A screenshot from Joseph DeLappe's "Dead_in_Iraq" project; one of the American Crusade satirical trading cards; (bottom) donation meter from the Buy Bush a PlayStation online campaign.

Source: Courtesy of Joseph DeLappe and Ted McManus.

heavily advertised at the time and suggested by donors as relevant titles. The accompanying letter to the White House also mentioned the inclusion of a second controller "for Mr. Cheney's use." The letter also stated the reasons for the campaign: "Given the amount of public speech and political rhetoric you have devoted to this issue in past months, it seems to us as though you are more interested in playing commando than in fighting an actual war with actual human casualties." In a matter of hours of the campaign's listing on the news aggregator, *Fark.com*, donations flooded in, and the campaign met its goal. Upon receipt, the White House gift office responded that the console was "being worked on" because of recent anthrax scares and that they would be sending a different response than usual. According to the website, Reparaz hoped that "different" did not involve black helicopters. As of July 7, 2004, Reparez had not received a response.[52] Still, the campaign did gather attention. The *Seattle Times* wondered if the Reparaz campaign had some effect on Sony's decision to drop their trademark on the term "shock and awe" as well as its plans to manufacture a war-themed game of the same name.[53]

Joseph DeLappe, an art professor at the University of Nevada, recognized that it only takes a few bodies to provoke a reality check. In 2006, DeLappe began performing what he called an "online gaming intervention" with the Pentagon-sponsored online game *America's Army*.[54] Signing in as "Dead_in-_Iraq," DeLappe dropped his cyber-rifle and began entering names of deceased US soldiers into the scrolling message bar that players use to converse. A typical entry included name, age, and date of death: "Dead_in_Iraq: JOHN DOE 21 MAY 4, 2004." By September, DeLappe had listed 1,273 of the 2,670 dead. The responses from some of the 6 million registered players of *America's Army* offer a sobering glimpse into the dissonance between the realism of the game and the realities of the ongoing war. As the names scroll up the screen, it eventually occurs to the players that they represent dead soldiers. One asks, "Are those real people?" Another dismisses the names as "propaganda," a curious word choice given the context. Another simply demands that Dead_in-_Iraq "Shut the f*** up!" DeLappe went on to exhibit the project around the country, choosing screen shots of the game that depict player comments, usually with a dead game character sprawled in the background. Some called the effort a clever use of digital tools to achieve a meaningful effect. Others dismissed the project as an empty artistic gesture that could have more directly commented on politics. Still others objected that the project unfairly used the names of dead soldiers to promote a message with which those soldiers themselves may not have agreed.[55] One of the project's most fascinating aspects, however, was that it did not state a "message" but only brought two quite accessible aspects of war culture into close proximity. Dead_in_Iraq was thus less about advocacy than about drawing attention to relationships among citizens, media, and war. According to DeLappe, "This game exists as a metaphor, not wanting us to see the carnage, the coffins coming home. It's been sanitized for us."[56] In the midst of the project, the Army released *America's Army: Real Heroes*, a game version that includes profiles of actual soldiers. Observing this development, DeLappe recognized that the project struck at the heart of the discourse of "realism" that animates the interactive war:

> Their intention to make the game more real is basically what I'm trying to do, but all the soldiers happen to still be alive. What's going to happen if one of them dies on another tour? Will they leave them in the game?[57]

While the Army likely took steps to make sure this never happened, the question draws attention to a defining instability of the interactive war.

Acceleration

If Delappe's project utilized a strategy of collapsing war back into its consumption, other artists and activists have waged powerful critiques of militainment by accelerating its own logics. Some of these have been done in the idiom of the spectacle. In late 2002, for example, as it began to appear likely that the Bush administration would go through with its plans to invade Iraq, *Mad* magazine issued an image that *Salon.com* called "one of the most widely circulated Photoshop images on the Internet."[58] The image is a coming attractions movie poster for a fictitious film called *Gulf Wars II: Clone of the Attack*. According to a *Pittsburgh Post-Gazette* editorial, the poster's aesthetic is a hybrid of *Star Wars*—especially the 2002 blockbuster sequel *Attack of the Clones*—and *Gone with the Wind*.[59] The would-be film casts George W. Bush as alpha-hero, Condoleezza Rice as heroine with flowing Scarlett O'Hara locks, Saddam Hussein as frumpy arch villain, George H.W. Bush as mentor, and a host of minor recurring characters: Donald Rumsfeld, Colin Powell, and Dick Cheney, the last of which emits an unearthly green glow from his head. Not pictured is Osama bin Laden, who, the poster tells us, represents the "Phantom Menace," a reference to a 1999 *Star Wars* installment. The credits read, "Produced by the military-industrial complex in association with Texaco, Mobil, Exxon, et al. The success of this military action has not yet been rated." Apart from such jabs, the image's power is its ability to provoke instant recognition of our position as citizen-spectators accustomed to the "war movie" since the first Gulf War.[60] The *Clone of the Attack* poster works to intensify the citizen-spectator's cinematic relationship to war past the point at which it had been comfortably naturalized. Instead of simply saying no to the war movie, this strategy harnesses its momentum to push it off a cliff.

Accelerating the logics of war-themed toys, *The Daily Show* did a short segment featuring the Military Forward Command Post, the playset that drew attention during the 2002 Christmas season. Correspondent Ed Helms suggested that the destroyed dollhouse come with a "War Widow Barbie" (complete with black veil) and a "Ballistic Projectile Action Lump" (a stone) as used by protesters in Gaza.[61] In another instance, artist Wayne Coe felt inspired to comment on war-themed model sets that flew off the shelves in 2003. Coe constructed model boxes—complete with cover art, logo, and age warning—with titles like "Guantanamo Guard Dog" and "I. E. D." (short for "improvised explosive device," a prime insurgent weapon and major cause of casualties among American troops in Iraq). Coe's box for "Human Pyramid" depicts an Abu Ghraib-style photo of a pile of naked bodies with a rubber-gloved thumbs-up in the foreground. The back of the box features schematic instructions for how to properly stack the humanoid game pieces

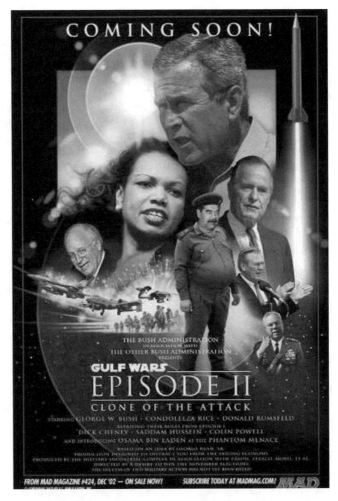

Figure 5.10 Mad Magazine's satirical movie poster.

supposedly in the box. Coe shrink-wrapped the convincing boxes and exhibited them in a New York festival that happened to grant him a 7 × 7-ft store display window on Division Street to display his work, an ideal venue for such merchandise.[62] One Los Angeles reviewer called the display "funny at first, but there is something ultimately chilling about seeing some of the most shameful scenes in America's history played out beneath that comfortingly familiar Revell logo."[63]

One of the most dramatic instances of acceleration strategy came in the form of an installation project entitled "Domestic Tension," created by Wafaa Bilal, an Iraqi-born artist living in Chicago. Bilal spent the entire month of May, 2007, in a small, white room in Chicago's Flatfile gallery, furnished with only a

Figure 5.11 "Human Pyramid" and "Guantanamo Guard Dog"—Wayne Coe's war model boxes on display.

Source: Photos courtesy of Wayne Coe.

white bed and a white lamp. A paintball gun loaded with yellow paintballs stood on a tripod near the edge of the room. Bilal wired the gun to the Internet through a webcam in a configuration similar to that pioneered for so-called "Internet hunting."[64] With this set-up, the website enabled visitors to remotely aim the gun through a webcam "sight" and squeeze off a round with the click of a mouse. A two-way link allowed Bilal to communicate with those on the shooting end of the transaction. Bilal also engineered the contraption to issue a loud gunshot sound with each round giving a shell-shocked quality to everyday life in the room in addition to the painful paintball welts. Life under these conditions was not easy. As Bilal described the experience, "They wait for me to let my guard down, like predators."[65] By the end of the project, the website had eighty million hits, and the gun had fired more than 65,000 shots.[66] Perhaps the site's biggest boost in traffic came when the project was reported on the bookmarking site, *Digg.com*. The majority of the comments left on the *Digg* story were hostile, such as "Dude get a decent server so we can play some Waffa [*sic*] Ball!" and "Too bad we can't waterboard him."[67] Comments comparing Bilal to a terrorist may have been in part a response to his choice to wear a Palestinian kuffiyeh scarf. Bilal explained, "I learned all these new things about myself. I learned I was a nigger, and a sand nigger. That I was gay. Part of it is demonization, then you can justify trying to shoot me."[68] There were inspiring moments as well. The day after a shooter successfully destroyed Bilal's lamp, a marine who had served in Iraq brought him a new one.[69]

Part of Bilal's stated purpose was to engage people who might not normally engage the conversation. Rather than moralize, "Domestic Tension" drew its conversant into a familiar but accelerated position. The view of the room from the website looked very much like that of a first-person shooter video game, with the muzzle of the gun protruding into the scene from the bottom of the frame. The webpage framed the screen with the outline of a globe, casting the

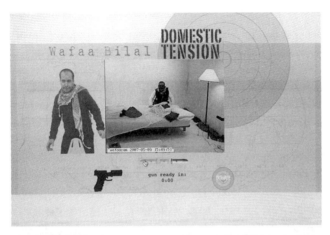

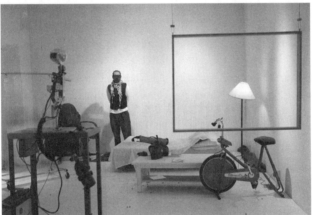

Figure 5.12 Wafaa Bilal's "Domestic Tension" project. (top) Website with webcam gunsight view; (bottom) Bilal under siege in his living quarters.

Source: Photos courtesy of Wafaa Bilal.

experience in geopolitical space or what Bilal called a "global shootout" in a
CBS News interview.[70] His own story drove the narrative home. Bilal grew up in
Iraq under Saddam Hussein, later fleeing to the US in 1991 after being labeled
a political dissident for refusing to be conscripted into the Iraqi army. As a
faculty member of Chicago's Art Institute during the build up to the US
invasion of Iraq in 2003, he experienced a daily dose of what he called
"domestic tension" on the street.[71] In 2005, he learned that a missile shot from
a Predator drone had killed his brother outside their family home in Najaf. A
few months later, his father was killed at a security checkpoint.[72] These tragedies
not only inspired "Domestic Tension" but also fed into its reception, giving the
accelerated "game" an undeniable critical force.

Reversal

Both spectacular and interactive consumption of war rely on constructing the imperialist subject and a demonized enemy. As such, simply reversing these positions can be a powerful strategy. Walking the streets of New York or a number of other world cities between 2005 and 2006, one may have spotted a poster for a film entitled *United We Stand*. With battleship, a squadron of fighter jets, and a background explosion, the poster may well have been another in a long line of post-9/11 Hollywood blockbusters. Looking closer, one may have noticed the slogan beneath the title: "Europe Has a Mission." The European Union flag billowing in the distance and a line-up of European actors—from Ewan McGregor to Penelope Cruz—complete the scene. "The clash of codes is almost palpable," wrote Ben Davis of *ArtNet*.[73] The poster was part of a larger effort by two Spanish artists, Eva and Franco Mattes, who go by the collective name of "0100101110101101.org." The duo enlisted collaborators worldwide to download and pin up the poster, erect billboards, run banner ads on websites, and place ads in magazines featuring the fictitious film. The ads by themselves did most of the work, but the "several hundred thousand" who visited the *United We Stand* website got a synopsis: "It is the year 2020. With the excuse of halting North Korea's nuclear program, the US invades China—a development long expected by international analysts. 'We have a problem. Make that Two: America and China'."[74] This tagline read very similarly to US Secretary of State Donald Rumsfeld's characterization of what he called "old Europe" in January of 2003: "Germany has been a problem, and France has been a problem."[75] Holland Cotter of the *New York Times* noted that the images mimicked "Hollywood-style propaganda-as-history," and though the film was fake, the poster campaign "may lodge in our consciousness all the same."[76] *United We Stand*'s reversals spoke to a broad audience, drawing into relief stark differences between American and European identity myths. Within a global milieu saturated with Hollywood films and other American cultural influences, the project's authors asked: "Why is the patriotic iconography of the USA commonly accepted, while when it is applied to Europe it completely changes its meaning and actually becomes ludicrous?"[77] The strategy of reversal tends to pose these kinds of questions, taking its prime target to be habitually rein-scribed notions of American exceptionalism. The deeper these subconscious symbolic practices, the greater the rupture when the terms are reversed.

The strategy of reversal is arguably more volatile in the interactive idiom. In 2003, for example, a 19-year-old from California named Jesse Petrilla created a game called *Quest for Saddam*. The game achieved modest popularity during the invasion and early occupation of Iraq. According to the game description, *Quest for Saddam* enabled one to "participate in the largest manhunt in history"

Figure 5.13 Movie poster for the fake film *United We Stand* and pedestrian contemplating the poster in New York City.

Source: Images courtesy of Eva Mattes and Franco Mattes of 0100101110101101.org.

at the same time that it played out on US television news.[78] Later, in 2006, while Petrilla was busy hanging an effigy of Osama bin Laden from a noose in front of a California mosque, his game again showed up in the news.[79] A group called the Global Islamic Media Front began distributing the game with certain modifications, including the replacement of Iraqi soldiers with American soldiers and Hussein's face with Bush's. Petrilla was "not flattered" by this act of imitation, which went by the name of *The Night of Bush Capturing* (AKA *Quest for Bush*).[80] Whereas CNN described *Quest for Saddam* with curiosity and praise, where "gamers hunt down the former Iraqi leader in tongue in cheek fashion," the same network covered the appearance of *Quest for Bush* with a good measure of panic, describing it as the "latest way Islamic radicals are using the Internet to spread their message of hate."[81]

Both games eventually drew the attention of Wafaa Bilal while he recovered from the trauma of his paintball project, "Domestic Tension." Noting the elegant symmetries of the scene, Bilal decided to test the public tolerance for reversal. In 2007, he integrated *Quest for Bush* into a project called "Virtual Jihadi," which he exhibited at Rensselaer Polytechnic Institute in Troy, New York. Bilal further modified the game so that his own face appeared as a playable screen character wearing a bomb vest. The object of the game remained the same as in *Quest for Bush*: to penetrate a bunker and kill President Bush. Virtual Jihadi showed for one day before it exploded into public controversy.

Rensselaer's College Republicans called the art department a "terrorist safe-haven," the FBI moved in to conduct an inquiry, and the school shut down the exhibit.[82] The act of censorship attracted national attention, achieving a major goal of the project. Bilal explained that the piece was not intended to glorify terrorism but rather to serve as a "platform for conversation" to reverse the "conflict zone" and the "comfort zone."[83] Moreover, by moving the game into a domestic context, Virtual Jihadi tested the convenient binary of "games we play" and "games they play."[84] The exhibit prompted questions such as why one game depicting the assassination of a state leader is a "terrorist game," while a game depicting the same for another state leader is quite acceptable.[85] With the lineage of *Quest for Bush* close at hand, Virtual Jihadi set a trap of sorts, flushing a public denunciation out into the open so as to force it to reckon with a pronounced double standard. Moreover, through Bilal and his on-screen avatar, the project turned the tables on the usual set of subjectivities, denaturalizing the "comfort zone" and asking what it means to be under siege, real and virtual.

A similar dynamic charged the Syrian publishing company Dar el Fikr, which in 2001 issued the first Arab-made 3D war video game *Under Ash*.[86] The game was a direct response to video games like *Jane's Israeli Air Force* (where the goal is to bomb Arab cities) and *Delta Force* (where Americans fight an enemy force comprised of Arabs). Hassan Salem, director of Dar el Fikr, said that no

Figure 5.14 (top) Screenshots from *Quest for Saddam* and *Quest for Bush*; (bottom) "Virtual Jihadi."

American company would sell them the basic graphics engine for the game, so it had to be built from scratch. Even so, the first pressing of ten thousand copies sold out in a week.[87] The game did not simply reverse characters. Game players take on the avatar of Ahmad, a young Palestinian, who has decided to resist and join the Intifada. Ahmad begins by throwing rocks at tanks and gradually progresses to armed conflict, engaging in missions to raid Israeli bases and settlements in the occupied territory, and take down Israeli flags. He rescues wounded Palestinians who have been shot by "Zionists" while praying at mosque in a reenactment of a 1994 massacre. The game is framed by its opening sequence, where Ahmad's grandfather tells the story about the rise of the Intifada and the restoration of hope while photos of conflict and repression somberly grace the screen. *Under Ash* has characteristics that set it apart from many first person shooters. There is no "winning" the game, so "the struggle" is portrayed as just that. Ahmad is not superhuman in any sense, and there are no medical kits that can magically restore his life. When he gets hit, he dies. If Ahmad shoots civilians, the game is over. There are no suicide bombings. Responding to complaints that the game is too difficult, the designer Radwan Qassmiyya stated:

> *Under Ash* is about history. In our modern history there is no solution to the conflict, so the game is a mirror. There is no solution for Ahmad's case. At the last level of the game, there will be no major victory, no reclaiming land or anything like that.[88]

Qassmiyya suggested instead that the game is about experiencing what it is to be a Palestinian in Jerusalem. As such, he suggested that the game should be viewed as a tool for those who sympathize with those under occupation but cannot help—a tool of "self-salvation." Part of the meaningfulness of the game thus comes from its ability to successfully turn the tables, breaking the spell that playing more mainstream titles like *Israeli Air Force* is a transparent, non-political, and private matter. *Under Ash* also introduces productive complexity into the field of war-themed video games. The game operates on a much different plane of reversal than, say, *Quest for Bush*—a game that Qassmiyya played and found to be "nothing but propaganda" and "hateful."[89] Rather than simply substituting one "side" for another, the game self-consciously assumes the tragic perspective of the powerless, the occupied, and the conquered. In doing so, it not only questions whether a war game ought to be "fun," but also shines a critical spotlight on the near monolithic empire of militainment produced and consumed by the winners in advance.

Figure 5.15 Screenshots from *Under Ash*. (left) Main character carrying a wounded comrade; (right) the portrayal of occupying Israeli Defense Forces.

Realism Versus Reality

If these interventions teach anything, it is that militainment culture is not unassailable. Indeed, it has taken some time for these many factors to align in the consumable war. The process has been building ever since the "Vietnam Syndrome" alerted policy planners that blind trust in government would not be enough to authorize war. Broadly speaking, militainment culture grew out of a shift in the locus of authorization, a shift from propaganda *per se* to the integration of war into existent practices of consumption. This has been extremely tricky business in that it has produced meanings always on the verge of self-negation. One outcome of this shift has been the development of the spectacular war. Here the unconsumable realities of war wait in the wings, occasionally wandering in at inopportune times to prick the conscience. The interactive war that arrived on its heels, however, pressed the unconsumable war into much closer proximity with practices of consumption, inviting one in with promises of authenticity and immersive experience. This raised the stakes. The greater the attempt at consumable "realism," the more vulnerable the discourse became to the intrusion of certain unconsumable realities. If the fault lines of the spectacular war were few and wide, the interactive war was comprised of a network of hairline fractures distributed throughout the system of meaning. Indeed, these fissures have infused the very identity of the virtual citizen-soldier, whose armor threatens to shatter at the least critical provocation. This chapter examined how a range of such provocations render their blows through strategies of collapse, acceleration, and reversal. In the interactive war, a well-placed precision strike is all it takes to activate these fissures, to initiate a systemic crisis that calls the entire experience into question. Doing so forces the culture to take a step back and reckon with the true somberness of state violence and our significant role as deliberative citizens.

Chapter 6

Debriefing

Previews to Postviews

In many ways, the wave of "militainment" culture that washed through the polity at the beginning of the new century can be represented by a short film produced by the Pentagon in 2002. Called *Enduring Freedom: The Opening Chapter*, the 4-minute film slipped itself in among the usual movie previews beginning in September, just as the Bush administration began beating the drums for the invasion of Iraq. In assuming the role of movie trailer, the film suggested that "Enduring Freedom," the mission name for the US incursion into Afghanistan, was only the "opening chapter" of the coming media event. The purpose of the film was ambiguous, however. Ed Halter of the *Village Voice* called it part of "the next generation of wartime propaganda" where "techno-jingoism" meets "jockish, Army of One-type sloganeering."[1] Indeed, *Enduring Freedom* freely mixed genres, delivering part recruitment ad, part documentary, part reality show, and part WWII-style propaganda film. Even its makers could not give a clear answer as to its function. According to the film's producer, Lt. Col. James Kuhn, *Enduring Freedom* was designed to "powerfully communicate to the American public what the Navy and Marine Corps team is and who we are."[2] He later elaborated: "The piece doesn't ask anyone to make a judgment or take an action. It's just saying, you're a taxpayer, here's a meaningful look at the military."[3] Indeed, the film did not ask its audience to take action—to brace for difficulty, buy war bonds, ration sugar, or even join the military. Like any self-respecting preview, its meaning instead resided in the phrase "the show is on its way." This could be heard in one on-screen soldier's words that "It's not a question of if we go to combat; it's a question of when." While taking on some of the features of the spectacle, however, *Enduring Freedom* sat perched on the cusp of the new interactive war. The film wasted no time in dropping the viewer into the boots of the soldier, as one of the "we" who are destined for combat. Beginning with an enlistee taking the oath of service, the film moved through 9/11 footage and the steely resolve of soldiers moving through their routines. *Enduring Freedom* swept the viewer up as a virtual recruit in a military preparing for imminent conflict. As one Marine notes in the video, "When you say send someone into war, they're not just some robot—these are people just like you." Though a preview of the war movie to come, the film's ultimate exhortation is not simply to witness the spectacular military machine in motion, but to virtually hop on board and into the skin of one of those "just like you."

This book has described the interactive war to which *Enduring Freedom* served as an "opening chapter." The case studies examined mainly focus on a narrow window of time, roughly from 9/11 through the invasion and subsequent occupation of Iraq. This period might be called the "militainment bubble," where audience attention, rallying effects, culture industry profit motives, and Pentagon interests aligned to produce a certain kind of consumable war. In many ways, this period represented a reprise and intensification of the 1991 Persian Gulf War. If the civic experience of Desert Storm followed the logics of the spectacle and political deactivation, however, the years following 9/11 featured certain institutional, political, technological, and cultural shifts that began to describe the "virtual citizen-soldier," a subject invited to step into a fantasy of first-person, interactive war. Sports discourses retooled the citizen's virtual proximity to death as an economy of pleasure consonant with the discourse of the "battlefield playground"; war journalism combined with the genre of reality television and its interactive logics; military recruitment broadened its cultural scope to create leisure environments; video games offered venues to play the war; the toy industry integrated military hardware and the television war in its ever closer collaborations with the Pentagon. As such, discourses of militainment have burrowed deeper into the capillaries of the subject, working internally to intensify a prescribed posture toward state violence and thereby widen the "coalition of the willing." These trends indicate a displacement of the democratic citizen who makes critical judgments about state policy with a citizen subject wired to consume and play out policies contrived and executed beyond the will of "the people." Much of this book has suggested that the appearance of the interactive war represents a more sophisticated and immersive regime of social control. The interactive war also harbors an array of instabilities, however. The will toward experiential realism inevitably brings it into contact with the realities of war, generating friction that threatens the cool mythologies that make war consumable in the first place. The interactive war thus represents the violent dissonance of the term "militainment" in its purest form. These contradictions exist as bundles of TNT in a war of representations, scattered in new authorial spaces for resistance.

Jean Baudrillard famously posed the question regarding late twentieth-century consumer excess: "What are you doing after the orgy?"[4] In regard to militainment and the consumption of war, it may be fair to say that the orgy has largely ended, the pyrotechnics of battle fading into sagging public approval numbers, a long occupation, conflicting success reports, rising casualty numbers, and a change of leadership in a nominally less belligerent direction. Having witnessed this militainment bubble as an historical episode, what can be said about its meaning and legacy? There are at least two ways to assess this question.

One approach is to conclude that certain realities have successfully challenged the ability to unproblematically consume war. The Iraq invasion eventually violated the American public's expectations of a quick and consequence-free repeat of Desert Storm. The Bush administration predicted the war to be a "cakewalk" that was supposedly to have ended under the "Mission Accomplished" banner on May Day 2003. Despite a long line-up of finish lines, the US deaths and injuries continued to rise, eventually making their presence felt among the general population. News of Iraqi civilian casualties—estimated at 100,000 in 2004 and 600,000 in 2006—may have sunk into public consciousness as well, despite the fact that these deaths have been consistently ignored by the press.[5] Because of its potential as a "quagmire" with a high soldier body count, discussions began among elites in 2005 of a potential "Iraq Syndrome" that might affect the public's future tolerance for elective military intervention.[6] Polls reflected this assessment. The percentage of Americans who agreed that the war was "worth fighting" topped out in April of 2003 at 70–75 percent after which they gently declined into the 50s, peaking briefly again at around 60 percent with the much hailed capture of Saddam Hussein. By 2006, approval ratings had flat-lined at around 30–35 percent.[7] It could be argued that the arrival of this "syndrome" signaled a collective critical awakening, one that increasingly questioned the underlying narratives that made the consumption of war possible. In other words, certain realities could no longer be held at bay, the field of deliberation and debate widened, and an increased skepticism toward wartime public relations took root. One may conclude that the consumption of war became an endeavor fraught with new complexity.

Certain signs seemed to point in this direction. In 2009, for example, Defense Secretary Robert Gates announced that he would lift the ban on press access to returning US coffins, giving families the choice to make funerals public.[8] Such gestures coincided with new public sensitivities to militainment culture as well. That same year, the National Football League announced that it would move away from describing football with war metaphors, though it continued with the practice of military flyovers and officer coin tosses.[9] In March of 2009, Konami Games announced it planned to release *Six Days in Fallujah*, what the company called a "docu-game" designed to reproduce the US siege of the city of Fallujah, Iraq, in 2004. By April, public outcry, including disapproval from veterans groups, had forced Konami to drop the project.[10] In

May, the Army Experience Center, a combination of video-game arcade and recruitment center in Philadelphia's Franklin Mills Mall, gained national attention. Veterans, religious leaders, and other protesters staged a theatrical demonstration citing incompatibility of war and its consumption as a game.[11] Events like these suggest that public debate has come to recognize these issues as a "front line."

From perhaps a less optimistic angle, the decline in militainment culture may have simply been a result of fatigue rather than a critical reassessment. That is, war may have simply played itself out and lost its novelty. The changing landscape of news from January of 2007 to March of 2008 seems to support this explanation. While the war itself did not undergo radical changes during this period, the Pew Research Center's Project for Excellence in Journalism found that coverage of the Iraq War plunged from 24 percent to four percent of the "newshole" across mass media outlets.[12] It is plausible that this massive tuning out first manifested in approval ratings, followed by a decrease in militainment-style programming, and finally the virtual elimination of Iraq from the news. Like a miniseries that had overstayed its welcome, the war had run its course—"jumped the shark" as it were—and the public changed the channel. Back to business as usual, attention moved to the failing economy, presidential primaries, and an election campaign in which even the candidates sidelined the tired issue of continued military occupation. This "fatigue" account is somewhat more disturbing in terms of democratic deliberation, because it suggests that in the era of militainment, the willingness to support a war is indistinguishable from a willingness to consume it.

Whatever the explanation for the decline, it is also the case that militainment culture has not entirely disappeared. Indeed, the explosion of militainment left behind a field of embers that continue to smolder for the time being. The interactive war has left its stamp on citizen identity, rewiring practices and identities among civic, media, and military spheres. A variety of indications suggest that militainment culture, though attenuated, is here to stay. Between 2005 and 2008, for example, the video game *America's Army* broadened its sphere of influence by strides, amassing 25 versions on all major game platforms, harvesting some nine million users by 2008, and holding steady at a rate of around one million new registered players a year.[13] The game has been a central fixture in the Army-hosted tournaments as well as its theme park-style "experience centers." Moreover, the Army has hooked its train to other popular games. In late 2007, for example, the Army teamed up with Microsoft and the popular *Halo* game franchise. *Halo 3*, a first-person shooter set on a futuristic world, had scheduled an online tournament for March of 2008. The Army not only sponsored the tournament but also offered "Basic Combat Training" sessions hosted on Xbox LIVE, including "sniper school," "vehicles," and "heavy weapons." These sessions featured combat strategies and advice from a cadre of real Army experts.[14] The Army had apparently taken a cue from the reality game *Kuma\War* and its mix of military experts and gameplay. The collaboration also showed the Army's willingness to extend its brand well beyond the realism and relevance of *America's Army*. The Army thus continued to cultivate an entertainment empire by colonizing ever larger and more diverse circles of leisure time. In this new landscape, the amusement park or a fantasy game has been recoded as yet another opportunity to play the war "over there."

In terms of journalism, a reprise of a main-event war as happened in 2003 is not likely for a decade or more. Instead, the occupations of Iraq and Afghanistan are likely to simmer in the background of public consciousness for the time being, given the Obama administration's reluctance to fully withdraw a US presence in Iraq and a willingness to ramp up the presence in Afghanistan. As the supposed "anti-war candidate," Obama seemed to serve as a short-term prophylactic against public opposition to the occupations. Suspended in this stasis, it is likely that an "Iraq Syndrome" will act as a light version of the "Vietnam Syndrome" that drove military intervention underground in the 1980s. Journalistic coverage of the war will continue to be determined by prevailing economic factors such as the public's disinterestedness in war coverage, the expense and danger of stationing reporters in these conflict zones, and the availability of services like DVIDS (the Pentagon's Digital Video Distribution System) that began providing free footage in lieu of the disappearing embedded reporter in 2004.[15] In the absence of any major Abu Ghraib-like scandals, these factors will likely maintain a protracted and cool status quo.

Though the military presence on reality television began a decline along with news coverage of the US presence in Iraq, it appears that military-themed shows will retain a limited role. In July of 2006, for example, NBC decided to host a special entitled *Military Fear Factor* among a number of other variations on its popular *Fear Factor* franchise. This show specifically sought out members of the Army, Navy, Air Force, and Marines who had recently served in Iraq. NBC shot the episode on the deck of the *U.S.S. Hornet*, an aircraft carrier permanently moored in San Francisco Bay and routinely loaned out for Pentagon-approved productions. Past credits included *xXx 2: State of the Union* (2005), *Rescue Dawn* (2007), an episode of *JAG*, and various commercials and television specials.[16] Contestants on *Military Fear Factor* launched themselves off the flight deck with a large slingshot, ate leeches from a mess tin, and unscrewed plastic hand grenades from the top of a truck before it plunged over the side of the ship—a strange tribute indeed to those who had risked life and limb at the behest of the country.[17]

One lasting residual effect of the entertaining war may have been its carving out a place on the cable and satellite TV dial. During the initial stages of the Iraq War, military-themed reality television and embedded reporting had been on a collision course. Though both genres appeared to quietly disappear as the occupation drew on, in reality, a hybrid of the two had migrated to a corner of the cultural landscape. In January of 2005, the *New York Times* announced, "Americans want their military TV."[18] That month, the aviation-themed Discovery Wings channel, which had been around since 1998, made the plunge into 24-hour militainment by rebranding itself The Military Channel.[19] The new channel promised to take viewers to the front lines, showcase new gadgets, and deliver the standard military history fare. The Military Channel premiered with a special entitled "Task Force Red Dog," where cameras followed around a Marine unit in Afghanistan, very much like the reality show *Profiles from the Front Line* that had inspired the embedding system.[20] A related program called *Delta Force* followed another Marine unit in Baghdad. In 2007, The Military Channel rolled out a *Military Diaries*-style show that showcased soldier-generated content. "The Military Channel at its essence is the voice of the troops," noted Discovery CEO David Zaslav. "We want to see the war through their eyes. That will help us understand what's going on there."[21] The new programming was part of a larger strategy to extend the channel's wild success by steering away from historical programming and toward shows that recounted first-person battlefield experiences and aerial dogfights in Iraq and elsewhere.[22] Two other channels followed the premiere of The Military Channel in 2005. A&E's History Channel spun off The Military History Channel, aiming more toward avid viewers of historical military documentaries. The Pentagon also launched its own ad-free cable channel aptly called The Pentagon Channel, whose audiences naturally spilled beyond military servicepersons and their families. The arrival and survival of these three cable channels suggest that reality-style militainment had settled into a more permanent niche.

Critical engagements of militainment found wider audiences, however, especially as war approval numbers dropped. Chapter 5 documented many of these, which experienced their own spike in visibility. The year 2008 saw perhaps one of the most pointed and public critiques of the entertaining war, John Cusack's project *War, Inc.* A richly dark satire, the film imagines a corporatized military occupation of the country of "Turaqistan." The "Tamerlane" company—a thinly veiled reference to Halliburton—runs the war with an absurdly effective public relations department. Military vehicles, for example, have been outfitted with commercial and sports logos, much like stock cars. In one trenchant scene, reporters stand in line to enter a briefing room. On the way in, a guard injects a chip into the necks of each of the "implanted reporters." Movie theater seats line the inside of the briefing room where the implants sit and put on 3D goggles. As the briefing starts, the room begins to shake and list from side to side like a Universal Studios simulator ride. The implants are clearly enjoying the experience, gasping and yelping with glee while rockets explode on screen. A more independently minded reporter (Marisa Tomei) sits next to an assassin-for-hire (John Cusack). She asks him about ways to get out of the "Emerald City" (a reference to the Green Zone in Baghdad) so that she may see "what's really going on." "Anything," she says, "has got to be better than this Xbox bull****." As they whisper about the level of death on the streets outside, one of the implants leans over and asks them to shut up: "We're trying to watch a battle here . . ." Moments later, as the action heats up on screen, this same reporter falls out of her seat, yelling in ecstasy, "I'm hit! I'm hit!" The film uses such juxtapositions to great effect. While a critique of the embedded reporter, the scene tapped into the deeper compulsions and contradictions of the virtual citizen-soldier. This put the film into direct visual conversation, for example, with the increasing presence of military theme parks that featured experiences not so different from the thrill ride of the film's "briefing room."

While predictions are always tenuous, all indicators suggest that the wake of the militainment bubble will be a complex field of tensions between the consumption of war and critical corrections. Because some version of the interactive war is here to stay, the "front lines" will continue to be negotiated. On the one hand will be the basic political responsibilities to the soldier, those at the other end of the gun, and deliberative democracy. On the other will be the seductions of the entertaining war. Part of the task in maintaining a robust and honest polity is to seek out these contradictions, expose them to the light, and force a confrontation so that the most defensible values persevere. Gilles Deleuze noted, "It is not a question of worrying or of hoping for the best, but of finding new weapons."[23] As the interactive war evolves, these weapons of critique will not always be obvious. They will always be present, however,

Figure 6.1 (left) "Implanted journalism" scene from *War, Inc.*; (right) the traveling Virtual Army Experience center in 2008 featuring Humvee and simulated M-4 rifles with realistic pneumatic recoil.

Source: The Virtual Army Experience page at http://www.vae.americasarmy.com/.

within the circulation of signs and within the citizen-subject. It is this citizen, after all, who holds the ultimate power to authorize state violence and to "pull the trigger." Our goal as a polity should be to cultivate a citizen conscious of the gravity of this responsibility, a citizen critical of the cultural forces that would turn real soldiers into pawns in a game and real civilians into fodder for a cynical pastime. Our goal should be to cultivate a civic culture where political energies are channeled into open democratic deliberation rather than siphoned off into consuming and re-enacting official policy. These are elemental values, but they are perhaps the only way to truly win the war.

Notes

The full form of the bibliographical entry is also given in the Bibliography.

Introduction

1 Rage Against the Machine, "No Shelter" (1998).
2 Thomas Hayden and Marc Silver, "Tanks for the Memories," *U.S. News and World Report*, June 6, 2005, D14.
3 Natalie Zmuda, "Are the Army's New Marketing Tactics a Little Too Kid-Friendly?," *Advertising Age*, September 8, 2008, 1. Carrie McLeroy, "Army Experience Center Opens in Philadelphia," *Army.Mil/News*, September 2, 2008. Online: http://www.army.mil/-news/2008/09/02/12072-army-experience-center-opens-in-philadelphia/. John Leland, "Urban Tool in Recruiting by the Army: An Arcade," *New York Times*, January 5, 2009, section 9, pg. 3.
4 Julie V. Iovine, "The Army Wants You for the Afternoon," *New York Times*, October 10, 2004, section 2, pg. 1.
5 Sam Keen, *Faces of the Enemy: Reflections of the Hostile Imagination* (San Francisco: Harper & Row, 1986), 10.
6 Judith Butler, "Contingent Foundations: Feminism and the Question of 'Postmodernism'," in *Feminists Theorize the Political*, ed. Judith Butler and Joan W. Scott (New York: Routledge, 1992), 10–12.
7 Caren Kaplan, "Precision Targets: GPS and the Militarization of Consumer Identity," *American Quarterly* 58, no. 3 (2006): 709.
8 For an historical treatment of the curious affinity between the medium of film and the subject of the atom bomb, see Jerome F. Shapiro, *Atomic Bomb Cinema: The Apocalyptic Imagination on Film* (New York: Routledge, 2002).
9 James Poniewozik and Jess Cagle, "That's Militainment!," *CNN.com*, February 25, 2002. Online: http://www.cnn.com/ALLPOLITICS/time/2002/03/04/militainment.html.
10 Steve Ford, "So Terrible We Can't Get Enough," *News and Observer*, March 23, 2003, A30.
11 These included The Military Channel (the rebranding of the Discovery Wings channel), The Military History Channel (an A&E/History Channel venture), and the Pentagon Channel (operated out of the Pentagon). Mark Glassman, "Military Channels Are Competing on Cable TV," *New York Times*, January 24, 2005, C8.
12 Jonathan Burston, "War and the Entertainment Industries: New Research Priorities in an Era of Cyber-Patriotism," in *War and the Media: Reporting Conflict 24/7*, ed. Daya Kishan Thussu and Des Freedman (Thousand Oaks, CA: Sage Publications, 2003), 169.
13 See the chapter "The Culture Industry: Enlightenment as Mass Deception," in Max

Horkheimer and Theodor Adorno, *Dialectic of Enlightenment*, trans. John Cumming (New York: Continuum, 1999), 120–67.

14 See http://www.cultureindustry.com.

15 Walter Benjamin, "The Work of Art in the Age of Mechanical Reproduction," in *Illuminations*, ed. Hannah Arendt (New York: Schocken Books, 1968), 241.

16 See Charles Harrison and Paul Wood, eds., *Art in Theory, 1900–2000: An Anthology of Changing Ideas* (Malden, MA: Blackwell Publishing, 2003), 147.

17 Quoted in Patrick Sloyan, "The War You Won't See: Why the Bush Administration Plans to Restrict Coverage of Gulf Combat," *Washington Post*, January 13, 1991, C2.

18 Benjamin, "The Work of Art in the Age of Mechanical Reproduction," 242.

19 See http://hotzone.yahoo.com.

20 For an extensive treatment of this transition, see Paul Virilio, *War and Cinema: The Logistics of Perception*, trans. Patrick Camiller (London: Verso, 1989).

21 Others include British films *Attack on a China Mission* (1900) about the Boxer Rebellion and *How a British Bulldog Saved the Union Jack* (1906) about the Zulu wars. Back in the US, Vitagraph presented *Scenes from a True Life* (1910) and D.W. Griffith's *The Battle* (1911). See Jeanine Basinger, *The World War II Combat Film: Anatomy of a Genre* (Middletown, CT: Wesleyan University Press, 2003), 347.

22 Susan Sontag, *Regarding the Pain of Others* (New York: Farrar Straus and Giroux, 2003), 24.

23 Susan Sontag, *On Photography* (New York: Farrar, Straus, and Giroux, 1977), 110–11.

24 Ibid., 86.

25 Lawrence Weschler, "Valkyries over Iraq," *Harper's*, November 2005, 69.

26 Ibid., 77.

27 Susan Sontag specifically draws attention to this descriptor, tying it to the tradition of disaster movies that preceded the event. Sontag, *Regarding the Pain of Others*, 22.

28 Slavoj Žižek, *Welcome to the Desert of the Real!: Five Essays on September 11 and Related Dates* (New York: Verso, 2002), 16.

29 Jean Baudrillard, *The Spirit of Terrorism; and Other Essays*, New ed. (London; New York: Verso, 2003), 5.

30 Todd J. Gillman and Carolyn Barta, "Bush Administration Getting Cozy with Hollywood," *Dallas Morning News*, November 22, 2001 (Lexis Nexis database).

31 Andy Seiler, "Hollywood Declares Time is Right for War Movies," *USA Today*, 27 November 2001, 1A.

32 Quoted in "Movie Theatres of War," *Advertiser*, 8 November 2001, 40. Film critic John Patterson also goes out of his way to note the phenomenon of audience cheering and applause at the film's opening. "Bottom Gun: John Patterson Takes a Look at this Week's US Movies, and Finds *Behind Enemy Lines* Serving up Jingoistic War Film Cliches," *Guardian*, December 3, 2001, 12.

33 For a complete history of early public relations, see Stuart Ewen, *PR!: A Social History of Spin*, 1st ed. (New York: Basic Books, 1996). See also Edward L. Bernays, *Propaganda* (Brooklyn, NY: Ig Publishing, 2005). Walter Lippmann, *Public Opinion* (New Brunswick, NJ: Transaction Publishers, 1991).

34 Such OWI collaborations were an effort to emulate the highly sophisticated and centralized German Ministry of Propaganda, which incidentally saw itself as locked in an "arms race" with the US to develop the much more compelling technology of color film. Eric Rentschler, *The Ministry of Illusion: Nazi Cinema and Its Afterlife* (Cambridge, MA: Harvard University Press, 1996), 203. The German director of *The Eternal Jew* (1940), Fritz Hippler, noted that total war had "forced us to reconsider our notions of 'weapons' and 'soldiers' " so that "all expression of national life become weapons of war." Quoted in Rentschler, *The Ministry of Illusion*, 202.

35 A history of this office along with a list of films supported and rejected by the Pentagon has been catalogued in David L. Robb, *Operation Hollywood: How the Pentagon Shapes and Censors the Movies* (New York: Prometheus Books, 2004).

36   Quoted in Allan M. Winkler, *The Politics of Propaganda: The Office of War Information, 1942–1945* (New Haven, CT: Yale University Press, 1978), 12.

37   Quoted in ibid., 61. Treasury Secretary Henry Morganthau, Jr. recognized there were faster ways of raising money, but that the bond campaign gave everyone a "financial stake in democracy" and "an opportunity to do something." John Morton Blum, *V Was for Victory: Politics and American Culture During World War II* (New York: Harcourt Brace Jovanovich, 1976), 17.

38   Harold Lasswell, "The Garrison State," *American Journal of Sociology* 46 (1941): 461.

39   A primary technique is what Lasswell describes as the "startle pattern," a punctuated adjustment to an assumed threat of danger (external or increasingly internal) expressed in the "authoritative manner that dominates military style," ibid.: 460. Such a state increasingly depends on war scares as well. For these war threats to remain solvent, Lasswell argued, they must be nourished from time to time with a bloodletting, a spectacular exercise in war. Finally, alongside this preoccupation with fighting, there is a tendency toward the repetition and ceremonialization of public martial rhetoric. Later, Lasswell clarified the model slightly to suggest that though democracy suffers under the garrison state, the appearance of democratic participation is sustained through a regular but empty invoking of its symbols. Lasswell, "The Garrison State Hypothesis Today," in *Changing Patterns of Military Politics*, ed. Samuel Huntington (New York: Free Press, 1962), 51–70. For follow-ups on Lasswell's ideas, see Vernon Dibble, "The Garrison Society," *New University Thought* 5 (1966–67), 106–15. See also an interesting analysis of Presidential State of the Union speeches, public opinion, and other indicators in Samuel Fitch, "The Garrison State in America: A Content Analysis of Trends in the Expectation of Violence," *Journal of Peace Research* 22 (1985), 31–45.

40   C. Wright Mills, *The Power Elite* (New York: Oxford University Press, 1956), 304.

41   Ibid., 315.

42   Dwight Eisenhower, "Farewell Address," January 17, 1961 (http://millercenter.org/scripps/archive/speeches/detail/3361). In an original draft of the speech, the term was to be the "military-industrial-congressional complex." The word "congressional" was struck to avoid baiting Congress. It should be noted that, though he held reservations, Eisenhower was one of the most ardent supporters of the permanent military, a position widely apparent in the context of his entire farewell address and other public statements. A. Duane Litfin, "Eisenhower on the Military-Industrial Complex: Critique of a Rhetorical Strategy," *The Central States Speech Journal* 25, no. 3 (1974), 198–209. The notion of the "military-industrial complex" persists to this day as a dominant critical term, appearing most prominently in the latter stages of unpopular wars. Critics of the Vietnam War repeatedly invoked the "military-industrial complex" along with Eisenhower's name and authority as a term of protest. The early half of the 1970s witnessed the materialization of an entire library shelf devoted to examinations of militarism and the workings of the military-industrial complex. See Seymour Melman, *Pentagon Capitalism: The Political Economy of War* (New York: McGraw-Hill, 1970). Adam Yarmolinsky, *The Military Establishment; Its Impacts on American Society*, 1st ed. (New York: Harper & Row, 1971). Steven Rosen, *Testing the Theory of the Military-Industrial Complex* (Lexington, MA: Lexington Books, 1973). Peter Wallensteen, Johan Galtung, and Carlos Portales, *Global Militarization*, Westview Special Studies in Peace, Conflict, and Conflict Resolution (Boulder, CO: Westview Press, 1985). James A. Donovan, *Militarism, U.S.A.* (New York: Scribner, 1970). Sidney Lens, *The Military-Industrial Complex* (Philadelphia, PA: Pilgrim Press, 1970). Carroll W. Pursell, *The Military-Industrial Complex* (New York: Harper & Row, 1972). Thereafter, the term largely fell out of the public lexicon only to be later resurrected in the wake of the 2003 invasion of Iraq. By June 2004, the portion of the population who approved of the occupation had fallen below half, making way once again for a critical eye. Linda Feldmann, "Why Iraq War Support Fell So Fast," *Christian Science Monitor*, November 21, 2005, 1. Two documentary films also hit the market in 2006 questioning the role of corporate profit in war-making. Eugene Jarecki's *Why We Fight* most directly invoked the notion of the military-industrial complex. The original limited release date was

January 17, 2005, exactly 45 years after Eisenhower's farewell address. The film self-consciously took its name from the well-known series of US government propaganda films produced during World War II as if to signal the complete overhauling of the question from that of national defense to corporate profits. Robert Greenwald's *Iraq for Sale* appeared the same year examining the invasion as a profitable business venture.

43 Eisenhower's concern that the military might be serving corporate rather than public interests had been predicted in 1937 by the most decorated marine of WWI, General Smedley Butler. Butler wrote in his famous tract, *War is a Racket*, that modern warfare was no more than a tool for protecting business interests abroad. For Butler, war functioned to transfer wealth from the citizenry to big business, a transaction signed with the blood of soldiers. Smedley Butler, *War Is a Racket* (Los Angeles: Feral House, 2003).

44 As Habermas puts it, out of the vibrant civil sphere formed "a repoliticized social sphere in which state and societal institutions fused into a single functional complex that could no longer be differentiated according to the criteria of public and private." Jürgen Habermas, *The Structural Transformation of the Public Sphere: An Inquiry into a Category of Bourgeois Society*, trans. Thomas Burger and Frederick Lawrence (Cambridge, MA: MIT Press, 1996), 148.

45 Hannah Arendt, *The Human Condition* (Chicago: University of Chicago Press, 1989), 181.

46 Ibid.

47 The War Powers Act of 1973 attempted to restore congressional control over the right to declare war and represented an exception to dominant trends toward separating citizen power from military power.

48 An early study of this phenomenon was Peter W. Singer, *Corporate Warriors: The Rise of the Privatized Military Industry*, Cornell Studies in Security Affairs (Ithaca, NY: Cornell University Press, 2003). Singer's groundbreaking work was followed by Chalmers A. Johnson, *The Sorrows of Empire: Militarism, Secrecy, and the End of the Republic*, 1st ed. (New York: Metropolitan Books, 2004). Perhaps signaling that the issue of private armies had gained widespread attention was the appearance of a more popular text, Jeremy Scahill, *Blackwater: The Rise of the World's Most Powerful Mercenary Army* (New York: Nation Books, 2007). The new phenomenon has also been called the "war service industry." Dina Rasor and Robert Bauman, *Betraying Our Troops: The Destructive Results of Privatizing War* (New York: Palgrave Macmillan, 2007).

49 Jeremy Scahill, "Bush's Mercenaries Thrive in Iraq," *Toronto Star*, January 29, 2007, A13.

50 Michael Hardt and Antonio Negri, *Multitude: War and Democracy in the Age of Empire* (New York: Penguin Press, 2004), 47.

51 The notion of the citizen-soldier extends back to the early Renaissance period, particularly Machiavelli. In his advice to the Medicis, Machiavelli argued that a primary threat to the stability of the state, be it principality or republic, is the practice of holding standing mercenary armies whose inherent disloyalty might cause them to rise up against the state at any moment. Mercenary armies, Machiavelli wrote, are "disunited, thirsty for power, undisciplined, and disloyal; they have no fear of God, they do not keep faith with their fellow men; they avoid defeat just so long as they avoid battle; in peacetime you are despoiled by them, and in wartime by the enemy." Niccolò Machiavelli, *The Prince*, trans. George Bull, New ed., Penguin Classics (New York: Penguin, 1999), 77. Machiavelli elaborated that there is a profound difference "between a happy army that fights for its own glory and one that is poorly organized and fights for the ambition of others." Niccolò Machiavelli, *Discourses on Livy*, trans. Julia Conaway Bondanella and Peter E. Bondanella (New York: Oxford University Press, 1997), 113. As such, Machiavelli argued for the distribution of military power through a more loyal militia of citizens-soldiers, who would then have a personal investment in the continuation of the state. For the aristocracy, the creation of a "republic" was a trade-off to be sure. In distributing the military power among citizen-soldiers, the ruling elite relinquished a measure of sovereignty in exchange for the stability of the state.

52 Through Machiavelli and a succeeding line of civic republican thinkers, the citizen-soldier took a central role in the revival of classical notions of participatory government, access

made possible by the acquisition of a military identity. In the lineage of civic republican thought, this has generally meant espousing the rule of law, participation, and an Aristotelian mixed government balanced between three parts: monarchy, oligarchy, and democracy. Civic republicanism can also be thought of as an update to "classical republicanism," but the word "republican" did not exist in either Ancient Greek or Roman times except in terms of the rather vague *res publica* (Latin: "the public thing"). Enlightenment eyes looked back to the Ciceronian Roman Republic as an ideal representation of Aristotle's mixed government. The Roman model was uniquely duplicated by the city-state of Venice (from roughly 1223–1600 C.E), what the Italians called the *Serenissima* (the "Serene State"). Civic republican thought was thus born in the shadow of ancient Rome, Renaissance Venice, and within the broader intellectual trends of humanism and scholasticism. This new technology of state also mirrored the Protestant Reformation's core concept of a "priesthood of all believers" that swept through Europe roughly the same time. In short, by gaining a military identity, the new citizen-soldier gained a hand in government. Iseult Honohan explains that the civic republican tradition, generally speaking, is a constellation of ideas regarding the preservation of a republic that finds its seeds in classical Greek and Roman thought (Aristotle and Cicero), beginning properly with Machiavelli and Harrington, and continuing through later thinkers such as Rousseau, Wollstonecraft, and Madison. "Emphasizing responsibility for common goods sets republicanism apart from libertarian theories centred on individual rights." Iseult Honohan, *Civic Republicanism* (New York: Routledge, 2002), 1. For a fine discussion of civic republicanism in Machiavelli and Rousseau, see R. Claire Snyder, *Citizen-Soldiers and Manly Warriors: Military Service and Gender in the Civic Republic Tradition* (Lanham, MD: Rowman & Littlefield Publishers, 1999), 45–55.

53 As Elaine Scarry notes, the Fifteenth Amendment (citizenship to Blacks), the Nineteenth Amendment (voting rights for women), and the Twenty-Sixth Amendment (lowering of voting age to eighteen) all passed with the acknowledgment that those groups in question had contributed militarily. Elaine Scarry, "Watching and Authorizing the Gulf War," in *Media Spectacles*, ed. Marjorie Garber, Jann Matlock, and Rebecca L. Walkowitz (New York: Routledge, 1993), 57–73. The Emancipation Proclamation included language that equated eligibility to serve with civic freedom. W.E.B. Du Bois, writing during World War I, demanded that Blacks be included in the draft as an essential step to full citizenship and equal rights. Similar arguments can be heard today in debates regarding the admittance of homosexuals into the military and women into combat roles. See John Whiteclay Chambers, *To Raise an Army: The Draft Comes to Modern America* (New York: Free Press, 1987), 156. Cynthia Enloe argues that the contemporary exclusion of women from the front line combat constitutes a wedge by which the patriarchy has traditionally asserted its civic superiority. Cynthia H. Enloe, *Does Khaki Become You?: The Militarisation of Women's Lives* (Boston, MA: South End Press, 1983), 15. Jody Cramsie makes a similar case: "To contribute to the defense of the nation is a fundamental civic obligation; it is participation in an essential national enterprise." See Jody Cramsie, "Gender Discrimination in the Military: The Unconstitutional Exclusion of Women from Combat," *Valparaiso University Law Review* 17, no. 2 (1983): 580. Registry for Selective Service remains a primary requirement for citizenship, and running for high political office, until relatively recently, meant that one must hold one's military credentials up to public scrutiny.

54 Challenges to the citizen-soldier ideal go back much further. John Whiteclay Chambers notes this evolution. While the citizen-soldier ideal made possible the state-building that emerged in sixteenth-century Europe, the ideal eventually gave way to the more centralized practices of mass conscription that provoked the Napoleonic Wars and World War I. Chambers suggests that the US lagged significantly behind its European progenitors, preferring the citizen-soldier model of the militia man to mass conscription out of a certain Jeffersonian suspicion of centralized control. In the Second Amendment, for example, the civic republican ideals of mixed government and military participation are condensed into their most essential form: "A well regulated Militia, being necessary to the security of a free State, the

right of the people to keep and bear Arms shall not be infringed." Chambers characterizes the pre-Revolutionary War *Zeitgeist*: a large professional army was a "vehicle for political corruption, manipulation, and tyranny of the State." Chambers, *To Raise an Army*, 19. The US Constitution specifically denies Congress the authority to fund a standing army. Article I, Section 8 of the US Constitution makes it clear that while Congress has the authority "To raise and support armies, but no appropriation of money to that use shall be for a longer term than two years." The standing army was instituted without amending the Constitution.

55 Scarry, "Watching and Authorizing the Gulf War." The loss of such fundamental aspects of citizenship leaves Scarry wondering what is in store for other civil rights and liberties.

56 George H.W. Bush, "The President's News Conference," *George Bush Presidential Library and Museum*, November 30, 1990. Online: http://bushlibrary.tamu.edu/research/public_papers.php?id=2516&year=1990&month=11.

57 Charles Rangel of New York, John Conyers of Michigan, and Pete Stark of California.

58 Rangel, a decorated veteran of the Korean War, stated, "If those calling for war knew their children were more likely to be required to serve, there would be more caution and a greater willingness to work with the international community in dealing with Iraq." Elise Young, "Talk of a Military Draft Has New Significance: Proposal to Require Service Alters Outlook for Some Youths," *Seattle Times*, February 2, 2003, A16.

59 Edward Epstein, "House Defeats Bill to Reintroduce Draft," *San Francisco Chronicle*, October 6, 2004, A1. See also Carl Hulse, "Threats and Responses: The Draft," *New York Times*, February 9, 2003, 17.

60 The WWI Committee on Public Information (CPI) and the WWII Office of War Information (OWI) were the main organs through which the military interfaced film and radio. In Nazi Germany, especially, such a melding had been primary goal of Propaganda Minister Josef Goebbels. Though Hitler preferred more hard-edged propaganda like *Triumph of the Will* (1935) and *The Eternal Jew* (1940), Goebbels preferred to work through existing entertainment genres, especially the musical. Goebbels saw the theater as a vital link to the popular mind, and he actively cultivated a habitually movie-going public who would be exposed to official ideas on a habitual basis. Indeed, after heavy bombing raids, Goebbels made it a priority to get the film houses up and running as soon as possible. Doob calls this Goebbels' principle of evoking interest in an audience by transmitting propaganda through an attention-getting medium. See Leonard W. Doob, "Goebbels' Principles of Propaganda," in *Public Opinion and Propaganda*, ed. Daniel Katz et al. (New York: Dryden Press, 1954), 513.

61 Robert Stam, "Mobilizing Fictions: The Gulf War, the Media, and the Recruitment of the Spectator," *Public Culture* 4, no. 2 (1992): 124.

62 Burston, "War and the Entertainment Industries: New Research Priorities in an Era of Cyber-Patriotism," 164.

63 Thomas and Virchow point out that, after years of cultural aversion, this same model has begun to take hold in Germany. Tanja Thomas and Fabian Verchow, "Banal Militarism and the Culture of War," in *Bring 'Em On: Media and Politics in the Iraq War*, ed. Lee Artz and Yahya R. Kamalipour (Lanham, MD: Rowman & Littlefield Publishers, 2005), 29.

64 Nick Turse, *The Complex: How the Military Invades Our Everyday Lives* (New York: Metropolitan Books, 2008).

65 The Bush administration appointed Charlotte Beers, who headed two top advertising firms in the US (Tatham-Laird & Kudner until 1992 and as CEO of Ogilvy & Mather until 1996) to Undersecretary of Public Diplomacy and Public Affairs from 2001 to 2003. Mark Andrejevic, "The Rehabilitation of Propaganda: Post 9/11 Media Coverage in the United States," in *Rhetorical Democracy: Discursive Practices of Civic Engagement: Selected Papers from the 2002 Conference of the Rhetoric Society of America*, ed. Gerard A. Hauser and Amy Grim (Mahwah, NJ: Lawrence Erlbaum, 2004), 88–89.

66 Gilles Deleuze and Félix Guattari, *A Thousand Plateaus: Capitalism and Schizophrenia* (Minneapolis: University of Minnesota Press, 1987), 75–110.

67 Allen Ginsburg, "Verses Written for Student Antidraft Registration Rally 1980," in *Collected Poems, 1947–1980* (Harper & Row, 1984), 730.

I All-Consuming War

1 Julia Malone, "POWs Top Allied Agenda," *Atlanta Journal and Constitution*, March 2, 1991, A1.

2 Ibid.

3 Ann Devroy and Guy Gugliotta, "Bush to 'Move Fast' on Mideast Peace," *Washington Post*, March 2, 1991, A1.

4 "Trust in Federal Government, 1958–2004," American National Election Studies. Online: http://www.electionstudies.org/nesguide/toptable/tab5a_1.htm.

5 Michael J. Arlen, *Living-Room War* (New York: Viking Press, 1969).

6 For a fine discussion of the Vietnam Syndrome's effect on subsequent media experimentation, see Susan L. Carruthers, *The Media at War: Communication and Conflict in the Twentieth Century* (New York: St. Martin's Press, 2000).

7 Ben H. Bagdikian, *The New Media Monopoly* (Boston: Beacon Press, 2004). Robert McChesney, *Rich Media, Poor Democracy: Communication Politics in Dubious Times* (Urbana: University of Illinois Press, 1999).

8 James W. Carey, "American Journalism on, before, and after September 11," in *Journalism after September 11*, ed. Barbie Zelizer and Stuart Allen (New York: Routledge, 2002).

9 John C. Stauber and Sheldon Rampton, *Toxic Sludge Is Good for You: Lies, Damn Lies, and the Public Relations Industry* (Monroe, ME: Common Courage Press, 1995). This development coincided with what scholars have recognized as an increase in executive branch power, the "rhetorical presidency," where presidents have successfully leveraged mass media to speak over the heads of the legislative branch and dominate policy questions through direct appeals to the people. See Jeffrey Tulis, *The Rhetorical Presidency* (Princeton, NJ: Princeton University Press, 1987).

10 In their "propaganda model," Chomsky and Herman cite access to news (what they call "sourcing") as one of five filters that help shape a news environment complicit with the interests of powerful institutions. See Chapter 1 of Edward S. Herman and Noam Chomsky, *Manufacturing Consent: The Political Economy of the Mass Media* (New York: Pantheon Books, 2002).For a discussion of the pooling system in comparison to other Pentagon-press relationships from Vietnam onward, see Carruthers, *The Media at War*.

11 Daniel C. Hallin and Todd Gitlin, "Agon and Ritual: The Gulf War as Popular Culture and as Television Drama," *Political Communication* 10 (1993): 411. In 2003, Operation Iraqi Freedom similarly launched Fox News into a primary role, demonstrating that the most commercially successful war coverage is one that best nuzzles the hand that feeds. This was widely known as the "Fox Effect," as it prompted other news sources to follow suit. Mike Tierney, "Fox Now the Big Dog in Cable News—and Growing," *Atlanta Journal and Constitution*, May 9, 2005, 1A.

12 Ernest Larsen, "Gulf War TV," *Jump Cut*, no. 36 (1991): 7–8.

13 In 2005, the Pentagon listed over 735 overseas bases. The true number is probably closer to 1000, according to Chalmers A. Johnson, *Nemesis: The Last Days of the American Republic*, The American Empire Project (New York: Metropolitan Books, 2006), 139–40.

14 Michael Hardt and Antonio Negri, *Multitude: War and Democracy in the Age of Empire* (New York: Penguin Press, 2004), 20.

15 For the earliest and clearest treatment of post-industrial socio-economics, see Daniel Bell, *The Coming of Post-Industrial Society: A Venture in Social Forecasting* (New York: Basic Books, 1976).

16 Indeed, the brand has become the *sine qua non* of consumer society. Jean Baudrillard was perhaps one of the first to perceive the sign as the fundamental unit of capitalistic exchange,

expressed most clearly in Jean Baudrillard, *For a Critique of the Political Economy of the Sign* (St. Louis, MO: Telos Press, 1981). With reference to the predominance of the brand, see Naomi Klein, *No Logo: Taking Aim at the Brand Bullies* (New York: Picador USA, 2000).

17 See Norman Solomon's discussion of how the material and economic imperatives of the Gulf War manifested in President Bush's public discourse. Norman Solomon, *War Made Easy: How Presidents and Pundits Keep Spinning Us to Death* (Hoboken, NJ: John Wiley, 2005), 87.

18 J.C. Herz, *Joystick Nation* (New York: Little, Brown, and Co., 1997), 197–213. James Der Derian, *Virtuous War: Mapping the Military-Industrial-Media-Entertainment Network* (Boulder, CO: Westview Press, 2001). Lisa Parks, *Cultures in Orbit* (Durham, NC: Duke University Press, 2005), 98.

19 Media scholar Daniel Hallin and historian William Hammond convincingly argue that the television depiction of Vietnam was relatively free of violent imagery, suggesting that this myth of a violence driven journalism served to justify later press controls. William M. Hammond, "The Press in Vietnam as Agent of Defeat: A Critical Examination," *Reviews in American History* 17, no. 2 (1989), 312–323. William M. Hammond, *Reporting Vietnam: Media and Military at War* (Lawrence, KS: University Press of Kansas, 1998). Daniel C. Hallin, *The "Uncensored War": The Media and Vietnam* (New York: Oxford University Press, 1986). Hallin notes that certain iconic violent images did make their way onto the screen late in the war (for example, the My Lai massacre and the famous "napalm girl" photo) but these had appeared after public opinion had fallen, not before.

20 Moreover, half of these American fatalities had been killed by friendly fire. Jean Baudrillard, *The Gulf War Did Not Take Place* (Bloomington: Indiana University Press, 1995), 69.

21 Dana Milbank, "Curtains Ordered for Media Coverage of Returning Coffins," *Washington Post*, October 21, 2003, A23. This policy was strengthened during the second Bush presidency for Operation Iraqi Freedom. In April of 2003, the issue was made public when a military contractor employee leaked photos of returning caskets to the *Seattle Times*.

22 Margot Norris, "Only the Guns Have Eyes: Military Censorship and the Body Count," in *Seeing through the Media: The Persian Gulf War*, ed. Susan Jeffords and Lauren Rabinowitz (New Brunswick, NJ: Rutgers University Press, 1994), 296.

23 Patrick Sloyan, "What Bodies?" in *The Iraq War Reader: History, Documents, Opinions*, ed. Michael L. Sifry and Christopher Cerf (New York: Touchstone Books, 2003), 130. Originally published as Patrick Sloyan, "What Bodies?" The Digital Journalist, November 2002. Online: http://www.digitaljournalist.org/issue0211/sloyan.html.

24 See Norris, "Only the Guns Have Eyes: Military Censorship and the Body Count." Sloyan, "What Bodies?" See also "How Many Iraqi Soldiers Died?" *Time*, June 17, 1991, 26.

25 Eric Schmitt and Thom Shanker, "A Nation Challenged: Body Count; Taliban and Qaeda Death Toll in Mountain Battle Is a Mystery," *New York Times*, March 14, 2002, A1.

26 General Franks stated, "I don't believe you have heard me or anyone else in our leadership talk about the presence of 1,000 bodies out there, or in fact how many have been recovered. You know we don't do body counts." Edward Epstein, "Success in Afghan War Hard to Gauge; U.S. Reluctance to Produce Body Counts Makes Proving Enemy's Destruction Difficult," *San Francisco Chronicle*, March 23, 2002, A1.

27 Busah Ebo, "War as Popular Culture: The Gulf Conflict and the Technology of Illusionary Entertainment," *Journal of American Culture* 18 (1995): 23–24.

28 Incidentally, the words "missile," "missive," and "message" share the same Latinate root, "mittere," which means "to send." Etymologically, the boundaries between the act of representation and the act of war are quite permeable.

29 Paul Fussell, *The Great War and Modern Memory* (New York: Oxford University Press, 1975), 22.

30 Elaine Scarry, *The Body in Pain: The Making and Unmaking of the World* (New York: Oxford University Press, 1985), 71.

31 The term "plausible deniability" comes from the world of covert operations. The term first emerged from the bowels of the CIA during the Church investigations of secret operations to assassinate world leaders such as Cuba's Fidel Castro and Chile's Salvador Allende. When

such assassinations are conducted, the doctrine of plausible deniability suggests they be commissioned to a third party such as the mafia so that the CIA can plausibly deny connection. See "Church Report: Covert Action in Chile 1963–1973," ed. Select Committee to Study Governmental Operations with Respect to Intelligence Activities (Washington, DC: US Government Printing Office, 1975).

32 Slavoj Žižek, "Passion: Regular or Decaf?" *In These Times*, March 29, 2004, 24. See also Žižek, *Welcome to the Desert of the Real!: Five Essays on September 11 and Related Dates*.

33 Asu Askoy and Kevin Robins, "Exterminating Angels: Morality, Violence, and Technology in the Gulf War," in *Triumph of the Image: The Media's War in the Persian Gulf*, ed. Hamid Mowlana, Herbert I. Schiller, and George Gerbner (Boulder, CO: Westview Press, 1992), 202–212. See also Douglas Kellner, *The Persian Gulf TV War* (Boulder, CO: Westview Press, 1992), 157–63.

34 Hallin and Gitlin, "Agon and Ritual: The Gulf War as Popular Culture and as Television Drama," 417.

35 Indeed, although *Top Gun* featured plenty of aerial dog fighting, the enemy was hardly named or identified, much less explained apart from scattered references to "MiG" aircraft, which were Soviet-made. The post-ideological flavor of *Top Gun* positions the film as a forerunner of what has been called the "new patriotism." See Frank J. Wetta and Martin A. Novelli, "'Now a Major Motion Picture': War Films and Hollywood's New Patriotism," *The Journal of Military History* 67, no. 3 (2003), 861–882. For a touchstone work regarding the post-Cold War political climate, see Daniel Bell, *The End of Ideology: On the Exhaustion of Political Ideas in the Fifties* (Cambridge, MA: Harvard University Press, 1988).

36 Paul Virilio, *Desert Screen: War at the Speed of Light* (New York: Continuum, 2002), 53.

37 See, for example, Robert L. Ivie, "Images of Savagery in American Justifications for War," *Communication Monographs* 47, no. 4 (1980), 279–292. Robert L. Ivie, "Savagery in Democracy's Empire," *Third World Quarterly* 26, no. 1 (2005), 55–65. Dana L. Cloud, "'To Veil the Threat of Terror': Afghan Women and the <Clash of Civilizations> in the Imagery of the U.S. War on Terrorism," *Quarterly Journal of Speech* 90, no. 3 (2004), 285–306. Stephen W. Silliman, "The 'Old West' in the Middle East: U.S. Military Metaphors in Real and Imagined Indian Country," *American Anthropologist* 110, no. 2 (2008), 237–47.

38 The suggestion that soldiers deployed themselves, of course, becomes most absurd when the majority of soldiers oppose official policy. In 2006, a Zogby poll found that 72 percent of US troops stationed in Iraq favored withdrawal. This period of low popularity was of course precisely the period when the call by many to "support the troops" (that is, support the policy) was the loudest on the home front. Richard Sisk, "70% of Troops Want out—Poll," *Daily News*, March 1, 2006, 10.

39 Juan de Onis, "Nixon Puts 'Bums' Label on Some College Radicals," *New York Times*, May 2, 1970, 1. See the discussion of these counterdemonstration tactics in Jerry Lembcke, *The Spitting Image: Myth, Memory, and the Legacy of Vietnam* (New York: New York University Press, 1998).

40 Helen Kennedy, "Kerry's Old Navy Foe Looks to Sink Senator," *Daily News*, May 4, 2004, 26.

41 H. Bruce Franklin, *Vietnam and Other American Fantasies* (Amherst, MA: University of Massachusetts Press, 2000), 174–201. See also Hallin, *The "Uncensored War": The Media and Vietnam*, 178.

42 Ronald Reagan, "Remarks on Presenting the Medal of Honor to Master Sergeant Roy P. Benavidez," *Ronald Reagan Presidential Library*, February 24, 1981. Online: http://www.reagan.utexas.edu/archives/speeches/1981/22481d.htm.

43 This image became a defining phenomenon of the U.S. experience of the Vietnam conflict, invoked in countless editorials, speeches, and popular films, and becoming most visible in the immediate build-up to Operation Desert Storm in 1991. Not only is there no evidence of such an event, people do not even begin to recount the story until many years after the last soldiers arrived home. Lembcke, *The Spitting Image: Myth, Memory, and the Legacy of*

Vietnam. A survey of newspaper coverage regarding anti-war protest came away with similar findings. Over half of coverage involving protesters and troops between 1990 and 1991 made reference to protesters' supposed anti-troop behavior during Vietnam. Looking back to coverage during the period 1965–1971, however, this same study found the actual incidence of anti-troop behavior or rhetoric to be negligible, while finding much stronger evidence of pro-troop and anti-elite rhetoric among demonstrators. Thomas D. Beamish, Harvey Molotch, and Richard Flacks, "Who Supports the Troops? Vietnam, the Gulf War, and the Making of Collective Memory," *Social Problems* 42, no. 3 (1995), 344–60.

44 See, for example, Robert Jensen, *Citizens of the Empire: The Struggle to Claim Our Humanity* (San Francisco: City Lights Books, 2004), 21. George Mariscal, "In the Wake of the Gulf War: Untying the Yellow Ribbon," *Cultural Critique*, no. 19 (1991): 112.

45 Andrew J. Bacevich, *The New American Militarism: How Americans Are Seduced by War* (New York: Oxford University Press, 2005), 108.

46 Guy Debord, *The Society of the Spectacle*, trans. Donald Nicholson-Smith (New York: Zone Books, 1994), Section 2.

47 Ibid., Section 24.

48 Ibid., Sections 25, 44.

49 Ibid., Section 21.

50 Ibid., Section 64.

51 This essay was one of three written for the French magazine *Liberation* between January and March of 1991. Along with "The Gulf War Will Not Take Place" and "The Gulf War: Is It Really Taking Place?," the three are collected in the published volume: Baudrillard, *The Gulf War Did Not Take Place*.

52 Logistically, the displacement of the "event" of war onto the screen manifested in the so-called "CNN effect," where real-time global broadcast of "the war" began to affect decisions made on the ground. See Steven Livingston, *Clarifying the CNN Effect: An Examination of Media Effects According to Type of Military Intervention* (Cambridge, MA: Joan Shorenstein Center on the Press Politics and Public Policy, John F. Kennedy School of Government, Harvard University, 1997). Piers Robinson, *The CNN Effect: The Myth of News, Foreign Policy and Intervention* (New York: Routledge, 2002).

53 Babak Bahador, *The CNN Effect in Action: How the News Media Pushed the West toward War in Kosovo*, Palgrave Macmillan Series in International Political Communication (New York: Palgrave Macmillan, 2007). Noam Chomsky, "The Media and War: What War?," in *Triumph of the Image: The Media's War in the Persian Gulf: A Global Perspective*, ed. Hamid Molwana, George Gerbner, and Herbert I. Schiller (Boulder, CO: Westview Press, 1992), 51.

54 George Gerbner, "Persian Gulf War, the Movie," in *Triumph of the Image: The Media's War in the Persian Gulf: A Global Perspective*, ed. Hamid Molwana, George Gerbner, and Herbert I. Schiller (Boulder, CO: Westview Press, 1992), 244.

55 Don Ohlmeyer, *The Heroes of Desert Storm* (NBC, 1991).

56 See a fine discussion of the Reagan rhetoric of the soldier in Bacevich, *The New American Militarism: How Americans Are Seduced by War*, 97–121.

57 After President George W. Bush appointed him to serve on the President's Committee on the Arts and Humanities, Chetwynd went on to direct *DC 9/11: Time of Crisis* (2003) for Showtime. This film focused on the heroism of President George W. Bush and his cabinet, what the *Independent* called "a piece of myth-making to put the propagandists of every tin-pot totalitarian regime to shame." Iain Miller, "Decisive, Determined and Articulate. Is That Really My Bush?" *Independent*, May 9, 2004, 24. (Strangely, the actor who played Bush in *DC 9/11*, Timothy Bottoms, had played the president prior on the satirical Comedy Central show by the creators of *South Park* called "That's My Bush.") Following *DC 9/11*, Chetwynd wrote the straight-to-video *Celsius 41.11: The Temperature at Which the Brain ... Begins to Die* (2004), a rejoinder to Michael Moore's 2003 theatrical release critical of the Bush administration, *Fahrenheit 9/11*.

58 Roger Stahl, "A Clockwork War: Rhetorics of Time in a Time of Terror," *Quarterly Journal of*

Speech 94, no. 1 (2007): 73. Ebo, "War as Popular Culture: The Gulf Conflict and the Technology of Illusionary Entertainment," 21.

59 Tom Engelhardt, "The Gulf War as Total Television," in *Seeing through the Media*, ed. Susan Jeffords and Lauren Rabinovitz (New Brunswick, NJ: Rutgers University Press, 1994), 81–96. Robert Jensen argues that the press build-up around the "Shock and Awe" blitzkrieg strategy used against Iraq in 2003 was similarly shot through with the pleasures of the spectacle and its anticipation. Concern for human life in Baghdad's streets and neighborhoods was just one of the casualties of this orientation. Robert Jensen, "The Military's Media," *The Progressive* (May 2003): 22–25.

60 Colin McInnes, *Spectator-Sport War: The West and Contemporary Conflict* (Boulder, CO: Lynn Rienner Publishers, 2002). Richard Keeble, *Secret State, Silent Press* (Bedfordshire: John Libby Media, 1997).

61 Christine Scodari, "Operation Desert Storm As 'Wargames': Sport, War and Media Intertextuality," *Journal of American Culture* 16, no. 1 (1993), 1–5.

62 Ebo, "War as Popular Culture: The Gulf Conflict and the Technology of Illusionary Entertainment," 20.

63 Kenon Breazeale, "Bringing the War Back Home: Consuming Operation Desert Storm," *Journal of American Culture* 17, no. 1 (1994): 31. See also Scott Shugar, "Operation Desert Store: First the Air War, Then the Ground War, Now the Marketing Campaign," *Los Angeles Times*, September 29, 1991, 18.

64 John Arquilla and David Ronfeldt, "Cyberwar Is Coming!" *Comparative Strategy* 12, no. 2 (1993), 141–168. See also John Arquilla et al., *The Advent of Netwar* (Santa Monica, CA: RAND, 1996).

65 The Office of Strategic Influence (OSI) created after 9/11 to conduct "black propaganda" operations in overseas media is a good example of this. James Dao and Eric Schmitt, "A Nation Challenged: Hearts and Minds; Pentagon Readies Effort to Sway Sentiment Abroad," *New York Times*, February 19, 2002, A1.

66 See the series of policy papers by the Joint Chiefs of Staff online at http://www.dtic.mil/futurejointwarfare/. In particular, see General Henry H. Shelton, *Joint Vision 2020* (Washington, DC: US Government Printing Office, 2000). This document is also archived online as of July 2007 at http://www.dtic.mil/jointvision/jv2020.doc.

67 Hardt and Negri, *Multitude: War and Democracy in the Age of Empire*, 41, 55. Drawing these trends together, they suggest that "war" after 9/11 underwent fundamental changes in meaning. Rising to absolute heights, war transcended its previous status as a "state of exception" to become a permanent and ubiquitous global condition. Plunging toward the mundane, war was simultaneously demoted into a police action. Hardt and Negri argue that Full Spectrum Dominance reverses Clausewitz's famous dictum that "war is politics by other means," suggesting instead that war is post-industrial society's primary organizational principle. They borrow this reversal of Clausewitz directly from Foucault. See Michel Foucault et al., *"Society Must Be Defended": Lectures at the College de France, 1975–76*, 1st ed., trans. David Macey (New York: Picador, 2003), 15–16. Though much of Foucault's work charts power through discursive formations, he suggested that "one's point of reference should not be to the great model of language (*langue*) and signs, but to that of war and battle. The history which bears and determines us has the form of a war rather than that of a language: relations of force, not relations of meaning." Michel Foucault, *Power/Knowledge: Selected Interviews and Other Writings, 1972–1977*, ed. and trans. Colin Gordon (New York: Pantheon Books, 1980), 114. Roland Barthes has made similar claims about the relationship between war and discourse, maintaining that "weapons and signs are essentially the same thing" and terrorism is at core a deployment of the signifier. *The Grain of the Voice: Interviews 1962–1980*, trans. Linda Coverdale (New York: Hill and Wang, 1985), 127, 160–61. Hardt and Negri's reversal of Clausewitz not only means that military power has infused the potitical sphere, but it also reverses the usual conception of power, drawing instead from Foucault's notion of "biopower," which he conceived neither as repressive nor conquering, but rather as an

immanent structure constitutive of life's production. See in particular the discussion of productive biopower in Michel Foucault, *The History of Sexuality*, vol. 1, trans. Robert Hurley (New York: Vintage Books, 1990). Elsewhere Foucault notes that it is "one of the essential traits of Western societies that the force relations which for a long time had found expression in war, in every form of warfare, gradually became invested in the order of political power." Foucault, *The History of Sexuality*, vol. 1, 102. Reframing this notion, Hardt and Negri write that post-industrial war has become a "regime of biopower," as much about the production of life as the production of death, what they name the "military-vital complex." Hardt and Negri, *Multitude: War and Democracy in the Age of Empire*, 13, 41.

68 For an analysis of the RMA and how these changes in military science and infrastructure have mirrored those of late twentieth-century capitalism, see Randy Martin, "Derivative Wars," *Cultural Studies* 20, no. 4–5 (2006), 459–76. Martin notes that the RMA imagines a condition after the Cold War where "imminent threat has been generalized" and military action, insofar as it opens up new avenues for investment, is translated into something of a futures forecast (471).

69 Ann Scott Tyson, "New US Strategy: 'Lily Pad' Bases," *Christian Science Monitor*, August 10, 2004, 6.

70 The Stockholm International Peace Research Institute (SIPRI) calculated that the regular U.S. military budget comprised 46 percent of total world military spending. With the added billions spent on incursions into Iraq and Afghanistan, the figure has well exceeded half since 2001. See http://SIPRI.org. See also David R. Francis, "It's Back: The Global Arms Race," *Christian Science Monitor*, March 26, 2007, 16.

71 Friedrich Nietzsche, *Beyond Good and Evil*, trans. Walter Kaufmann (New York: Vintage Books, 1989), 81.

72 See for example Paul Virilio and Sylvere Lotringer, *Pure War*, trans. Mark Polizotti (New York: Semiotexte, 1983). "[I]t is no longer exo-colonization (the age of extending world conquest) but the age of intensiveness and endo-colonization. Now one colonizes one's own population" (95). See also Paul Virilio, *The Art of the Motor*, trans. Julie Rose (Minneapolis, MN: University of Minnesota Press, 1995), 109–12.

73 Donald Rumsfeld, "Transforming the Military," *Foreign Affairs* 81, no. 3 (2002), 20–32.

74 The proposed safety precaution accompanied the department's raising of the terrorist threat level to "orange" or high. The announcement conveniently helped attenuate a massive anti-war protest scheduled for February 15, 2003, in New York City, the very day and city most likely to be hit by a terrorist attack, according to Ridge. Mark Lepage, "New York Ducts and Covers," *Montreal Gazette*, February 17, 2003.

75 As far back as WWII, air power obliterated spatial boundaries between home front and battlefield, turning civilians and factory infrastructure into valuable targets. The ratio of soldiers to civilians killed in wars has steadily risen since. Chris Hables Gray, *Cyborg Citizen: Politics in the Posthuman Age* (New York: Routledge, 2001), 55–58. The Cold War that followed created a civic field unified under the terrible specter of the nuclear bomb.

76 James Hay, "Designing Homes to Be the First Line of Defense," *Cultural Studies* 20, no. 4–5 (2006): 372.

77 Jean Baudrillard, *The Spirit of Terrorism; and Other Essays*. New ed. (New York: Verso, 2003), 4.

78 Geoff King, "'Just Like a Movie': 9/11 and Hollywood Spectacle," in *The Spectacle of the Real*, ed. Geoff King (Portland, OR: Intellect, 2005), 47–57.

79 Debord, *The Society of the Spectacle*, Section 64.

80 Matthew T. Hall, "Military Re-Enlistments Rise in Response to Devastation," *San Diego Union-Tribune*, September 30, 2001, B1.

81 George W. Bush, "Address Before a Joint Sessions of Congress," September 20, 2001, http://www.gpoaccess.gov/wcomp/v37no38.html.

82 Tillman was killed in April of 2004 in what the Pentagon described as a heroic fight with the enemy. A month later it was revealed that Tillman had died in a round of "friendly fire." The case comprised one of the more visible controversies of the post-9/11 wars in Afghanistan

and Iraq. Claudia Lauer and Johanna Neuman, "Rumsfeld Denies Tillman Coverup," *Los Angeles Times*, August 2, 2007, A12.

83 It should be noted that a form of embedding had been used by the US military during WWII but mainly as a method of archival documentation and on a limited scale. See Carruthers, *The Media at War: Communication and Conflict in the Twentieth Century*, 79.

84 Victor J. Caldarola, "Time and the Television War," *Public Culture* 4, no. 2 (1992): 130.

85 Stam, "Mobilizing Fictions: The Gulf War, the Media, and the Recruitment of the Spectator," 104.

86 Ibid.: 102.

87 See, for example, his discussion of the clean war in Kellner, *The Persian Gulf TV War*, 157.

88 See Sam Brenton and Reuben Cohen, *Shooting People: Adventures in Reality TV* (New York: Verso, 2003), 166–73. Robin Andersen, "That's Militainment! The Pentagon's Media-Friendly 'Reality' War," *Extra!* 2003, 6–9. James Compton, "Shocked and Awed: The Convergence of Military and Media Discourse," in *Global Politics in the Information Age*, ed. Mark J. Lacy and Peter Wilkin (Manchester: Manchester University Press, 2005), 54.

89 Robin Andersen, *A Century of Media, a Century of War* (New York: Peter Lang, 2006), 217–19.

90 Ibid., 234–35.

91 Ibid., 244.

92 Ibid., 299.

93 At the time, of course, it was the breaching of the clean war—in the form of a dead U.S. soldier being dragged through the streets of Mogadishu—that compelled the Clinton administration to pull out of the Somalia intervention.

94 The CBC produced a candid documentary of these tensions in Douglas Arrowsmith, *Deadline Iraq: Uncensored Stories of the War* (CBC Films, 2003).

95 Franklin, *Vietnam and Other American Fantasies*, 23–24.

96 Donna Miles, "Military, Hollywood Team up to Create Realism, Drama on Big Screen," *American Forces Press Service*, June 8, 2007. Online: http://www.defenselink.mil/news/newsarticle.aspx?id=46352.

97 "Raytheon Sarcos Exoskeleton Robotic Suit Linked to Iron Man Superhero," *PR Newswire*, May 2, 2008 (Lexis Nexis database).

98 Paul Virilio, *Desert Screen: War at the Speed of Light*, trans. Michael Degener (New York: Continuum, 2002).

99 Norris, "Only the Guns Have Eyes: Military Censorship and the Body Count," 289.

2 Sports and the Militarized Body Politic

1 Jim Castonguay, "The Gulf War TV Super Bowl," *Bad Subjects*, no. 35 (1997). Online: http://bad.eserver.org/issues/1997/35/castonguay.html. See also Sue Curry Jansen and Don Sabo, "The Sport/War Metaphor: Hegemonic Masculinity, the Persian Gulf War, and the New World Order," *Sociology of Sport Journal*, no. 11 (1994): 5.

2 Scott Shugar, "Operation Desert Store: First the Air War, Then the Ground War, Now the Marketing Campaign," *Los Angeles Times*, September 29, 1991, 18.

3 George W. Bush, "Presidential Address to the Nation," October 7, 2001. Online: http://www.whitehouse.gov/news/releases/2001/10/20011007–8.html.

4 R.W. Jr. Apple, "Home Front: Edgy Sunday," *New York Times*, October 8, 2001, A1.

5 Scott Stossel, "Sports: War Games," *American Prospect*, November 19, 2001. Online: http://www.prospect.org/cs/articles?articleId=5978.

6 David Kindred, "An Army and Navy of One," *Sporting News*, December 10, 2001, 64.

7 William C. Rhoden, "Sports of the Times; Metaphors, Realities and Football," *New York Times*, January 29, 2003, D1.

8 Bob Keefe, "Super Bowl XXXVII: Security's Super Tight for Big Game," *Atlanta Journal and Constitution*, January 26, 2003 6D.

9 Gary West, "Fort Worth Game Tries to Put Fun Back into the Bowls," *Fort Worth*

Star-Telegram, December 22, 2006 (Lexis Nexis database). See also Eric Bailey, "Iron Man," *Tulsa World*, December 22, 2006, B1.

10 Christine Scodari, "Operation Desert Storm As 'Wargames': Sport, War and Media Intertextuality," *Journal of American Culture* 16, no. 1 (1993): 1–5.

11 Jansen and Sabo, "The Sport/War Metaphor: Hegemonic Masculinity, the Persian Gulf War, and the New World Order," 4. In 2003, such military experts would be "embedded" in the studio as part of a White House initiative to influence coverage. David Barstow, "Behind TV Analysts, Pentagon's Hidden Hand," *New York Times*, April 20, 2008, A1.

12 Matthew Nadelhalft, "Metawar: Sports and the Persian Gulf War," *Journal of American Culture* 16, no. 4 (1993), 25–33. General Norman Schwarzkopf famously described the entire US plan of attack as a "Hail Mary." See Jansen and Sabo, "The Sport/War Metaphor: Hegemonic Masculinity, the Persian Gulf War, and the New World Order," 3. See also Jeffrey O. Segrave, "The Sports Metaphor in American Cultural Discourse," *Culture, Sport, and Society* 3, no. 1 (2000): 49–50.

13 "War by appointment" is a phrase borrowed from William J. Small, "The Gulf War: Mass Media Coverage and Restraints," in *The 1,000 Hour War: Communication in the Gulf*, ed. Thomas A. McCain and Leonard Shyles (Westport, CT: Greenwood Press, 1994), 3.

14 George W. Bush, "President Says Saddam Hussein Must Leave Iraq within 48 Hours," March 17, 2003. Online: http://www.whitehouse.gov/news/releases/2003/03/20030317–7.html.

15 Assuming war with Iraq to be inevitable, one site, MarchToWar.com, took wagers on when the invasion would commence. The site's introduction read "That's right, we're giving away free gasoline to the winner of our Baghdad Bonanza Betting pool. So fire up the S.U.V.—it won't be long now." Farah Stockman, "On the Internet, Betting on Hussein's Fate Is Heavy, Cyberspace Wagering Seen as Good Predictor," *Boston Globe*, March 11, 2003, B1. See also Philip Klein, "Gamblers Place Wagers on Saddam's Demise," *Reuters*, March 24, 2003 (Lexis Nexis database).

16 Jack Wilkinson, "March Madness: NCAA: Show Must Go On," *Atlanta Journal and Constitution*, March 19, 2003, 1C.

17 Richard Sandomir, "The Decline and Fall of Sports Ratings," *New York Times*, September 10, 2003, D1.

18 Dario Del Corno, "Games and War in Ancient Greece," in *War and Games*, ed. Tim Cornell and Thomas B. Allen (Rochester, NY: Boydell Press, 2002), 20.

19 Johan Huizinga, *Homo Ludens*, trans. George Steiner (London: Maurice Temple Smith, 1970), 110.

20 Quoted in Dave Zirin and John Cox, "Hey Guys, It's Just a Game," *The Nation*, June 20, 2006. Online: http://www.thenation.com/doc/20060703/zirin.

21 Varda Burstyn, *The Rites of Men: Manhood, Politics, and the Culture of Sport* (Toronto: University of Toronto Press, 1999), 165.

22 Thorstein Veblen, *The Theory of the Leisure Class* (Boston: Houghton Mifflin, 1973), 170–76.

23 George Orwell, *The Collected Essays, Journalism, & Letters, George Orwell*, ed. Sonia Orwell and Ian Angus, vol. 4 (Boston: David R. Godine, 2000), 42.

24 Chomksy argues that the general population's level of expertise concerning spectator sports shows that the problem is not that people are unable to govern themselves, but rather that they are encouraged to expend their intellectual capacities elsewhere. Noam Chomsky, *Understanding Power*, ed. Peter R. Mitchell and John Schoeffel (New York: The New Press, 2002), 99–101. Allan Guttman suggests that this "neo-Marxist" argument is not supported by the sociological research. Those that play sports have been found to be more active in all parts of life, including politics, than those who do not. The data for sports spectators are less conclusive, however. Allan Guttman, *Sports Spectators* (New York: Columbia University Press, 1986), 153–54.

25 Nadelhalft, "Metawar: Sports and the Persian Gulf War," 28.

26 A top official in the Bush II administration even acknowledged Operation Iraqi Freedom in

2003 to have been illegal. Richard Perle, Assistant Secretary of Defense, told a British audience, "I think in this case international law stood in the way of doing the right thing." Oliver Burkeman and Julian Borger, "Bush in Britain: War Critics Astonished as US Hawk Admits Invasion Was Illegal," *Guardian*, November 20, 2003, 4.

27 Gilles Deleuze, *Negotiations: 1972–1990*, trans. Martin Joughin (New York: Columbia University Press, 2002), 180.

28 Michael Hardt and Antonio Negri, *Empire* (Cambridge, MA: Harvard University Press, 2000), 9.

29 Ibid., 13.

30 Donald Rumsfeld, "A New Kind of War," *New York Times*, September 27, 2001, A21.

31 Hardt and Negri, *Empire*, 23. The notion of the control society is an extension of Foucault's "biopower" or the regulation and administration of life through its interior. Michel Foucault, *The History of Sexuality*, vol. 1, trans. Robert Hurley (New York: Vintage Books, 1990), 140–41.

32 Part of this process is an increasing saturation of life with visibility such that the body becomes a system of exposed surfaces. Biopower complicates the idea of "the body" as a discrete unit of ontological knowledge, and for this reason Hardt and Negri offer Donna Haraway's "cybernetic organism" as a way of understanding corporeality within the logics of Empire. Haraway's ontology describes the integration of the individual body into a network of machines, discourses, and other social and biological structures all the way down to genomics. Donna Haraway, *Simians, Cyborgs, and Women: The Reinvention of Nature* (New York: Routledge, 1991), 149–81.

33 Virilio, *Desert Screen: War at the Speed of Light*, 30.

34 George H.W. Bush, "Address to a Joint Session of Congress and the Nation," September 11, 1990, http://millercenter.org/scripps/archive/speeches/detail/3425. See also the op-ed by Rumsfeld, "A New Kind of War."

35 Peter Donnelly, "Vertigo in America: A Social Comment," in *Sport, Culture, and Society*, ed. John W. Loy, Jr., Gerald S. Kenyon, and Barry D. McPherson (Philadelphia, PA: Lea & Febiger, 1981), 308–313.

36 Journalist and cultural critic Jeff Howe lamented that the power of naming and self-definition was lost when his adolescent pastime skateboarding was subsumed under the rubric of extreme sports. Jeff Howe, "Drawing Lines: A Report from the Extreme World," in *To the Extreme: Alternative Sports Inside and Out*, ed. Robert E. Rinehardt and Synthia Sydnor (Albany, NY: State University of New York Press, 2003), 253–72.

37 The list has expanded to include hang gliding, mountain biking, and every possible combination: sky surfing, boardsailing, wake boarding, mountainboarding, and even what has come to be known as free-style walking. Long-standing thrill sports like spelunking, water and snow skiing, scuba and free diving, snorkeling, street biking, snow shoeing, open water swimming, tight-rope walking, and hot-air ballooning have been folded into the mix.

38 Between 1999 and 2000, snowboarding climbed to 7 million participants and skateboarding to 12 million, a 51 percent gain compared with tackle football, which grew 15 percent to 6 million. Sandra Yin, "Going to Extremes," *American Demographics*, June, 2001, 26. Baseball participation dropped 13 percent from 1995 to 2000. Andrea Graham, "PR Pros Find Extreme Sports Less Elusive," *O'Dwyers PR Services Report*, December 2002, 1.

39 "Surfing the Wave," *Sports Marketing*, November 19, 2001, 14.

40 FOX launched its 24-hour extreme sports network Fuel in 2003. The distribution outfit X-Dream International launched the Extreme Sports Channel in Western Europe in May 1999 after which it opened up markets in North and South America with shows like "Not Recommended Behavior" and "Rebel TV." Such efforts opened the way for EXPN and FOX's Fuel, both lifestyle channels in the tradition of MTV with fashion and music as integral elements. Extreme sports broadcasting also paved the way for web-TV services such as X-Dream's Extreme.com, extreme sports brand Bluetorch, the EXPN and Fuel websites, and High.tv. Such venues have provided distribution for companies like Planet X, an extreme

sports producer that began distributing their programming in 1995 on the Fox Sports Network. Janis Mara, "IQ News: Earthlink, Sprint Go to Extreme," *Adweek*, September 11, 2000 (Lexis Nexis database). Allison Romano, "New Fox Net Dubbed 'Fuel'," *Broadcasting and Cable*, April 14, 2003, 33. Monica Hogan, "Comcast, ESPN Go to Extremes for X-Games," *Multichannel News*, August 13, 2001, 16. "Web-Only TV Channel Launches for Extreme Sport Market," *New Media Age*, June 26, 2003, 4. Andy Fry, "X-Dream Coasts on Extreme Sports Wave," *TeenScreen*, March 1, 2000, 16. "Fox Announces Extreme Sports Network," *TV Meets the Web*, December 3, 2002 (Lexis Nexis database). Thomas Umstead, "New ESPN Service Goes to Extremes," *Multichannel News*, April 29, 2002, 3. "Surfing the Wave," 14.

41 Allen Guttman, *From Ritual to Record* (New York: Columbia University Press, 1978).

42 In so doing, they fall into a category that Roger Caillois calls "games of simulation" and "vertigo sports," which, as opposed to games of chance and competition, he takes to be characteristic of primitive societies. Roger Caillois, *Man, Play, and Games* (New York: Free Press of Glencoe, 1961), 87. More commercialized stadium events like ESPN's X-Games or the roving Gravity Games have attempted to retain the accoutrements of modern competition by importing tournament structures, judges, and creative systems of record-keeping. Extreme sports' resistance to canonization, however, made this a tenuous endeavor. Arlo Eisenberg, a pioneer of in-line skating, noted this tension: "The television producers are defining rollerblading now; the corporate sponsors are. The focus of rollerblading is moving away from the personal goals of the individual and quickly moving toward winning championships and training to win championships. How do we get it back?" Arlo Eisenberg, "Psychotic Rant," in *To the Extreme: Alternative Sports, inside and Out*, ed. Robert E. Rinehart and Synthia Sydnor (Albany, NY: State University of New York Press, 2003), 25. As Eisenberg suggests, the soul of extreme sports does not lie in competition and overcoming opponents, but rather in identifying and meeting the limits of the body.

43 Traditional sports generally take up the torch of the polis and are invoked in metaphors of conquest: Houston takes on Chicago, LA ransacks Miami, and so forth. The modern Olympics, during the world wars or the rivalries of the cold war, had a pronounced and often vicious geographical politics that may have been, in some sense, a cathartic substitute for actual geopolitical hot war and possible nuclear annihilation. Peter Beck describes the post-WWII optimism that institutions like the international Olympics could serve as a cathartic substitute for war and thus forestall nuclear holocaust. Peter Beck, "Confronting George Orwell: Philip Noel-Baker on International Sport, Particularly the Olympic Movement, as Peacemaker," in *Militarism, Sport, Europe: War without Weapons*, ed. J.A. Mangan (Portland, OR: Frank Cass, 2003), 187–207.

44 Haraway, *Simians, Cyborgs, and Women: The Reinvention of Nature*, 164. In the case of skateboarding, the cityscape is the sport itself, a coupling of body and architecture. Railings, empty pools, and city drainage pipes become "rules" for bending creatively and spectacularly. Higher tech games like motorcross stunt jumping are defined by a different set of psychological, corporeal, machine, and geophysical boundaries.

45 Jeff Howe, "Drawing Lines: A Report from the Extreme World," in *To the Extreme: Alternative Sports Inside and Out*, ed. Robert E. Rinehardt and Synthia Sydnor (Albany, NY: State University of New York Press, 2003), 368.

46 For example, in his introduction to the coffee table book, *The Ultimate Encyclopedia of Extreme Sports*, Joe Tomlinson asks, "What are extreme sports all about? What is it that gets athletes charged up enough to put their lives at risk?" Tomlinson reveals a central feature of extreme sports: flirtation with death, injury, and the accompanying adrenaline rush. He continues, "[Athletes] can successfully do things that could kill those unfamiliar with their particular sports because they have dedicated themselves to performing within their limits, even while they have consistently challenged themselves to redefine those limits." Joe Tomlinson, *The Ultimate Encyclopedia of Extreme Sports* (London: Carleton, 1996), 7.

47 David Le Breton, "Playing Symbolically with Death in Extreme Sports," *Body and Society* 6, no. 1 (2000): 6.

48 Georges Bataille, *Theory of Religion*, trans. Robert Hurley (New York: Zone Books, 1992), 19.

49 Mihaly Csikszentmihalyi, *Beyond Boredom and Anxiety* (San Francisco: Jossey-Bass, 2000).

50 According to Bataille, sacrificial practices developed in early societies alongside the human world of usefulness. The tool, that which separates human existence from animal existence, creates an ecology of subject–object divisions that constitute the world of utility. When perfectly useful goods, animals, or humans are destroyed in the sacrificial ceremony, a society gains a mystical glimpse into the unified primeval world beyond utility, what Bataille argues is a basic human drive. "Beyond our immediate ends, man's activity in fact pursues the useless and infinite fulfillment of the universe." Georges Bataille, *The Accursed Share*, vol. 1, trans. Robert Hurley (New York: Zone Books, 1991), 21. This could involve the actual destruction of actual useful objects (such as in the Native American potlatch ceremony) or a purely symbolic gesture (such as a Christian's weekly meditation on a blameless, crucified body). The sacrifice is the violence that fulfills a kind of holy immanence, the irrational merger with the divine brought on by the momentary eradication of subject–object relations. The built-in necessity for sacrifice, Bataille suggests, arises from an excess that goads itself into its "luxurious expenditure" in the ecstatic moment. Bataille further argues that sacrifice disappeared with the rise of the "military order," a social system whose violence is projected outward upon the other (imperialism, capitalism, proselytism, expansion) rather than expended upon itself via the sacrificial urge: "The principle of military order is the methodical diversion of violence to the outside. If violence rages within, it opposes that violence to the extent it can. And it subordinates the diversion to a real end." Bataille, *Theory of Religion*, 65.

51 Hardt and Negri write that post-industrial war has become a "regime of biopower," as much about the production of life as the production of death. Hardt and Negri, *Multitude: War and Democracy in the Age of Empire*, 13, 41.

52 Stuart J. Murray, "Thanatopolitics: On the Use of Death for Mobilizing Political Life," *Polygraph* 18 (2006), 191–215.

53 Jeremy Packer, "Becoming Bombs: Mobilizing Mobility in the War on Terror," *Cultural Studies* 20, no. 4–5 (2006): 378.

54 This drama is mainly played out symbolically, distributed as a recurring theme in mass media. Indeed, Paul Virilio argues that such "suicidal experiments" act as a kind of antidote to the hypermediated abstraction of the physical world, fulfilling the wish to rediscover the weight of the body. Paul Virilio, *Open Sky*, trans. Julie Rose (London: Verso, 1997), 30–31.

55 John Stewart, *The Daily Show*, Comedy Central, November 1, 2007.

56 Ed Halter, "Hard Knoxville," *Village Voice*, November 5, 2002, 132.

57 John Stewart, *The Daily Show*, Comedy Central, January 18, 2007.

58 Greta Van Susteren and Steve Harrigan, "The Waterboarding Experience," *Fox on the Record with Greta van Susteren*, November 3, 2006 (Lexis Nexis database).

59 The cultural fascination with the masochistic testing of *non-lethal* weaponry in particular is indicative of the biopolitical logics of *Empire*. The taser's major function, like the cattle prod, is not to kill, but rather to distribute a productive mode of violence and control through populations and bodies.

60 This is perhaps why the Mel Gibson film *The Passion of the Christ* (2004) appeared when it did. An exercise in extreme masochism, the film truncates the story of Christ to solely feature his excruciating torture. Inflected through standard Christian theology and point-of-view camerawork, the film invites the viewer to occupy a relentlessly tortured body. In its larger context, such a symbolic exercise had strong political undertones. Icon Productions released the film during the summer of 2004 alongside Michael Moore's anti-Bush polemic, *Fahrenheit 9/11*. The two films became popular references for describing the demographics of the so-called "blue state/red state" political divide in the immediate aftermath of the US invasion of Iraq. While *Fahrenheit* found its ethos in anti-war defiance, *The Passion* offered up a body through which one could see "what it was like" by vicariously experiencing one's own torture and death. In this sense, the film performed Walter Benjamin's observation that the

trajectory of contemporary life points toward a culture whereby one's own destruction is elevated to the highest entertainment. Benjamin, "The Work of Art in the Age of Mechanical Reproduction," in *Illuminations*, ed. Hannah Arendt (New York: Schocken Books, 1968), 242.

61 For example, one of the first academic treatments of extreme sports was the edited volume, Belinda Wheaton, *Understanding Lifestyle Sports: Consumption, Identity, and Difference* (New York: Routledge, 2004).

62 See, for example, Naomi Klein, *No Logo: Taking Aim at the Brand Bullies* (New York: Picador USA, 2000).

63 Thomas Frank, *The Conquest of Cool* (Chicago: University of Chicago Press, 1998).

64 Major soft drinks like Coca-Cola and Pepsi have opted out of the extreme sports advertising game for fear that their corporate names might interfere with their street credibility. *Sports Marketing* magazine puts it this way: with extreme sports "money doesn't necessarily impress, and corporate size is likely to work against you." See "Surfing the Wave," 14.

65 The X achieved the level of catch-all cultural iconograph since the popularization of the term Generation X in the 1990s. Joseph Kahn of the *Boston Globe* explores the paradoxes of its use—somewhere between Christ and *Hustler Magazine*, between evolution and annihilation. We have seen the popularity of the X-Men, *The X Files*, Sony's video game station the X-Box, the short-lived XFL football league, pop tart temptress Christina Aguilera's transformation to Xtina, and drugs like Ecstasy ("X") and Xanax. Kahn notes that advertisers in particular have caught the X-wave and cultivated its mystique. Joseph P. Kahn, "X-Communication: Hot Products and Artists with 'X' in Their Names Are Everywhere—and It's No Accident, Say Marketing Experts," *Boston Globe*, May 3, 2003, D1.

66 Colin Grimshaw, "Living Dangerously—It Is Not Always the Advertisers You Would Normally Expect That Are Trying to Associate Themselves with Extreme Sports", *Campaign*, March 29, 2002, 35. Paul Virilio also associates the ecstaticism of extreme sports with an "addiction" to hallucinogens. See Virilio, *Desert Screen: War at the Speed of Light*, 30. The popularity of so-called "energy drinks" (laced with taurine, ginseng, guarana, ephedra and caffeine) like Red Bull, Erectus, Venom, and Liquid X has furthered the association with the drug ecstasy. The extreme marketing aesthetic is often characterized by graininess, static, digital scratchwork, and the jagged discontinuity of missing frames. Fashion, too, has a corresponding aura of delinquency, typified by the skateboard kid look: hooded sweatshirts, knit caps, and baggy jeans.

67 Mountain Dew decided to drop its long-time extreme marketing in 2006 after it was decided that "people in their fifties are doing extreme stuff." Kenneth Hein, "Not So Extreme: Dew Retooling Image," *Brandweek*, October 23, 2006 (Lexis Nexis database).

68 The SUV is a paradoxical cultural artifact that exists in the liminal space between dialectics of "dominion/harmony," "tame/wild," "familiarity/novelty," and "material/spiritual." See this argument in Richard K. Olsen, Jr., "Living above It All: The Liminal Fantasy of Sports Utility Vehicle Advertisements," in *Enviropop*, ed. Mark Meister and Phyllis Japp (Westport, CT: Praeger Publishers, 2002), 175–196.

69 James G. Cobb, "Hummer H2: An Army of One," *New York Times*, April 6, 2003, sec. 12, p. 1.

70 See Fred Barnes, *Rebel-in-Chief: Inside the Bold and Controversial Presidency of George W. Bush* (New York: Crown Forum, 2006).

71 Jim Verniere, "Excruciating: Diesel-Powered 'xXx' Results in Spontaneous Combustion," *Boston Globe*, August 9, 2002, S5.

72 Maureen Dowd on *Larry King Live*, November 6, 2004, CNN News Network.

73 "'xXx'treme Action Blurs Good, Evil, Fuels Diesel's Unlikely Hero," *Milwaukee Journal Sentinel*, August 9, 2002, 4E.

74 In the Fall of 1990, the World Freestyle Federation staged its championships in the Texas skies, introducing for the first time the "team video concept." In this idiom, the sky surfer jumps with a partner equipped with a helmet camera. Both work in tandem to produce a video of the jump that is shown in real-time on the ground for spectators and judges. The innovation of this technique is found in the collapse of subject and object as the camera-flyer

is implicated in the event. The cameraperson must maneuver and stay in-synch with the sky surfer to produce spectacular shots, angles, and an array of aerial acrobatics. The artistry of the image on the television is the object of judging, not the skydivers themselves. Tomlinson, *The Ultimate Encyclopedia of Extreme Sports*, 43.

75 The film was inspired by the much publicized June 1995 shooting down of Air Force flyer Scott O'Grady, who hid from Serbs for six days while eating bugs and grass and drinking rainwater before being rescued by Marines. The film is an extremely loose translation of the events of O'Grady's time on the ground as he did not encounter anyone in the field. In 2001, O'Grady resigned from the Air Force to perform full time as a motivational speaker. The "eventual heat" did come down in 2002 when O'Grady filed a lawsuit against Twentieth Century Fox for defaming his name and jeopardizing his career as a speaker. According to the suit, "Captain O'Grady was also troubled that the 'hero' in the Fox movie used foul language, was portrayed as a 'hot dog' type pilot, and disobeyed orders, unlike O'Grady." See "U.S. Pilot O'Grady Sues Film-Makers," *Montreal Gazette*, August 21, 2002, F7.

76 See David L. Robb, *Operation Hollywood: How the Pentagon Shapes and Censors the Movies* (New York: Prometheus Books, 2004), 181.

77 Quoted in ibid.

78 Jim Slotek, "Making War Look Good: Behind Enemy Lines Director Admits the Camera Exaggerates," *Toronto Sun*, December 3, 2001, 38.

79 Tanya Irwin, "Navy Offers Action in Campaign: Debut from CEA Suggests Enlisting Will 'Accelerate Your Life'," *Adweek*, March 19, 2001 (Lexis Nexis database).

80 Susan Greene, "Recruiting Pitch Draws Fire: Guard Tries 'Escape from Reality' Tactic," *Denver Post*, October 5, 2001, A18. In a related matter, the Pentagon experimented in 1999 with what it called the "Urban Combat Skateboard," a standard issue skateboard intended to assist with door-to-door searches. See "Operation / Series: Urban Warrior '99," Department of Defense, online: http://www.dodmedia.osd.mil/DVIC_View/Still_Details. cfm?SDAN=DMSD0002959&JPGPath=/Assets/2000/Marines/DM-SD-00-02959.JPG.

81 Tan Vinh, "Sporting Events Offer 'Gold Mine' for Army Recruiters," *Seattle Times*, July 25, 2005, B1.

82 Natalie Zmuda, "Are the Army's New Marketing Tactics a Little Too Kid-Friendly?" *Advertising Age*, September 8, 2008, 1. See also McLeroy, "Army Experience Center Opens in Philadelphia." This military publication specifically touts the placement of the center: "Located near a popular entertainment facility [Dave & Buster's] and an indoor skate park, the AEC features a number of interactive simulations and online educational opportunities."

83 The switch in campaign themes was accompanied by the near doubling of the advertising budget—from $85 million in 2000 to $150 million in 2001. Jane Weaver, "Advertising for the Army," *MSN News*, March 13, 2003. Online: https://www.msnbc.com/news/884250.asp.

84 Kevin Baker, "We're in the Army Now," *Harper's*, October 2003, 35–46.

85 "Residents Dispute Idea That Bomber Suspect Lived Amid Sympathizers," *Grand Rapid Press*, June 2, 2003, A5.

86 Quoted in James Dao, "Ads Now Seek Recruits for 'An Army of One'," *New York Times*, January 9, 2001, A1.

87 In 2006, the Army changed their slogan to "Army Strong," likely due to pressure from those who believed that "Army of One" did not promote military values.

88 See George Coryell, "'Army of One' Defends Ad Spots," *Tampa Tribune*, May 6, 2001, 1.

89 Zmuda, "Are the Army's New Marketing Tactics a Little Too Kid-Friendly?", 1. Dao, "Ads Now Seek Recruits for 'An Army of One'," A1.

90 Dave Trimmer, "Tapping New Market: Team to Compete as 'Army of One'," *Spokesman Review*, July 5, 2004, C1. Lauren Gregory, "Competition Fierce in Wartime Recruiting," *Chattanooga Times Free Press*, October 18, 2008, 0. Both the Marines and the Coast Guard dropped their NASCAR teams in 2006 after determining that such advertising was not as

effective as it had been for the other branches, especially the Army. See James W. Crawley, "Gentlemen, Rethink Your Logos; the Coast Guard and the Marines Are Dropping NASCAR Sponsorships," *Richmond Times Dispatch*, November 15, 2006, A4.

3 Reality War

1 Matthew Gilbert, "Double Vision: The TV Landscape Is One Unsettling Blur of News and Entertainment," *Boston Globe*, April 2, 2003, C1.

2 Lisa de Moraes, "'Reality' TV Is Marching to the Military's Tune," *Washington Post*, March 19, 2002, C7.

3 Bob Houlihan, "MTV's Extreme Challenge," *All Hands*, March 2001, 40–43. Online: http://www.news.navy.mil/media/allhands/acrobat/ah200103.pdf.

4 Ibid. The documents surrounding the Navy–Hollywood *Hunt for Red October* deal are instructive. After assisting in the film's production, the Navy considered putting a recruiting ad in the film's video release as well as using outtakes from the film in its own ads. This was rejected, however, at the advice of one of the Navy's ad agencies, who wrote in a memo, "Both movies [*The Hunt for Red October* and *Flight of the Intruder*] are already wonderful recruiting tools for the military, particularly the Navy, and to add a recruiting commercial onto the head of what is already a two-hour recruiting commercial is redundant." David L. Robb, *Operation Hollywood: How the Pentagon Shapes and Censors the Movies* (New York: Prometheus Books, 2004), 181.

5 Mark Haviland, "Road Rulers Meet AF During Show's Taping," *DCMilitary.com* (2001). Online: http://www.dcmilitary.com/dcmilitary_archives/stories/111401/11956-1. shtml.

6 Steve Oxman, "War Games," *Daily Variety*, March 28, 2001, 24.

7 Catherine Bacon, "Online War Game to Promote TV Special," *Streamingmedia.com* (2001). Online: http://www.streamingmedia.com/article.asp?id=6839.

8 Bill Carter, "Reality TV Goes Back to Basic," *New York Times*, April 2, 2001, C1.

9 *Boot Camp*'s resemblance to *Survivor* provoked a CBS lawsuit against Fox, which was later dropped. Bill Carter, "'Survivor' V. 'Boot Camp' in Latest TV Lawsuit," *New York Times*, April 11, 2001, C2. In fact, *Boot Camp*'s executive producer, Scott Messick, had also produced *Survivor* alongside the show's creator, Mark Burnett.

10 David Wood, "Operation Makeover; Military Gets Real; Survival Themes Aim to Jazz Up Image," *New Orleans Times-Picayune*, April 1, 2001, 29.

11 Ibid.

12 Donna Petrozzello, "War on Terror, the TV Series," *Daily News*, February 21, 2002, 100.

13 Columnist Dave Walker of the *New Orleans Times-Picayune* suggests that the real stars of *Boot Camp* were not the contestants, but rather the drill instructors. That is, the show's most remarkable feature was the unrelenting bark of the drill instructor's voice. Walker identifies the main points of reference to be Jack Web in the 1952 film *The D.I.*, the 1960s television series *Gomer Pyle, USMC*, the drill instructor in *Stripes* (1981) opposite Bill Murray's character, Louis Gossett Jr. in *An Officer and a Gentleman* (1982), and perhaps the defining picture of the drill instructor, R. Lee Ermey's portrayal in *Full Metal Jacket* (1987). Dave Walker, "Listen up, Maggots! The Drill Instructors Are the Real Stars in 'Boot Camp'—and Don't You Forget It," *Times-Picayune*, April 10, 2001, 1. The success of the drill instructor at this time coincided with a rash of "authority figure" television shows such as *Judge Judy, Dr. Phil*, and others.

14 Francine Prose, "Voting Democracy Off the Island," *Harper's*, March, 2004, 61.

15 Bill Keveney, "Military Is Up to These Challenges," *USA Today*, December 5, 2001, 4D.

16 Don Oldenburg, "And Now, 'Rudy, the Ultimate Seal'," *Washington Post*, February 13, 2001, C4.

17 Jeremy Scahill, "Blood Is Thicker Than Blackwater," *Nation* (2006). Online: http://www.thenation.com/doc/20060508/scahill.

18 "Former Leesburg Resident One of Civilians Killed in Iraq," *Associated Press State and Local Wire*, April 1, 2004 (Lexis Nexis database).

19   de Moraes, "'Reality' TV Is Marching to the Military's Tune," C7.

20   Robert Bianco, "'Top Gun' Meets MTV with 'AFP'," *USA Today*, March 29, 2002, 7E.

21   de Moraes, "'Reality' TV Is Marching to the Military's Tune," C7.

22   Marc Silver and Betsy Streisand, "Hollywood at War," *U.S. News and World Report*, March 11, 2002, 76.

23   See a discussion of this rhetorical strategy in H. Bruce Franklin, *Vietnam and Other American Fantasies* (Amherst, MA: University of Massachusetts Press, 2000), 174–201.

24   Karen Rasmussen and Sharon Downey, "Dialectical Disorientation in Vietnam War Films: Subversion of the Mythology of War," *Quarterly Journal of Speech* 77 (1991).

25   None of these films featured female soldiers.

26   Wetta and Novelli, "'Now a Major Motion Picture': War Films and Hollywood's New Patriotism," *The Journal of Military History* 67, no. 3 (2003), 861–82.

27   Wetta and Novelli reference the treatment of the American Revolution, *The Patriot* (2000). Here the eponymous main character played by Mel Gibson takes up arms not out of loyalty to country or the cause of independence, but rather out of personal revenge for the murder of his two sons. "Nowhere in the film," Wetta and Novelli point out, "does Gibson utter a single word on behalf of the struggle against the British for independence," a strange omission considering the title of the film. Ibid.: 871.

28   Stephen A. Klein, "Public Character and the Simulacrum: The Construction of the Soldier Patriot and Citizen Agency in *Black Hawk Down*," *Critical Studies in Media Communication* 22, no. 5 (2005), 427–49.

29   For an explanation of the Hollywood Liaison Office, its function, and the films it has both materially supported and rejected, see Robb, *Operation Hollywood: How the Pentagon Shapes and Censors the Movies*.

30   Jacqueline Garrelts, "Army Lends Aid to Hollywood," *Army News Service*, July 29, 2004. Online: http://www.militaryinfo.com/news_story.cfm?textnewsid=1098.

31   Questions about the Lynch story began to arise quickly after the initial press conference. Lynch later revealed that she was not being held captive and that the hospital was not occupied by Iraqi troops at the time of the rescue. In fact, hospital staff gave her special care and surgery even with a shortage of staff and beds. One hospital employee reported having attempted to return Lynch to US forces in an ambulance, but he had to turn back after US forces allegedly fired shots at him. See Hugh Dellios and E.A. Torriero, "Myth: How the Jessica Lynch Story Turned into a Fable," *San Diego Union-Tribune*, June 1, 2003, G6. When Diane Sawyer asked her if the Pentagon portrayal bothered her, Lynch said, "Yeah, it does. It does that they used me as a way to symbolize all this stuff. Yeah, it's wrong." David D. Kirkpatrick, "Jessica Lynch Criticizes U.S. Accounts of Her Ordeal," *New York Times*, November 7, 2003, A25. Stateside hospital records confirmed the allegation that Lynch had been raped, a fact revealed in her authorized biography *I Am a Soldier, Too*. The Iraqi doctors who treated her, however, claimed they did not see any evidence of rape. See William Branigin, "New Biography Indicates Lynch Was Raped by Captors," *Washington Post*, November 7, 2003, A24. David Weber, "Iraq Doctors Say Lynch Didn't Suffer Sex Assault," *Boston Herald*, November 8, 2003, 6.

32   Mark Andrejevic, *Reality TV: The Work of Being Watched* (Lanham, MD: Rowman & Littlefield Publishers, 2003), 9, 11.

33   See a discussion of reality television's democratization of fame in Susan Holmes, "'All You've Got to Worry About Is the Task, Having a Cup of Tea, and Doing a Bit of Sunbathing': Approaching Celebrity in Big Brother," in *Understanding Reality Television*, ed. Susan Holmes and Deborah Jermyn (New York: Routledge, 2004).

34   Andrejevic, *Reality TV: The Work of Being Watched*.

35   Harry Levins, "Strange Bedfellows Militarymediamilitary," *St. Louis Post-Dispatch*, February 16, 2003, B1. It should be noted that the embedding system was not strictly new. During WWII, the U.S. Department of War had stationed a handful of individual reporters within the ranks. Susan Carruthers, *The Media at War: Communication and Conflict in the Twentieth*

Century (New York: St. Martin's Press, 2000), 54–107. The increase in size, scope, and technological integration distinguished the practice in 2003.

36 Tom Brokaw, "Pentagon Recommends Boot Camp for Journalists Covering War," *NBC Nightly News*, February 10, 2003.

37 For a list of these films, see Robb, *Operation Hollywood: How the Pentagon Shapes and Censors the Movies*.

38 Judith S. Gillies, "Putting a Face on Those Who Serve," *Washington Post*, March 9, 2003, Y7.

39 "Series Eyes U.S. Military," *Montreal Gazette*, February 22, 2002, D11. See also Robb, *Operation Hollywood: How the Pentagon Shapes and Censors the Movies*.

40 Niyirah was the 15-year-old supposed hospital worker who testified on such atrocities in front of Congress. A year later the tale was revealed to have been entirely concocted by the Hill and Knowlton group on behalf of the Kuwaiti government. Moreover, Nayirah was found to be none other than the Kuwaiti ambassador's daughter. See John R. MacArthur, *Second Front: Censorship and Propaganda in the Gulf War* (New York: Hill and Wang, 1992), 54–60. See also Stauber and Rampton, *Toxic Sludge Is Good for You: Lies, Damn Lies, and the Public Relations Industry*, 167–74.

41 Torie Clarke, *Lipstick on a Pig: Winning in the No-Spin Era by Someone Who Knows the Game* (New York: Free Press, 2006).

42 Matthew Creamer, "Transparency—Embedded Reporters May Help Corporations Open Up," *PR Week*, May 19, 2003, 9.

43 Petrozzello, "War on Terror, the TV Series," 100.

44 " 'Front Line' a Questionable Dose of Reality," *Alameda Times-Star*, February 27, 2003 (Lexis Nexis database).

45 "Series Eyes U.S. Military," D11.

46 Carruthers, *The Media at War: Communication and Conflict in the Twentieth Century*, 108–62.

47 John Leland, "Cultural Studies: Glued to Public Seduction TV," *New York Times*, February 23, 2003, section 9, pg. 3.

48 Danny Schechter, "Independent Press Was a Target in Iraq," *Television Week*, February 28, 2005, 8. The origin of the phrase "fourth front" is unclear, but it does appear a decade earlier in Paul Virilio's appraisal of the first Gulf War, *Desert Screen*. Virilio writes:

> Already, the "fourth power" dissolves in the procedures of instantaneous information for which nobody is truly responsible, the notions of media and mediation tend themselves to disappear in a short circuit, a feedback that definitely nullifies the necessary independence of the news, especially its rational interpretation. And so the formidable spectre of a "fourth front" looms up on the horizon, where weapons of communication would no longer have anything in common with our current means of information and whose purely technical imperialism will come with a return of a feudalism where the old dungeon of the lords of the land would be advantageously replaced by the satellite.
>
> (Paul Virilio, *Desert Screen: War at the Speed of Light*, trans. Michael Degener (New York: Continuum, 2002), 134–35)

Since Virilio is read as a military theorist as much as a cultural critic, it is likely that he has a part in the etymology of the phrase.

49 Gillies, "Putting a Face on Those Who Serve," Y07.

50 Kathleen Obrien, "Most Wanted: Drilling Down/Television; the Other Reality," *New York Times*, March 31, 2003, C9.

51 Susan Crabtree, "Pentagon Enlists Reality TV Producer," *Daily Variety*, April 25, 2003, 4.

52 Thomas Rid, *War and Media Operations: The U.S. Military and the Press from Vietnam to Iraq* (New York: Routledge, 2007), 153. See also Gina Kim and Mark Ramirez, "Judging Embedded Reporting: The Experts," *Seattle Times*, March 26, 2003. Online: http://community. seattletimes.nwsource.com/archive/?date=20030326&slug=embedded26.

53 Andrew Hoskins, *Televising War: From Vietnam to Iraq* (New York: Continuum, 2004), 47.

54 Ibid.

55 "Embedded Reporting: What Are Americans Getting?" *Project for Excellence in Journalism*, April 3, 2003. Online: http://journalism.org/node/211.

56 W. Lance Bennett, *News, the Politics of Illusion*, 2nd ed. (New York: Longman, 1988). Kathleen Hall Jamieson, *Eloquence in an Electronic Age: The Transformation of Political Speechmaking* (New York: Oxford University Press, 1988).

57 Richard Roeper, "TV Reporters Lack Sense to Come In Out of the Rain," *Chicago Sun-Times*, September 22, 2003, 11.

58 Lori Montgomery, "Paying Tribute to the Chroniclers of War," *Washington Post*, October 2, 2003, B01.

59 Bryan Bender, "War Journalists Honored at Memorial," *Boston Globe*, October 2, 2003, A12.

60 Ibid.

61 Between March 20 and the fall of the Saddam Hussein statue on April 9, fourteen journalists had been killed in Iraq, only four of which were embedded. By the end of the year, 21 press workers had been killed in Iraq, sixteen of which were unilaterals and the majority of which had been killed by Western coalition forces. Peter Wilson, "Iraq Inquest," *Australian*, April 8, 2004, 20.

62 Robert Menard, head of the press freedom group Reporters Sans Frontières, said "Many journalists have come under fire, others have been detained and questioned for several hours and some have been mistreated, beaten and humiliated by Coalition forces," ibid., 20. In January of 2005, CNN executive Eason Jordan commented at the World Economic Forum conference in Switzerland that he believed coalition forces intentionally targeted and killed journalists. Jordan resigned from his position shortly after the comments went public "Bloggers Go Big Game Hunting," *Toronto Star*, February 20, 2005, A10.

63 Montgomery, "Paying Tribute to the Chroniclers of War," B01.

64 Andrea Stone, "Lights, Cameras Get Ready for War," *USA Today*, March 10, 2003, 3D.

65 Sig Christenson, "Pentagon Plan Opens Combat News Coverage," *San Antonio Express-News*, January 15, 2003, 4A.

66 Bob von Sternberg, "The Pentagon Gives Reporters Front Seats but Not Free Reign," *Star Tribune*, March 7, 2003, 1A.

67 Fox News reprimanded embedded journalist Geraldo Rivera for drawing a map of troop locations in the sand. CNN fired veteran journalist Peter Arnett after he did an interview on Iraqi television. CNN first defended Arnett's interview before firing him twelve hours later. Jack Shafer, "Sacking Arnett for the Wrong Reason," *Slate*, March 31, 2003. Online: http://www.slate.com/id/2080947. The US military ordered unilateral reporter Philip Smucker of the *Christian Science Monitor* to leave Iraq, accusing him of divulging troop locations; Rob Owen, "Reporters Get Yanked by Brass and Bosses," *Pittsburg Post-Gazette*, April 1, 2003, A1.

68 Wayne Woolley, Military Goes High-Tech to Spread 'Good News'," *Star-Ledger*, July 23, 2007, 1. Anyone can register at the DVIDS website and gain access to a growing library of high-quality, approved DoD B-roll and full stories. Online: http://www.dvidshub.com. Stauber and Rampton, *Toxic Sludge Is Good for You: Lies, Damn Lies, and the Public Relations Industry*, 184–85.

69 Robert Asen, "A Discourse Theory of Citizenship," *Quarterly Journal of Speech* 90, no. 2 (2004): 191, 203.

4 War Games

1 "Export Controls Put on 'Military' Playstation2," *Electronics Times*, April 26, 2000, 4. "Military Fears over Playstation2," *BBC NewsOnline, Asia-Pacific*, April 17, 2000. Online: http://news.bbc.co.uk/1/low/world/asia-pacific/716237.stm.

2 William L. Hamilton, "Toymakers Study Troops, and Vice Versa," *New York Times*, March 30, 2003, section 9, pg. 1.

3 William Saletan, "War Is Halo," *Slate Magazine*, July 22, 2008. Online: http://www.slate.com/id/2195751.

4 Quoted in J. C. Herz, *Joystick Nation* (New York: Little, Brown and Co., 1997), 197.

5 Janice Kennedy, "Virtual Hell," *Ottawa Citizen*, May 29, 2003, E5.

6 Michael Medved, "Zap! Have Fun and Help Defeat Terrorists, Too," *USA Today*, October 30, 2001, 15A.

7 Ronald Reagan, "Remarks During a Visit to Walt Disney World's Epcot Center near Orlando, Florida," *Ronald Reagan Presidential Library*, March 8, 1983. Online: http://www.reagan.utexas.edu/archives/speeches/1983/30883a.htm.

8 The most comprehensive treatment of military simulation is Der Derian, *Virtuous War: Mapping the Military-Industrial-Media-Entertainment Network*. The book constitutes a walk-through of the world of training simulation, what he calls the military-industrial-media-entertainment network.

9 Amy Harmon, "More Than Just a Game, but How Close to Reality?," *New York Times*, April 3, 2003, G1.

10 Quoted in John Crace, "War Game: Tap, Tap—You're Dead! How Computer Games Became the Army's Latest Training Tool," *Guardian*, July 9, 2002, 42.

11 Steve Silberman, "The War Room," *Wired Online*, September 2004. Online: http://www.wired.com/wired/archive/12.09/warroom_pr.html. See also Amit Asaravala, "When War Games Meet Video Games," *Wired Online*, October 20, 2004. Online: http://www.wired.com/news/tecnology/0,1282,65403,00.html.

12 Harmon, "More Than Just a Game, but How Close to Reality?," G1.

13 Herz, *Joystick Nation*. Der Derian, *Virtuous War: Mapping the Military-Industrial-Media-Entertainment Network*.

14 Herz, *Joystick Nation*, 209.

15 Marc Saltzman, "Army Enlists Simulation to Help Tackle Terrorists," *USA Today*, October 2, 2001, 3D.

16 Quoted in Tom Luftus, "War Games in a Time of War," *MSNBC.com*, July 18, 2004. Online: http://www.msnbc.msn.com/id/5318462.

17 Steve O'Hagan, "Recruitment Hard Drive: The US Army Is the World's Biggest Games Developer, Pumping Billions into New Software," *Guardian*, June 19, 2004, 12.

18 Andy Walker, "U.S. Army Scores Hit in Kinder, Gentler War Games," *Toronto Star*, May 19, 2003, D1.

19 Rick Rogers, "Video Game Brings the Fight to the Marines," *San Diego Union-Tribune*, June 3, 2005, A1.

20 Alexander R. Galloway, "Social Realism in Gaming," *Game Studies* 4, no. 1 (2004). Online: http://www.gamestudies.org/0401/galloway/.

21 Rob Riddell, "Doom Goes to War," *Wired*, May 4, 1997. Online: http://www.wired.com/archive/5.04/ff-doom.html.

22 Saltzman, "Army Enlists Simulation to Help Tackle Terrorists," 3D.

23 See Michael Peck, "Battlefield Gamers," *Defense Technology International*, September 1, 2007, 12.

24 Crace, "War Game: Tap, Tap—You're Dead! How Computer Games Became the Army's Latest Training Tool," 42.

25 Mike Snider, "Spies Will Learn Craft Via Games," *USA Today*, June 16, 2005, 5D.

26 Sharon Waxman, "Thinking Outside the Tank; California's Institute for Creative Technologies Puts Tinseltown Talent to Work on Military Defense," *Washington Post*, May 7, 2003, C1.

27 Noah Shachtman, "Army Sets up New Office of Video Games," *Wired*, December 12, 2007. Online: http://www.wired.com/dangerroom/2007/12/armys-new-offic.

28 Suneel Ratan, "War Games Come Marching In," *Wired*, December 9, 2003. Online: http://www.wired.com/news/games/0,2101,61515,00.html.

29 Don Oldenburg, "New Video War Games Give a Taste of Combat—for Fun," *Washington Post*, December 10, 2002, C1.

30 "Freedom isn't free" is a curious phrase, resonating with the Orwellian line, "Freedom is slavery." The Fox News Channel, beginning in 2001, has run a financial news magazine

called "The Cost of Freedom," suggesting that freedom is an economic calculation or perhaps that freedom itself runs at a negative cost to the economy.

31 Quoted in Ben Berkowitz and Jean Yoon, "In Wake of Attacks, Industry Weighs Video Game Violence," *San Diego Union-Tribune*, September 18, 2001, 4.

32 During this period, the Blackwater USA corporation was one of the largest of the private mercenary forces hired by the Pentagon. The skyrocketing use of private corporate mercenary forces by the US as security forces and in battle is documented extensively by Peter W. Singer (2003). See also Chalmers Johnson (2004). The online video game, *Kuma\War*, has developed a mission where one can play at being a soldier of the famed Blackwater USA corporation.

33 Derrick J. Lang, "'Army of Two,' 'Turning Point' and 'Kwari' Take New Aim at the Shooter Genre," *Associated Press*, November 21, 2007 (Lexis Nexis database).

34 Ibid.

35 Patrick Crogan, "Gametime: History, Narrative, and Temporality in Combat Flight Simulator II," in *The Video Game Theory Reader*, ed. Mark J. P. Wolf and Bernard Perron (New York: Routledge, 2003), 280.

36 See Roger Stahl, "A Clockwork War: Rhetorics of Time in a Time of Terror," *Quarterly Journal of Speech* 94, no. 1 (2007), 73–99.

37 Gerbner, "Persian Gulf War, the Movie."

38 Apart from the examples discussed here are numerous other war games with themes to match current events. Dozens of crude anti-Saddam Hussein and anti-Osama bin Laden games were distributed through the Internet in the years following September 11, 2001.

39 "The Games People Slay," *Wired*, April 1, 2003. Online: http://www.wired.com/news/culture/0,1284,58314,00.html.

40 Walker, "U.S. Army Scores Hit in Kinder, Gentler War Games," D1.

41 According to a search at the US Patent and Trademark Office database (http://www.uspto.gov), showed that "Shock and Awe" has been trademarked for products ranging from "The Shock and Awe Tour" for music promotion to sportswear, mugs, umbrellas and greeting cards. See also Julia Day, "Sony to Cash in on Iraq with 'Shock and Awe' Game," *Guardian Online*, April 10, 2003. Online: http://media.guardian.co.uk/print/0,,4644696-105237,00.html. "Sony Drops 'Shock and Awe' for Playstation Games," *USA Today Online*, April 16, 2003. Online: http://www.usatoday.com/tech/world/iraq/2003-04-16-shock-sony_x.htm. "No 'Shock and Awe' for Sony," *CNN.com*, April 16, 2003. Online: http://robots.cnn.com/2003/TECH/biztech/04/16/japan.sony.reut/index.html.

42 Ben Fritz, "Holiday Fuels Activision," *Daily Variety*, February 8, 2008, 4.

43 See Seth Schiesel, "Facing the Horrors of Distant Battlefields with a TV and Console," *New York Times*, March 19, 2008, E3.

44 Abbey Klaassen, "Media Morph: Episodic Games," *Advertising Age*, August 20, 2007, 15.

45 Quoted in Josh Sims, "When Reality Is Just an Illusion," *Independent*, March 29, 2004, 4.

46 Brian Crecente, "Fighting Reality: Military Games Entertain, Disturb with Creative Depictions of Modern Warfare," *Rocky Mountain News*, April 30, 2004, 29D.

47 Hiawatha Bray, "Online, They're Already Fighting the Last War," *Boston Globe*, March 3, 2004, C1.

48 Ibid.

49 Sims, "When Reality Is Just an Illusion," 5.

50 Ibid., 4.

51 Ibid., 40–47.

52 Sims, "When Reality Is Just an Illusion," 5. What "fun" means and what kind of violence games are likely to adopt in the future is an open question. Eidos Games introduced *ShellShock: 'Nam 67* in the summer of 2004, which "dares to go where no other war game has gone before" to deliver an "uncensored depiction of the Vietnam experience." Crecente, "Fighting Reality: Military Games Entertain, Disturb with Creative Depictions of Modern Warfare," 29D. Given Vietnam's distance and the growing market for gaming gore, this

should not be surprising, but it begs the question as to how the level of tolerance for gore will evolve in the future and how this will affect the appearance of more recent conflicts in games.

53 Stanley A. Miller, "War Game: Army Deploys to L.A. To Capture the Attention of America's Gamers," *Milwaukee Journal Sentinel*, May 12, 2003, 1A.

54 In 1999, the military hit a low water mark in recruiting. Because of this, the Department of Defense recruiting budget was nearly doubled from $299 to $592 million from 1998–2003 according to the General Accounting Office. "Military Recruiting: DoD Needs to Establish Objectives and Measures to Better Evaluate Advertising's Effectiveness," ed. United States General Accounting Office. Report to Senate and House Committees on Armed Services (2003). Compared to private corporate ad expenditures, the US military ranks 34, right behind McDonald's. Jim Edwards, "Uncle Sam Ups Ante for Recruiting Effort," *Adweek*, November 29, 2004 (Lexis Nexis database).

55 O'Hagan, "Recruitment Hard Drive," 12.

56 Quoted in Jacob Hodes and Emma Ruby-Sachs, "'America's Army' Targets Youth," *The Nation*, August 23, 2002. Online: http://www.thenation.com/doc/20020902/hodes20020823.

57 Shawn Jeffords, "Army Game Enlists 'Soft Sell' for Recruitment," *Chicago Sun-Times*, November 25, 2003, 20.

58 Dwight N. Odelius, "These Games Provide Funky Fun, and One's Free," *The Houston Chronicle*, December 25, 2003, 4.

59 Quoted in Wayne Woolley, "From 'Army of One' to Army of Fun," *New Orleans Times-Picayune*, September 7, 2003, 26.

60 Kennedy, "Virtual Hell," E5.

61 Maria Aspan, "A Game with Real Soldiers," *New York Times*, September 18, 2006. Natalie Zmuda, "Are the Army's New Marketing Tactics a Little Too Kid-Friendly?," *Advertising Age*, September 8, 2008, 1.

62 Jim Edwards, "Uncle Sam Ups Ante for Recruiting Effort." *Adweek*, November 29, 2004.

63 Miller, "War Game: Army Deploys to L.A.," 1A.

64 Julian E. Barnes, "The New Action Heroes," *U.S. News & World Report*, November 21, 2005, 53.

65 Josh White, "It's a Video Game, and an Army Recruiter," *Washington Post*, May 27, 2005, A25.

66 Wayne Woolley, "From 'Army of One' to Army of Fun," *New Orleans Times-Picayune*, September 7, 2003, 26.

67 Ibid., 26.

68 Barnes, "The New Action Heroes," 53.

69 Tina Susman, "Military Wins with Recruiting Game," *Newsday*, October 29, 2003, A7.

70 Woolley, "From 'Army of One' to Army of Fun," 26.

71 Marc Saltzman, "Army Gives New Meaning to War Games—on a PC," *USA Today Online*, May 2, 2002. Online: http://www.usatoday.com/tech/techreviews/2002/4/22/army-game. htm.

72 Kris Oser, "Big Guns Fall in Line Behind Army's Adver-Game," *Advertising Age*, April 11, 2005, 83.

73 Ibid., 83.

74 Arthur Asa Berger, *Video Games: A Popular Culture Phenomenon* (New Brunswick, NJ: Transaction Publishers, 2002), 14.

75 Kennedy, "Virtual Hell," E5.

76 Galloway, "Social Realism in Gaming."

77 A detailed analysis of the concept of technological fetishism and its relationship to virtue and barbarism in the Persian Gulf War can be found in Askoy and Robins, "Exterminating Angels: Morality, Violence, and Technology in the Gulf War."

78 Der Derian, *Virtuous War: Mapping the Military-Industrial-Media-Entertainment Network*, xvii.

5 Toying with Militainment

1 "Patriotism Fuels Flag Purchases," *USA Today*, 10 September 2002, 1D.

2 For a sense of the range of post-9/11 patriotic merchandise, see Richard Roeper, "Nothing Is So Sacred It Can't Be Marketed," *Chicago Sun-Times*, December 3, 2001, 11.

3 Jennifer Scanlon, " 'Your Flag Decal Won't Get You into Heaven Anymore': U.S. Consumers, Wal-Mart, and the Commodification of Patriotism," in *The Selling of 9/11: How a National Tragedy Became a Commodity*, ed. Dana Heller (New York: Palgrave Macmillan, 2005), 174–199.

4 George W. Bush, "At O'Hare, President Says 'Get on Board'," September 27, 2001. *White House Press Releases* (Lexis Nexis database).

5 Patrick Burns, "Some Easter Baskets Carry Military Theme This Year," *Intelligencer Journal*, April 4, 2003, A1. See also "Military Hamsters Capture Toy Sales," *Seattle Times*, 3 April 2003, C1.

6 "Iraq Faces Massive U.S. Missile Barrage," *CBSNews.com*, January 24, 2003. Online: http://www.cbsnews.com/stories/2003/01/24/eveningnews/printable/537928.shtml.

7 Napa Valley Worldwise Wholesalers. Online: http://www.napavalleywww.com/shockandawe.htm. Accessed April 17, 2005.

8 Bartosiewicz, "From G.I. Joe to Tora Bora Ted." *Salon.com*, September 11, 2003.

9 Merle English, "He Wrote the Book on G.I. Joe," *Newsday*, May 23, 2004, G3. Bo Emerson, "G.I. Joe Still Says Home to Troops, Collectors," *Atlanta Journal-Constitution*, March 31, 2003, 1E. William L. Hamilton, "Toymakers Study Troops, and Vice Versa," *New York Times*, March 30, 2003, section 9, pg. 1.

10 Quoted in Hamilton, "Toymakers Study Troops, and Vice Versa," section 9, pg. 1.

11 Hamilton, "Toymakers Study Troops, and Vice Versa," section 9, pg. 1.

12 Quoted in Bartosiewicz, "From G.I. Joe to Tora Bora Ted."

13 Brit Hume of Fox News, and Pat Buchanan and Keith Olbermann of MSNBC showed a particular preference for the term "Saddamite." For an analysis of the sexual symbolism and demonization of Hussein in Gulf War I, see Douglas Kellner, *The Persian Gulf TV War* (Boulder, CO: Westview Press, 1992), 65–66. See also Stam, "Mobilizing Fictions: The Gulf War, the Media, and the Recruitment of the Spectator," 120–21. Merchandising the evil Hussein was also a popular pastime of Desert Storm. See David Prochaska, " 'Disappearing' Iraqis," *Public Culture* 4, no. 2 (1992), 89–92.

14 Josefina Loza, "War on Terror Playing Out through New Fireworks," *Associated Press State and Local Wire*, July 2, 2004, (Lexis-Nexis database).

15 George Stephanopoulos, *Good Morning America*, ABC, May 2, 2003.

16 Quoted in "Bush—the Doll—Ready to Fly Plane Again," *Chicago Sun-Times*, August 14, 2003, 5. Also see Elaine Monoghan, "Bush's Landing on Aircraft Carrier Inspires Presidential Action Figure: Doll Draws Protests from War Veterans," *Ottawa Citizen*, August 13, 2003, D18.

17 Michael McWhertor, "America's Army Deployed to Toy Aisles [Bureau of Licensing]," *Kotaku*, November 15, 2007 (Lexis Nexis darabase).

18 Jackie Sindrich, "Topps Turns Attack into Trading Cards," *San Diego Union-Tribune*, November 9, 2001, E7.

19 Frank Green, "Upper Deck to Issue Patriotic Trading Cards; 'United We Stand' Line Contains Images from Sept. 11 Terror Attacks," *San Diego Union-Tribune*, November 10, 2001, C1.

20 Karen Herschenson, "Terrorist Cards Tout Tastelessness," *Contra Costa Times*, January 4, 2002, A3.

21 Matthew Preusch, "Games: An Army of Fun," *Newsweek*, November 28, 2005, 8.

22 Scott Shugar, "Operation Desert Store: First the Air War, Then the Ground War, Now the Marketing Campaign," *Los Angeles Times*, September 29, 1991.

23 Hamilton, "Toymakers Study Troops, and Vice Versa," section 9, pg. 1.

24 Ibid.
25 Ibid.
26 Miriam Fam, "Iraqi President Says U.S. Troops Should Stay; Election Workers Begin Final Tally of Historic Vote," *Associated Press*, February 1, 2005 (Lexis Nexis database).
27 Jim Krane, "Insurgency-Friendly Web Sites Valuable to Rebels, Reporters and U.S. Military—and Prone to Hoaxes," *Associated Press*, February 3, 2005 (Lexis Nexis database).
28 Dana Milbank, "No Crawfishing from a Unique Vernacular," *Washington Post*, September 10, 2002, A13. See also "Quotation of the Day," *New York Times*, September 7, 2002, A2.
29 See Krissah Williams, "Barbie Doesn't Play Here; War Toys Spur Debate Over Harmless Fantasy vs. Violent Reality," *Washington Post*, 22 December 2002, H5; Also Bartosiewicz, "From G.I. Joe to Tora Bora Ted."
30 "Forward Command Post," *Snopes.com*. Online: http://www.snopes.com/politics/military/commandtoy.asp.
31 Mary Morgan Edwards, "Military Easter Baskets Come under Fire," *Columbus Dispatch*, April 12, 2003, 1B.
32 Burns, "Some Easter Baskets Carry Military Theme This Year," A1. "Military Hamsters Capture Toy Sales," *Seattle Times*, April 3, 2003, C1.
33 Theresa Howard, "Walgreens Won't Sell Easter Baskets with Toy Soldiers," *USA Today*, March 7, 2003, 1B. See also Erik Baard, "Full Metal Bonnet," *Village Voice*, March 11, 2003, 39.
34 Patrick M. Regan, "War Toys, War Movies, and the Militarization of the United States, 1900–1985," *Journal of Peace Research* 31, no. 1 (1994), 45–58.
35 Kenneth D. Brown, "Modelling for War? Toy Soldiers in Late Victorian and Edwardian Britain," *Journal of Social History* 24, no. 2 (1990): 237–39.
36 Ibid.: 244–47.
37 Susan Sontag, *Regarding the Pain of Others* (New York: Farrar, Straus, and Giroux, 2003), 14.
38 Jeffrey Verhey, *The Spirit of 1914: Militarism, Myth, and Mobilization in Germany*, Studies in the Social and Cultural History of Modern Warfare (Cambridge, MA: Cambridge University Press, 2000), 225.
39 In 1982, Friedrich's heirs reopened the museum at another location in Berlin. See description at "Anti-Kriegs-Museum." Online: http://www.anti-kriegs-museum.de/english/start1.html.
40 Karen J. Hall, "A Soldier's Body: GI Joe, Hasbro's Great American Hero, and the Symptoms of Empire," *Journal of Popular Culture* 38, no. 1 (2004), 34–54.
41 Ibid.
42 Petra Bartosiewicz, "From G.I. Joe to Tora Bora Ted," *Salon.com*, September 11, 2003 (Lexis Nexis database).
43 Ibid.
44 A hack might make a player invincible or able to fire without missing a target. They are freely available on the Internet and, according to the *Guardian*, represent an "epidemic" that has infected the most popular online games. David McCandless, "Make Cheats, Not War," *Guardian*, May 22, 2003, 23.
45 Anne-Marie Schleiner, "Cracking the Maze Online Exhibit: Game Plug-Ins and Patches as Hacker Art," *Switch*, no. 12 (1999). Online: http://switch.sjsu.edu/nextswitch/switch_engine/front/front.php?
46 Nick Wadhams, "Online Games Increasingly a Place for Protest, Social Activism," *Associated Press*, February 6, 2003 (Lexis Nexis database).
47 "Velvet Strike Flamer Gallery," online: http://www.opensorcery.net/velvet-strike/mailgallery.html. See also Jennifer Buckendorff, "The 'Velvet-Strike' Underground," *Salon.com*, May 4, 2004 (Lexis Nexis database).
48 Buckendorff, "The 'Velvet-Strike' Underground."
49 Christine Harold, "Pranking Rhetoric: 'Culture Jamming' as Media Activism," *Critical Studies in Media Communication* 21, no. 3 (2004): 190.
50 Ibid.

51 Bill Berkowitz, "Collect Them All," *In These Times*, June 24, 2002, 8.

52 See Reparez's site, "The Buy Bush a PlayStation 2 Campaign." Online: http://www.evilninja.net/buybush.htm.

53 "*Seattle Times* Tech News Column," *Seattle Times*, April 21, 2003 (Lexis Nexis database).

54 Dead_in_Iraq. Online: http://www.unr.edu/art/DELAPPE/Gaming/Dead_In_Iraq/dead_in_iraq%20JPEGS.html

55 Kathleen Craig, "Dead in Iraq: It's No Game," *Wired.com*, June 6, 2006. Online: http://www.wired.com/gaming/gamingreviews/news/2006/06/71052. See also Rebecca Clarren, "Virtually Dead in Iraq," *Salon.com*, September 16, 2006 (Lexis Nexis database).

56 Craig, "Dead in Iraq: It's No Game."

57 This hypothetical situation hints at a limitation to the strategy of collapse. While the purpose of the strategy may be to inject a "reality check" into a fantasy world, the persistent absurdity of the "war without war" may have attenuated the power of the witness by de-realizing death itself. That is, perhaps such an event would not threaten the integrity of the game in an environment where the realism of the interactive, simulacra clean war threatens to overwhelm the reality of war. Clarren, "Virtually Dead in Iraq."

58 Corrie Pikul, "The Photoshopping of the President," *Salon.com*, July 1, 2004 (Lexis Nexis database).

59 Ann McFeatters, "Laughter in a Time of War," *Pittsburgh Post-Gazette*, March 30, 2003. Online: http://www.post-gazette.com/forum/cd/20030330edann30p3.asp.

60 Chuck Roberts, *CNN Headline News*, March 20, 2003 (Lexis Nexis database).

61 *The Daily Show*, Comedy Central, 19 December 2002.

62 Meg Linton, "Wayne Coe, American Hero," *Juxtapoz Magazine*, December 2006, http://www.waynecoe.com/press.html. The store owner, at odds with Coe's work, took the display down very early in the exhibition and did not return the boxes.

63 Greg Stacy, "Atrocity Becomes Art at OCCCA's 'Just How Does a Patriot Act?' Show," *OC Weekly*, October 16, 2008 (Lexis Nexis database).

64 Mary Vallis, "In Texas, a Mouse Can Kill a Deer; Web Site Would Give Hunters an Online Shot at Animals," *Chicago Sun-Times*, November 19, 2004, 46. "Computer-assisted hunting" was later banned in many states. Zachary M. Seward, "Internet Hunting Nipped in Bud," *Seattle Times*, August 12, 2007, A9.

65 Kari Lydersen, "Antiwar Art in a New Medium: Paintball-on-Web; Iraqi Dodges Projectiles at Chicago Gallery to Illustrate His People's Plight," *Washington Post*, May 29, 2007, A2.

66 Stevenson Swanson, "Iraqi Artist Claims 'Censorship'," *Chicago Tribune*, March 11, 2008, 3.

67 Kari Lydersen, "In the Crosshairs," *In these Times*, July, 2007, 48. Indeed, Bilal later constructed an online project called "Dog or Iraqi" in which he asked people to vote whether he or a canine should be waterboarded. The dog won. Bilal underwent a filmed waterboarding conducted by a man in a Santa Claus suit, which was then posted on the site www.dogoriraqi.com. See Robin Shulman, "Terror-Themed Game Suspended; Iraqi-Born Artist Asserts Censorship after Exhibit Is Shut Down," *Washington Post*, March 8, 2008, A3.

68 Lydersen, "In the Crosshairs," 48.

69 Lydersen, "Antiwar Art in a New Medium."

70 "Wafaa Bilal Sits in Small Room with a Paint Ball Gun While Visitors to His Web Site Take Shots at Him," *CBS News*, May 31, 2007 (Lexis Nexis database).

71 William Walker, "So Many Fears for Such a Beautiful Afternoon," *Toronto Star*, November 17, 2002, B3.

72 Lydersen, "Antiwar Art in a New Medium."

73 Ben Davis, "Pop Life," *Artnet.com*, December 16, 2005. Online: http://www.artnet.com/magazineus/reviews/davis/davis12-16-05.asp.

74 "United We Stand." Online: http://www.unitedwestandmovie.com/.

75 Kim Housego, "Rumsfeld's Remarks Draw Anger in France," *Associated Press*, January 23, 2003 (Lexis Nexis database).

76 Holland Cotter, "The Collective Conscious," *New York Times*, March 5, 2006, sec. 2, pg. 1.

77 "United We Stand." Online: http://www.0100101110101101.org/home/unitedwestand/ story.html.
78 See "Quest for Saddam: Die with Laughter as Action-Packed 3D Shooter Lets You Hunt Down The 'Butcher of Baghdad'," *Market Wire*, May 12, 2003 (Lexis Nexis database).
79 Achieving a level of notoriety from the game, Petrilla formed a political group called the United American Committee. Among its public stunts, in 2006 the group hung an effigy of Osama bin Laden from a noose in front of a mosque in Culver City, California in order to remind Americans of "the threat that radical Islam poses to all of us." Jose Antonio Vargas, "Way Radical, Dude; Now Playing: Video Games with an Islamist Twist," *Washington Post*, October 9, 2006, C1.
80 Ibid.
81 Carol Costello and Eric Horng, "Waiting Finally over for 'Matrix' Fans," *CNN*, May 15, 2003 (Lexis Nexis database). Wolf Blitzer et al., "Bush Administration Reacts to Iranian Showdown; President Bush Hails Global Literacy as Weapon against Terrorism; President Chirac Says France Willing to Work with U.S. on Iraq," *CNN*, September 18, 2006 (Lexis Nexis database).
82 Swanson, "Iraqi Artist Claims 'Censorship'."
83 Ibid.
84 *Quest for Bush* was only the latest addition to a growing catalog of games that play to nationalist and fundamentalist elements of Arab culture. For example, in 2004 the Lebanese Hizbollah government released *The Children of Jerusalem*, a *Space Invaders*-style game that features deadly stars of David and spiders with Ariel Sharon's face. Hizbollah also sponsored the release of *Special Force*, a technically sophisticated first-person shooter in which players can join with the Islamic resistance to fight Israeli soldiers who occupied Lebanon in 2000. The sequel, *Special Force 2*, deals with the Israeli invasion of 2006. The US-based game company IslamGames devised a number of low-tech games akin to those of the first-generation Nintendo. In *Ummah Defense I* and *II*, players defend an Islamic Earth in 2114 from an army of robots created by a lone infidel. Another title by IslamGames called *Islamic Fun* features basic puzzles and games to teach elements of Islam including one game called "The Resistance," where the player can act as a Lebanese farmer fighting an invading Israeli army. Rebecca Armstrong, "Jihad: Play the Game," *Independent*, August 17, 2005, 38–39. Games like this began to receive publicity in the US in 2005 after the July 7 London commuter bombings that killed fifty. *New York Times* columnist Thomas Friedman wondered if Islam-Games, distributed by a Muslim bookstore in Leeds, might have played a part in the bombings. Thomas L. Friedman, "Giving the Hatemongers No Place to Hide," *New York Times*, July 22, 2005, A19.
85 As an editorial put it, "RPI's apprehensions about of Bilal's 'Virtual Jihadi,' but not 'Quest for Saddam,' further legitimizes that the assassination of the Muslim leader of a sovereign Middle East nation is acceptable entertainment, but that a provocative work of art questioning the same notion about the U.S. president is not." Owen Goldfarb, " 'Virtual Jihadi' Creator Achieves His Objective," *Times Union*, March 20, 2008, A10. The director of the art department, Kathy High, expressed a similar response: "The original game was 'Quest for Saddam,' and this is a mimic of that game. Nobody seemed to protest 'Quest for Saddam,' and now they're questioning this game. So it seems OK to hunt down another head of state, but not the U.S. president." Swanson, "Iraqi Artist Claims 'Censorship'."
86 In 2005, the company released the sequel, *Under Siege*, which focuses on the lives of Palestinian characters during the second Intifada, between 1999 and 2002.
87 Kim Ghattas, "Video Game Features Virtual Intifada," *Inter Press Service*, 9 July 2002 (Lexis-Nexis Database).
88 Quoted in Ghattas, "Video Game Features Virtual Intifada."
89 Vargas, "Way Radical, Dude; Now Playing: Video Games with an Islamist Twist," C1.

6 Debriefing

1 Ed Halter, "War Games," *Village Voice*, November 13–19, 2002. Online: http:// www.villagevoice.com/print/issues/0246/halter.php.

2 "'Enduring Freedom' Short Film to be Released in Theaters," *Navy News Stand*, December 21, 2002. Online: http://www.news.navy.mil/search/display.asp?story_id=5094.

3 Quoted in Halter, "War Games."

4 Jean Baudrillard, "What Are You Doing after the Orgy?," *Artforum* 22, no. 2 (1983), 42–46.

5 Les Roberts et al., "Mortality before and after the 2003 Invasion of Iraq: Cluster Sample Survey," *Lancet* 364, no. 9448 (2004) 1857–1864. Gilbert Burnham et al., "Mortality after the 2003 Invasion of Iraq: A Cross-Sectional Cluster Sample Survey," *Lancet* 368, no. 9545 (2006), 1421–1428. A study by the World Health Organization estimated the number of dead as from 104,000 to 223,000 for the period between 2003 and 2006. Amir H. Alkhuzai et al., "Violence-Related Mortality in Iraq from 2002 to 2006," *New England Journal of Medicine* 358, no. 5 (2008), 484–93. See also coverage in the popular press: Lawrence K. Altman, Richard A. Oppel, Jr., and Gardiner Harris, "W.H.O. Says Iraq Civilian Death Toll Higher Than Cited," *New York Times*, January 10, 2008, A14.

6 John Mueller, "The Iraq Syndrome," *Foreign Affairs* 84, no. 6 (2005). (Lexis Nexis database).

7 ABC News/Washington Post Poll, *Pollingreport.com*. Online: http://www.pollingreport. com/iraq2.htm. The numbers are similar whether one asks whether President Bush has done a good job, whether the war was right or a "mistake," or whether it was "worth fighting" in terms of costs and benefits to the US. Virtually no poll asks whether the invasion was morally, ethically, or legally right or wrong—a question that appears to be off limits.

8 Julian E. Barnes, "U.S. Lifts Photo Ban on Fallen," *Los Angeles Times*, February 17, 2009, A10.

9 Les Carpenter, "NFL Orders Retreat from War Metaphors," *Washington Post*, February 1, 2009, D1.

10 Jamin Brophy-Warren, "Iraq, the Videogame," *Wall Street Journal Online*, April 7, 2007. Online: http:// online.wsj.com/article/SB123902404583292727.html#mod=rss_ Lifestyle.

11 Robert Watson, "Bare Knuckles: War Games Trigger an Ethical Conflict," *Philadelphia Inquirer*, May 8, 2009, W31.

12 "Iraq War Coverage Plunges," *Pew Research Center's Project for Excellence in Journalism*, March 25, 2008. Online: http://www.journalism.org/node/10345. Awareness of US troop fatalities also diminished in kind during this same period. "Awareness of Iraq War Fatalities Plummets," *Pew Research Center's Project for Excellence in Journalism*, March 12, 2008. Online: http://people-press.org/report/401/awareness-of-iraq-war-fatalities-plummets.

13 Maria Aspan, "A Game with Real Soldiers," *New York Times*, September 18, 2006, C6. Natalie Zmuda, "Are the Army's New Marketing Tactics a Little Too Kid-Friendly?" *Advertising Age*, September 8, 2008.

14 Nick Gillett, "Military Operations," *Guardian*, January 19, 2008, 30.

15 "US to Air Own Military News, Pentagon Wants More Control of Iraq, Afghanistan Reports," *Seattle Post-Intelligencer*, February 28, 2004, A4. Wayne Woolley, "Military Goes High-Tech to Spread 'Good News'," *Star-Ledger*, July 23, 2007.

16 A list of projects can be found on the *USS Hornet* website. "TV & Movie Film Production Opportunities," USS Hornet Museum. Online: http://www.hornetevents.com/film/ index.html.

17 Hanna Tamrat, "Hornet Hosts 'Fear Factor'," *Inside Bay Area*, July 16, 2006 (Lexis Nexis database).

18 Mark Glassman, "Military Channels Are Competing on Cable TV," *New York Times*, January 24, 2005, C8.

19 *The Military Channel* had been launched after the first Gulf War, but the cable channel went bankrupt in 1999. The Discovery network bought and revitalized the brand in 2005. This of course indicates that interest in such programming is directly dependent on proximity to a recent conflict.

20 The channel's first live programming was, appropriately enough, the Army-Navy football game.
21 David Lieberman, "Military Channel to Be 'Voice of Troops'," *USA Today*, February 5, 2007, 5B.
22 Ibid.
23 Gilles Deleuze, *Negotiations: 1972–1990*, Trans. Martin Joughin (New York: Columbia University Press, 2002), 179.

Bibliography

Alkhuzai, Amir H., Ihsan J. Ahmad, Mohammed J. Hweel, Thakir W. Ismail, Hanan H. Hasan, Abdul Rahman Younis, Osman Shawani, Vian M. Al-Jaf, Mahdi M. Al-Alak, Louay H. Rasheed, Suham M. Hamid, Naeema Al-Gasseer, Fazia A. Majeed, Naira A. Al Awqati, Mohamed M. Ali, J. Ties Boerma, and Colin Mathers. "Violence-Related Mortality in Iraq from 2002 to 2006." *New England Journal of Medicine* 358, no. 5 (2008): 484–93.

Altman, Lawrence K., Richard A. Oppel, Jr., and Gardiner Harris. "W.H.O. Says Iraq Civilian Death Toll Higher Than Cited." *New York Times*, January 10, 2008, A14.

Andersen, Robin. "That's Militainment! The Pentagon's Media-Friendly 'Reality' War." *Extra!*, 2003, 6–9.

——— . *A Century of Media, a Century of War.* New York: Peter Lang, 2006.

Andrejevic, Mark. *Reality TV: The Work of Being Watched.* Lanham, MD: Rowman & Littlefield Publishers, 2003.

——— . "The Rehabilitation of Propaganda: Post 9/11 Media Coverage in the United States." In *Rhetorical Democracy: Discursive Practices of Civic Engagement: Selected Papers from the 2002 Conference of the Rhetoric Society of America*, ed. Gerard A. Hauser and Amy Grim, 85–90. Mahwah, NJ: Lawrence Erlbaum, 2004.

"Anti-Kriegs-Museum." http://www.anti-kriegs-museum.de/english/start1.html.

Apple, R.W. Jr. "Home Front: Edgy Sunday." *New York Times*, October 8, 2001, A1.

Arendt, Hannah. *The Human Condition.* Chicago: University of Chicago Press, 1989.

Arlen, Michael J. *Living-Room War.* New York: Viking Press, 1969.

Armstrong, Rebecca. "Jihad: Play the Game." *Independent*, August 17, 2005, 38–39.

Arquilla, John, and David Ronfeldt. "Cyberwar Is Coming!" *Comparative Strategy* 12, no. 2 (1993): 141–68.

Arquilla, John, David F. Ronfeldt, United States. Dept. of Defense, and National Defense Research Institute (US). *The Advent of Netwar.* Santa Monica, CA: RAND, 1996.

Arrowsmith, Douglas. "Deadline Iraq: Uncensored Stories of the War." 60 minutes: CBC Films, 2003.

Asaravala, Amit. "When War Games Meet Video Games." *Wired Online*, October 20, 2004. http://www.wired.com/news/tecnology/0,1282,65403,00.html.

Asen, Robert. "A Discourse Theory of Citizenship." *Quarterly Journal of Speech* 90, no. 2 (2004): 189–211.

Askoy, Asu, and Kevin Robins. "Exterminating Angels: Morality, Violence, and

Technology in the Gulf War." In *Triumph of the Image: The Media's War in the Persian Gulf*, ed. Hamid Mowlana, Herbert I. Schiller and George Gerbner, 202–12. Boulder, CO: Westview Press, 1992.

Aspan, Maria. "A Game with Real Soldiers." *New York Times*, September 18, 2006, C6.

"Awareness of Iraq War Fatalities Plummets." *Pew Research Center's Project for Excellence in Journalism*, March 12, 2008. http://people-press.org/report/401/awareness-of-iraq-war-fatalities-plummets.

Baard, Erik. "Full Metal Bonnet." *Village Voice*, March 11, 2003, 39.

Bacevich, Andrew J. *The New American Militarism: How Americans Are Seduced by War*. New York: Oxford University Press, 2005.

Bacon, Catherine. "Online War Game to Promote TV Special." *Streamingmedia.com* (2001), http://www.streamingmedia.com/article.asp?id=6839.

Bagdikian, Ben H. *The New Media Monopoly*. Boston: Beacon Press, 2004.

Bahador, Babak. *The CNN Effect in Action: How the News Media Pushed the West toward War in Kosovo*. New York: Palgrave Macmillan, 2007.

Bailey, Eric. "Iron Man." *Tulsa World*, December 22, 2006, B1.

Baker, Kevin. "We're in the Army Now." *Harper's*, October, 2003, 35–46.

Barnes, Fred. *Rebel-in-Chief: Inside the Bold and Controversial Presidency of George W. Bush*. New York: Crown Forum, 2006.

Barnes, Julian E. "The New Action Heroes." *U.S. News & World Report*, November 21, 2005, 53.

––––– . "U.S. Lifts Photo Ban on Fallen." *Los Angeles Times*, February 17, 2009, A10.

Barstow, David. "Behind TV Analysts, Pentagon's Hidden Hand." *New York Times*, April 20, 2008, A1.

Barthes, Roland. *The Grain of the Voice: Interviews 1962–1980*. Trans. Linda Coverdale. New York: Hill and Wang, 1985.

Bartosiewicz, Petra. "From G.I. Joe to Tora Bora Ted." *Salon.com*, September 11, 2003 (Lexis Nexis database).

Basinger, Jeanine. *The World War II Combat Film: Anatomy of a Genre*. Middletown, CT: Wesleyan University Press, 2003.

Bataille, Georges. *The Accursed Share*, vol. 1, trans. Robert Hurley. New York: Zone Books, 1991.

––––– . *Theory of Religion*. Trans. Robert Hurley. New York: Zone Books, 1992.

Baudrillard, Jean. *For a Critique of the Political Economy of the Sign*. St. Louis, MO: Telos Press, 1981.

––––– . "What Are You Doing after the Orgy?" *Artforum* 22, no. 2 (1983): 42–46.

––––– . *The Gulf War Did Not Take Place*. Bloomington: Indiana University Press, 1995.

––––– . *The Spirit of Terrorism; and Other Essays*. New ed. New York: Verso, 2003.

Beamish, Thomas D., Harvey Molotch, and Richard Flacks. "Who Supports the Troops? Vietnam, the Gulf War, and the Making of Collective Memory." *Social Problems* 42, no. 3 (1995): 344–60.

Beck, Peter. "Confronting George Orwell: Philip Noel-Baker on International Sport, Particularly the Olympic Movement, as Peacemaker." In *Militarism, Sport, Europe: War without Weapons*, ed. J.A. Mangan, 187–207. Portland, OR: Frank Cass, 2003.

Bell, Daniel. *The Coming of Post-Industrial Society: A Venture in Social Forecasting*. New York: Basic Books, 1976.

——— . *The End of Ideology: On the Exhaustion of Political Ideas in the Fifties*. Cambridge, MA: Harvard University Press, 1988.

Bender, Bryan. "War Journalists Honored at Memorial." *Boston Globe*, October 2, 2003, A12.

Benjamin, Walter. "The Work of Art in the Age of Mechanical Reproduction." In *Illuminations*, ed. Hannah Arendt. New York: Schocken Books, 1968.

Bennett, W. Lance. *News, the Politics of Illusion*. Second edn. New York: Longman, 1988.

Berger, Arthur Asa. *Video Games: A Popular Culture Phenomenon*. New Brunswick, NJ: Transaction Publishers, 2002.

Berkowitz, Ben, and Jean Yoon. "In Wake of Attacks, Industry Weighs Video Game Violence." *San Diego Union-Tribune*, September 18, 2001, 4.

Berkowitz, Bill. "Collect Them All." *In These Times*, June 24, 2002, 8.

Bernays, Edward L. *Propaganda*. Brooklyn, NY: Ig Publishing, 2005.

Bianco, Robert. " 'Top Gun' Meets MTV with 'AFP'." *USA Today*, March 29, 2002, 7E.

Blitzer, Wolf, Jamie McIntyre, Suzanne Malveaux, Andrea Koppel, Jack Cafferty, Zain Verjee, Ted Rowlands, Mary Snow, Michael Ware, Abbi Tatton, Paula Zahn, and Jeanne Moos. "Bush Administration Reacts to Iranian Showdown; President Bush Hails Global Literacy as Weapon against Terrorism; President Chirac Says France Willing to Work with U.S. on Iraq." *CNN*, September 18, 2006 (Lexis Nexis database).

"Bloggers Go Big Game Hunting." *Toronto Star*, February 20, 2005, A10.

Blum, John Morton. *V Was for Victory: Politics and American Culture During World War II*. New York: Harcourt Brace Jovanovich, 1976.

Branigin, William. "New Biography Indicates Lynch Was Raped by Captors." *Washington Post*, November 7, 2003, A24.

Bray, Hiawatha. "Online, They're Already Fighting the Last War." *Boston Globe*, March 3, 2004, C1.

Breazeale, Kenon. "Bringing the War Back Home: Consuming Operation Desert Storm." *Journal of American Culture* 17, no. 1 (1994): 31–37.

Brenton, Sam, and Reuben Cohen. *Shooting People: Adventures in Reality TV*. New York: Verso, 2003.

Brokaw, Tom. "Pentagon Recommends Boot Camp for Journalists Covering War." *NBC Nightly News*, February 10, 2003 (Lexis Nexis database).

Brown, Kenneth D. "Modelling for War? Toy Soldiers in Late Victorian and Edwardian Britain." *Journal of Social History* 24, no. 2 (1990): 237–54.

Buckendorff, Jennifer. "The 'Velvet-Strike' Underground." *Salon.com*, May 4, 2004 (Lexis Nexis database).

Burkeman, Oliver, and Julian Borger. "Bush in Britain: War Critics Astonished as Us Hawk Admits Invasion Was Illegal." *Guardian*, November 20, 2003, 4.

Burnham, Gilbert, Riyadh Lafta, Shannon Doocy, and Les Roberts. "Mortality after the 2003 Invasion of Iraq: A Cross-Sectional Cluster Sample Survey." *Lancet* 368, no. 9545 (2006): 1421–28.

Burns, Patrick. "Some Easter Baskets Carry Military Theme This Year." *Intelligencer Journal*, April 4, 2003, A1.

Burston, Jonathan. "War and the Entertainment Industries: New Research Priorities in an Era of Cyber-Patriotism." In *War and the Media: Reporting Conflict 24/7*, ed. Daya Kishan Thussu and Des Freedman, 163–75. Thousand Oaks, CA: Sage Publications, 2003.

Burstyn, Varda. *The Rites of Men: Manhood, Politics, and the Culture of Sport*. Toronto: University of Toronto Press, 1999.

Bush, George H.W. "Address to a Joint Session of Congress and the Nation." September 11, 1990. http://millercenter.org/scripps/archive/speeches/detail/3425.

——— . "The President's News Conference." *George Bush Presidential Library and Museum*, November 30, 1990. http://bushlibrary.tamu.edu/research/public_papers.php?id=2516&year=1990&month=11.

Bush, George W. "At O'Hare, President Says 'Get on Board'." September 27, 2001. *White House Press Releases* (Lexis Nexis database).

——— . "President Says Saddam Hussein Must Leave Iraq within 48 Hours." March 17, 2003. http://www.gpoaccess.gov/wcomp/v39no12.html.

——— . "Presidential Address to the Nation." October 7, 2001. http://www.gpoaccess.gov/wcomp/v37no41/.html.

——— . "Address Before a Joint Session of Congress." September 20, 2001. http://www.gpoaccess.gov/wcomp/v37no38.html.

Butler, Judith. "Contingent Foundations: Feminism and the Question of 'Postmodernism'." In *Feminists Theorize the Political*, ed. Judith Butler and Joan W. Scott, 3–21. New York: Routledge, 1992.

Butler, Smedley. *War Is a Racket*. Los Angeles: Feral House, 2003.

Caillois, Roger. *Man, Play, and Games*. New York: Free Press of Glencoe, 1961.

Caldarola, Victor J. "Time and the Television War." *Public Culture* 4, no. 2 (1992): 127–36.

Carey, James W. "American Journalism on, before, and after September 11." In *Journalism after September 11*, ed. Barbie Zelizer and Stuart Allen, 71–90. New York: Routledge, 2002.

Carpenter, Les. "NFL Orders Retreat from War Metaphors." *Washington Post*, February 1, 2009, D1.

Carruthers, Susan. *The Media at War: Communication and Conflict in the Twentieth Century*. New York: St. Martin's Press, 2000.

Carter, Bill. "Reality TV Goes Back to Basic." *New York Times*, April 2, 2001, C1.

——— . " 'Survivor' V. 'Boot Camp' in Latest TV Lawsuit." *New York Times*, April 11, 2001, C2.

Castonguay, Jim. "The Gulf War TV Super Bowl." *Bad Subjects* no. 35 (1997). http://bad.eserver.org/issues/1997/35/castonguay.html.

Chambers, John Whiteclay. *To Raise an Army: The Draft Comes to Modern America*. New York: Free Press, 1987.

Chomsky, Noam. "The Media and War: What War?" In *Triumph of the Image: The Media's War in the Persian Gulf: A Global Perspective*, ed. Hamid Molwana, George Gerbner and Herbert I. Schiller, 51–63. Boulder, CO: Westview Press, 1992.

——— . *Understanding Power*. Ed. Peter R. Mitchell and John Schoeffel. New York: The New Press, 2002.

Christenson, Sig. "Pentagon Plan Opens Combat News Coverage." *San Antonio Express-News*, January 15, 2003, 4A.

"Church Report: Covert Action in Chile 1963–1973." ed. Select Committee to Study Governmental Operations with Respect to Intelligence Activities. Washington, DC: U.S. Government Printing Office, 1975.

Clarke, Torie. *Lipstick on a Pig: Winning in the No-Spin Era by Someone Who Knows the Game*. New York: Free Press, 2006.

Clarren, Rebecca. "Virtually Dead in Iraq." *Salon.com*, September 16, 2006 (Lexis Nexis database).

Cloud, Dana L. " 'To Veil the Threat of Terror': Afghan Women and the <Clash of Civilizations> in the Imagery of the U.S. War on Terrorism." *Quarterly Journal of Speech* 90, no. 3 (2004): 285–306.

Cobb, James G. "Hummer H2: An Army of One." *New York Times*, April 6, 2003, section 12, pg. 1.

Compton, James. "Shocked and Awed: The Convergence of Military and Media Discourse." In *Global Politics in the Information Age*, ed. Mark J. Lacy and Peter Wilkin, 39–62. Manchester: Manchester University Press, 2005.

Coryell, George. " 'Army of One' Defends Ad Spots." *Tampa Tribune*, May 6, 2001, 1.

Costello, Carol, and Eric Horng. "Waiting Finally over for 'Matrix' Fans." *CNN*, May 15, 2003 (Lexis Nexis database).

Cotter, Holland. "The Collective Conscious." *New York Times*, March 5, 2006, section 2, pg. 1.

Crabtree, Susan. "Pentagon Enlists Reality TV Producer." *Daily Variety*, April 25, 2003, 4.

Crace, John. "War Game: Tap, Tap—You're Dead! How Computer Games Became the Army's Latest Training Tool." *Guardian*, July 9, 2002, 42.

Craig, Kathleen. "Dead in Iraq: It's No Game." *Wired.com*, June 6, 2006. http://www.wired.com/gaming/gamingreviews/news/2006/06/71052.

Cramsie, Jody. "Gender Discrimination in the Military: The Unconstitutional Exclusion of Women from Combat." *Valparaiso University Law Review* 17, no. 2 (1983): 547–88.

Crawley, James W. "Gentlemen, Rethink Your Logos; the Coast Guard and the Marines Are Dropping NASCAR Sponsorships." *Richmond Times Dispatch*, November 15, 2006, A4.

Creamer, Matthew. "Transparency—Embedded Reporters May Help Corporations Open Up." *PR Week*, May 19, 2003, 9.

Crecente, Brian. "Fighting Reality: Military Games Entertain, Disturb with Creative Depictions of Modern Warfare." *Rocky Mountain News*, April 30, 2004, 29D.

Crogan, Patrick. "Gametime: History, Narrative, and Temporality in Combat Flight Simulator II." In *The Video Game Theory Reader*, ed. Mark J. P. Wolf and Bernard Perron, 275–302. New York: Routledge, 2003.

Csikszentmihalyi, Mihaly. *Beyond Boredom and Anxiety*. San Francisco: Jossey-Bass, 2000.

Dao, James. "Ads Now Seek Recruits for 'An Army of One'." *New York Times*, January 9, 2001, A1.

Dao, James, and Eric Schmitt. "A Nation Challenged: Hearts and Minds; Pentagon Readies Effort to Sway Sentiment Abroad." *New York Times*, February 19, 2002, A1.

Davis, Ben. "Pop Life." *Artnet.com* December 16, 2005. http://www.artnet.com/magazineus/reviews/davis/davis12–16–05.asp.

Day, Julia. "Sony to Cash in on Iraq with 'Shock and Awe' Game." *Guardian Online*, April 10, 2003. http://media.guardian.co.uk/print/0,,4644696–105237,00.html.

Debord, Guy. *The Society of the Spectacle*. Trans. Donald Nicholson-Smith. New York: Zone Books, 1994.

Del Corno, Dario. "Games and War in Ancient Greece." In *War and Games*, ed. Tim Cornell and Thomas B. Allen, 17–36. Rochester, NY: Boydell Press, 2002.

Deleuze, Gilles. *Negotiations: 1972–1990*. Trans. Martin Joughin. New York: Columbia University Press, 2002.

Deleuze, Gilles, and Félix Guattari. *A Thousand Plateaus: Capitalism and Schizophrenia*. Trans. Brian Massumi. Minneapolis: University of Minnesota Press, 1987.

Dellios, Hugh, and E.A. Torriero. "Myth; How the Jessica Lynch Story Turned into a Fable." *San Diego Union-Tribune*, June 1, 2003, G6.

de Moraes, Lisa. " 'Reality' TV Is Marching to the Military's Tune." *Washington Post*, March 19, 2002, C7.

de Onis, Juan. "Nixon Puts 'Bums' Label on Some College Radicals." *New York Times*, May 2, 1970, 1.

Der Derian, James. *Virtuous War: Mapping the Military-Industrial-Media-Entertainment Network*. Boulder, CO: Westview Press, 2001.

Devroy, Ann, and Guy Gugliotta. "Bush to 'Move Fast' on Mideast Peace." *Washington Post*, March 2, 1991, A1.

Dibble, Vernon. "The Garrison Society." *New University Thought* 5, (1966–67): 106–15.

Donnelly, Peter. "Vertigo in America: A Social Comment." In *Sport, Culture, and Society*, ed. John W. Loy, Jr., Gerald S. Kenyon and Barry D. McPherson, 308–13. Philadelphia, PA: Lea & Febiger, 1981.

Donovan, James A. *Militarism, U.S.A.* New York: Scribner, 1970.

Doob, Leonard W. "Goebbels' Principles of Propaganda." In *Public Opinion and Propaganda*, ed. Daniel Katz, Dorwin Cartwright, Samuel Eldersveld and Alfred McClung Lee, 508–22. New York: Dryden Press, 1954.

Ebo, Busah. "War as Popular Culture: The Gulf Conflict and the Technology of Illusionary Entertainment." *Journal of American Culture* 18, (1995): 19–25.

Edwards, Jim. "Uncle Sam Ups Ante for Recruiting Effort." *Adweek*, November 29, 2004 (Lexis Nexis database).

Edwards, Mary Morgan. "Military Easter Baskets Come under Fire." *Columbus Dispatch*, April 12, 2003, 1B.

Eisenberg, Arlo. "Psychotic Rant." In *To the Extreme: Alternative Sports, Inside and Out*, ed. Robert E. Rinehart and Synthia Sydnor, 21–26. Albany, NY: State University of New York Press, 2003.

Eisenhower, Dwight. "Farewell Address." January 17, 1961. http://millercenter.org/scripps/archive/speeches/detail/3361.

"Embedded Reporting: What Are Americans Getting?". *Project for Excellence in Journalism*, April 3, 2003. http://journalism.org/node/211.

Enloe, Cynthia H. *Does Khaki Become You?: The Militarisation of Women's Lives*. Boston, MA: South End Press, 1983.

Epstein, Edward. "Success in Afghan War Hard to Gauge; U.S. Reluctance to Produce Body Counts Makes Proving Enemy's Destruction Difficult." *San Francisco Chronicle*, March 23, 2002, A1.

——— . "House Defeats Bill to Reintroduce Draft." *San Francisco Chronicle*, October 6, 2004, A1.

Ewen, Stuart. *PR!: A Social History of Spin*. 1st ed. New York: Basic Books, 1996.

"Export Controls Put on 'Military' Playstation2." *Electronics Times*, April 26, 2000, 4.

Fam, Miriam. "Iraqi President Says U.S. Troops Should Stay; Election Workers Begin Final Tally of Historic Vote." *Associated Press*, February 1, 2005 (Lexis Nexis database).

Feldmann, Linda. "Why Iraq War Support Fell So Fast." *Christian Science Monitor*, November 21, 2005, 1.

Fitch, Samuel. "The Garrison State in America: A Content Analysis of Trends in the Expectation of Violence." *Journal of Peace Research* 22, (1985): 31–45.

Fontenot, Gregory, E.J. Degen, David Tohn, and Tommy Franks. *On Point: The U.S. Army in Operation Iraqi Freedom*. Edited by Office of the Chief of Staff. Fort Leavenworth, KS: Combat Studies Institute Press, 2003.

Ford, Steve. "So Terrible We Can't Get Enough." *News and Observer*, March 23, 2003, A30.

"Former Leesburg Resident One of Civilians Killed in Iraq." *The Associated Press State and Local Wire*, April 1, 2004 (Lexis Nexis database).

Foucault, Michel. *The History of Sexuality*, vol. 1. Trans. Robert Hurley. New York: Vintage Books, 1990.

Foucault, Michel, Mauro Bertani, Alessandro Fontana, François Ewald, and David Macey. *"Society Must Be Defended": Lectures at the College de France, 1975–76*. Trans. David Macey. 1st edn. New York: Picador, 2003.

Foucault, Michel. *Power/Knowledge: Selected Interviews and Other Writings, 1972–1977*. Ed. and Trans. Colin Gordon. New York: Pantheon Books, 1980.

"Fox Announces Extreme Sports Network." *TV Meets the Web*, December 3, 2002 (Lexis Nexis database).

Francis, David R. "It's Back: The Global Arms Race." *Christian Science Monitor*, March 26, 2007, 16.

Frank, Thomas. *The Conquest of Cool*. Chicago: University of Chicago Press, 1998.

Franklin, H. Bruce. *Vietnam and Other American Fantasies*. Amherst, MA: University of Massachusetts Press, 2000.

Friedman, Thomas L. "Giving the Hatemongers No Place to Hide." *New York Times*, July 22, 2005, A19.

Fritz, Ben. "Holiday Fuels Activision." *Daily Variety*, February 8, 2008, 4.

"'Front Line' a Questionable Dose of Reality." *Alameda Times-Star*, February 27, 2003 (Lexis Nexis database).

Fry, Andy. "X-Dream Coasts on Extreme Sports Wave." *TeenScreen*, March 1, 2000, 16.

Fussell, Paul. *The Great War and Modern Memory*. New York: Oxford University Press, 1975.

Galloway, Alexander R. "Social Realism in Gaming." *Game Studies* 4, no. 1 (2004). http://www.gamestudies.org/0401/galloway/

"Games People Slay." *Wired*, April 1, 2003. http://www.wired.com/news/culture/0,1284,58314,00.html.

Garrelts, Jacqueline. "Army Lends Aid to Hollywood." *Army News Service*, July 29, 2004. http://www.militaryinfo.com/news_story.cfm?textnewsid=1098.

Gerbner, George. "Persian Gulf War, the Movie." In *Triumph of the Image: The Media's War in the Persian Gulf: A Global Perspective*, ed. Hamid Molwana, George Gerbner and Herbert I. Schiller, 243–65. Boulder, CO: Westview Press, 1992.

Gilbert, Matthew. "Double Vision: The TV Landscape Is One Unsettling Blur of News and Entertainment." *Boston Globe*, April 2, 2003, C1.

Gillett, Nick. "Military Operations." *Guardian*, January 19, 2008, 30.

Gillies, Judith S. "Putting a Face on Those Who Serve." *Washington Post*, March 9, 2003, Y7.

Gillman, Todd J., and Carolyn Barta. "Bush Administration Getting Cozy with Hollywood." *Dallas Morning News*, November 22, 2001 (Lexis Nexis database).

Glassman, Mark. "Military Channels Are Competing on Cable TV." *New York Times*, January 24, 2005, C8.

Goldfarb, Owen. "'Virtual Jihadi' Creator Achieves His Objective." *Times Union*, March 20, 2008, A10.

Graham, Andrea. "PR Pros Find Extreme Sports Less Elusive." *O'Dwyers PR Services Report*, December 2002, 1.

Gray, Chris Hables. *Cyborg Citizen: Politics in the Posthuman Age*. New York: Routledge, 2001.

Green, Frank. "Upper Deck to Issue Patriotic Trading Cards; 'United We Stand' Line Contains Images from Sept. 11 Terror Attacks." *San Diego Union-Tribune*, November 10, 2001, C1.

Greene, Susan. "Recruiting Pitch Draws Fire Guard Tries 'Escape from Reality' Tactic." *Denver Post*, October 5, 2001, A18.

Gregory, Lauren. "Competition Fierce in Wartime Recruiting." *Chattanooga Times Free Press*, October 18, 2008, 0.

Grimshaw, Colin. "Living Dangerously—It Is Not Always the Advertisers You Would Normally Expect That Are Trying to Associate Themselves with Extreme Sports." *Campaign*, March 29, 2002, 35.

Guttman, Allen. *From Ritual to Record*. New York: Columbia University Press, 1978.

——— . *Sports Spectators*. New York: Columbia University Press, 1986.

Habermas, Jürgen. *The Structural Transformation of the Public Sphere: An Inquiry into a Category of Bourgeois Society*. Trans. Thomas Burger and Frederick Lawrence. Cambridge, MA: MIT Press, 1996.

Hall, Karen J. "A Soldier's Body: GI Joe, Hasbro's Great American Hero, and the Symptoms of Empire." *Journal of Popular Culture* 38, no. 1 (2004): 34–54.

Hall, Matthew T. "Military Re-Enlistments Rise in Response to Devastation." *San Diego Union-Tribune*, September 30, 2001, B1.

Hallin, Daniel C. *The "Uncensored War": The Media and Vietnam*. New York: Oxford University Press, 1986.

Hallin, Daniel C., and Todd Gitlin. "Agon and Ritual: The Gulf War as Popular Culture and as Television Drama." *Political Communication* 10, (1993): 411–24.

Halter, Ed. "Hard Knoxville." *Village Voice*, November 5, 2002.

Hamilton, William L. "Toymakers Study Troops, and Vice Versa." *New York Times*, March 30, 2003, section 9, pg. 1.

Hammond, William M. "The Press in Vietnam as Agent of Defeat: A Critical Examination." *Reviews in American History* 17, no. 2 (1989): 312–23.

——— . *Reporting Vietnam: Media and Military at War*. Lawrence, KS: University Press of Kansas, 1998.

Haraway, Donna. *Simians, Cyborgs, and Women: The Reinvention of Nature*. New York: Routledge, 1991.

Hardt, Michael, and Antonio Negri. *Empire*. Cambridge, MA: Harvard University Press, 2000.

——— . *Multitude: War and Democracy in the Age of Empire*. New York: Penguin Press, 2004.

Harmon, Amy. "More Than Just a Game, but How Close to Reality?" *New York Times*, April 3, 2003, G1.

Harold, Christine. "Pranking Rhetoric: 'Culture Jamming' as Media Activism." *Critical Studies in Media Communication* 21, no. 3 (2004): 189–211.

Harrison, Charles, and Paul Wood, eds. *Art in Theory, 1900–2000: An Anthology of Changing Ideas*. Malden, MA: Blackwell Publishing, 2003.

Haviland, Mark. "Road Rulers Meet AF During Show's Taping." *DCMilitary.com* (2001), http://www.dcmilitary.com/dcmilitary_archives/stories/111401/11956–1.shtml.

Hay, James. "Designing Homes to Be the First Line of Defense." *Cultural Studies* 20, no. 4–5 (2006): 349–77.

Hayden, Thomas, and Marc Silver. "Tanks for the Memories." *U.S. News and World Report*, June 6, 2005, D14.

Hein, Kenneth. "Not So Extreme: Dew Retooling Image." *Brandweek*, October 23, 2006 (Lexis Nexis database).

Herman, Edward S., and Noam Chomsky. *Manufacturing Consent: The Political Economy of the Mass Media*. New York: Pantheon Books, 2002.

Herschenson, Karen. "Terrorist Cards Tout Tastelessness." *Contra Costa Times*, January 4, 2002, A3.

Hersh, Seymour. "The Coming Wars: What the Pentagon Can Now Do in Secret." *New Yorker*, January 24, 2005, 40–47.

Herz, J.C. *Joystick Nation*. New York: Little, Brown, and Co., 1997.

Hodes, Jacob, and Emma Ruby-Sachs. "'America's Army' Targets Youth." *The Nation*, August 23, 2002. http://www.thenation.com/doc/20020902/hodes20020823.

Hogan, Monica. "Comcast, ESPN Go to Extremes for X-Games." *Multichannel News*, August 13, 2001, 16.

Holmes, Susan. "'All You've Got to Worry About Is the Task, Having a Cup of Tea, and Doing a Bit of Sunbathing': Approaching Celebrity in Big Brother." In *Understanding Reality Television*, ed. Susan Holmes and Deborah Jermyn, 111–135. New York: Routledge, 2004.

Honohan, Iseult. *Civic Republicanism*. New York: Routledge, 2002.

Horkheimer, Max, and Theodor Adorno. *Dialectic of Enlightenment*. Trans. John Cumming. New York: Continuum, 1999.

Hoskins, Andrew. *Televising War: From Vietnam to Iraq*. New York: Continuum, 2004.

Houlihan, Bob. "MTV's Extreme Challenge." *All Hands*, March 2003, 40–43.

Housego, Kim. "Rumsfeld's Remarks Draw Anger in France." *Associated Press*, January 23, 2003 (Lexis Nexis database).

"How Many Iraqi Soldiers Died?" *Time*, June 17, 1991, 26.

Howard, Theresa. "Walgreens Won't Sell Easter Baskets with Toy Soldiers." *USA Today*, March 7, 2003, 1B.

Howe, Jeff. "Drawing Lines: A Report from the Extreme World." In *To the Extreme: Alternative Sports Inside and Out*, ed. Robert E. Rinehardt and Synthia Sydnor, 253–72. Albany, NY: State University of New York Press, 2003.

Huizinga, Johan. *Homo Ludens*. Trans. George Steiner. London: Maurice Temple Smith, 1970.

Hulse, Carl. "Threats and Responses: The Draft." *New York Times*, February 9, 2003, 17.

Iovine, Julie V. "The Army Wants You for the Afternoon." *New York Times*, October 10, 2004, section 2, pg. 1.

"Iraq War Coverage Plunges." *Pew Research Center's Project for Excellence in Journalism*, March 25, 2008. http://www.journalism.org/node/10345.

Irwin, Tanya. "Navy Offers Action in Campaign: Debut from CEA Suggests Enlisting Will 'Accelerate Your Life'." *Adweek*, March 19, 2001 (Lexis Nexis database).

Ivie, Robert L. "Images of Savagery in American Justifications for War." *Communication Monographs* 47, no. 4 (1980): 279–91.

——— . "Savagery in Democracy's Empire." *Third World Quarterly* 26, no. 1 (2005): 55–65.

Jamieson, Kathleen Hall. *Eloquence in an Electronic Age: The Transformation of Political Speechmaking.* New York: Oxford University Press, 1988.

Jansen, Sue Curry, and Don Sabo. "The Sport/War Metaphor: Hegemonic Masculinity, the Persian Gulf War, and the New World Order." *Sociology of Sport Journal* vol. 11 no. 1 (1994): 1–17.

Jeffords, Shawn. "Army Game Enlists 'Soft Sell' for Recruitment." *Chicago Sun-Times,* November 25, 2003, 20.

Jensen, Robert. *Citizens of the Empire: The Struggle to Claim Our Humanity.* San Francisco: City Lights Books, 2004.

Johnson, Chalmers A. *The Sorrows of Empire: Militarism, Secrecy, and the End of the Republic.* 1st edn. New York: Metropolitan Books, 2004.

——— . *Nemesis: The Last Days of the American Republic.* New York: Metropolitan Books, 2006.

Kahn, Joseph P. "X-Communication: Hot Products and Artists with 'X' in Their Names Are Everywhere—and It's No Accident, Say Marketing Experts." *Boston Globe,* May 3, 2003, D1.

Kaplan, Caren. "Precision Targets: GPS and the Militarization of Consumer Identity." *American Quarterly* 58, no. 3 (2006): 693–713.

Keefe, Bob. "Super Bowl XXXVII: Security's Super Tight for Big Game." *Atlanta Journal-Constitution,* January 26, 2003.

Keen, Sam. *Faces of the Enemy: Reflections of the Hostile Imagination.* San Francisco: Harper & Row, 1986.

Kellner, Douglas. *The Persian Gulf TV War.* Boulder, CO: Westview Press, 1992.

Kennedy, Helen. "Kerry's Old Navy Foe Looks to Sink Senator." *Daily News,* May 4, 2004, 26.

Kennedy, Janice. "Virtual Hell." *Ottawa Citizen,* May 29, 2003, E5.

Keveney, Bill. "Military Is up to These Challenges." *USA Today,* December 5, 2001, 4D.

Kim, Gina, and Mark Ramirez. "Judging Embedded Reporting: The Experts." *Seattle Times,* March 26, 2003. http://community.seattletimes.nwsource.com/archive/?date=20030326&slug=embedded26.

Kindred, David. "An Army and Navy of One." *Sporting News,* December 10, 2001, 64.

King, Geoff. " 'Just Like a Movie': 9/11 and Hollywood Spectacle." In *The Spectacle of the Real,* ed. Geoff King, 47–57. Portland, OR: Intellect, 2005.

Kirkpatrick, David D. "Jessica Lynch Criticizes U.S. Accounts of Her Ordeal." *New York Times,* November 7, 2003, A25.

Klaassen, Abbey. "Media Morph: Episodic Games." *Advertising Age,* August 20, 2007, 15.

Klein, Naomi. *No Logo: Taking Aim at the Brand Bullies.* New York: Picador USA, 2000.

Klein, Philip. "Gamblers Place Wagers on Saddam's Demise." *Reuters,* March 24, 2003 (Lexis Nexis database).

Klein, Stephen A. "Public Character and the Simulacrum: The Construction of the Soldier Patriot and Citizen Agency in *Black Hawk Down.*" *Critical Studies in Media Communication* 22, no. 5 (2005): 427–49.

Krane, Jim. "Insurgency-Friendly Web Sites Valuable to Rebels, Reporters and U.S. Military—and Prone to Hoaxes." *Associated Press,* February 3, 2005 (Lexis Nexis database).

Lang, Derrick J. " 'Army of Two,' 'Turning Point' and 'Kwari' Take New Aim at the Shooter Genre." *Associated Press*, November 21, 2007 (Lexis Nexis database).

Larsen, Ernest. "Gulf War TV." *Jump Cut* no. 36 (1991): 3–10.

Lasswell, Harold. "The Garrison State." *American Journal of Sociology* 46, (1941): 455–68.

——— . "The Garrison State Hypothesis Today." In *Changing Patterns of Military Politics*, ed. Samuel Huntington, 51–70. New York: Free Press, 1962.

Lauer, Claudia, and Johanna Neuman. "Rumsfeld Denies Tillman Coverup." *Los Angeles Times*, August 2, 2007, A12.

Le Breton, David. "Playing Symbolically with Death in Extreme Sports." *Body and Society* 6, no. 1 (2000): 1–11.

Leland, John. "Cultural Studies: Glued to Public Seduction TV." *New York Times*, February 23, 2003, section 9, pg. 3.

——— . "Urban Tool in Recruiting by the Army: An Arcade." *New York Times*, January 5, 2009, section 9, pg. 3.

Lembcke, Jerry. *The Spitting Image: Myth, Memory, and the Legacy of Vietnam*. New York: New York University Press, 1998.

Lens, Sidney. *The Military-Industrial Complex*. Philadelphia, PA: Pilgrim Press, 1970.

Lepage, Mark. "New York Ducts and Covers." *Montreal Gazette*, February 17, 2003, A1.

Levins, Harry. "Strange Bedfellows Militarymediamilitary." *St. Louis Post-Dispatch*, February 16, 2003, B1.

Lieberman, David. "Military Channel to Be 'Voice of Troops'." *USA Today*, February 5, 2007, 5B.

Linton, Meg. "Wayne Coe, American Hero." *Juxtapoz Magazine*, December 2006. http://www.waynecoe.com/press.html.

Lippmann, Walter. *Public Opinion*. New Brunswick, NJ: Transaction Publishers, 1991.

Litfin, A. Duane. "Eisenhower on the Military-Industrial Complex: Critique of a Rhetorical Strategy." *The Central States Speech Journal* 25, no. 3 (1974): 198–209.

Livingston, Steven. *Clarifying the CNN Effect: An Examination of Media Effects According to Type of Military Intervention*. Cambridge, MA: Joan Shorenstein Center on the Press Politics and Public Policy John F. Kennedy School of Government Harvard University, 1997.

Luftus, Tom. "War Games in a Time of War." *MSNBC.com*, July 18, 2004. http://www.msnbc.msn.com/id/5318462.

Lydersen, Kari. "Antiwar Art in a New Medium: Paintball-on-Web; Iraqi Dodges Projectiles at Chicago Gallery to Illustrate His People's Plight." *Washington Post*, May 29, 2007, A2.

——— . "In the Crosshairs." *In these Times*, July, 2007, 48.

MacArthur, John R. *Second Front: Censorship and Propaganda in the Gulf War*. New York: Hill and Wang, 1992.

Machiavelli, Niccolò. *Discourses on Livy*. Trans. Julia Conaway Bondanella and Peter E. Bondanella. New York: Oxford University Press, 1997.

——— . *The Prince*. Trans. George Bull. New edn. Penguin Classics. New York: Penguin, 1999.

Malone, Julia. "POWs Top Allied Agenda." *Atlanta Journal and Constitution*, March 2, 1991, A1.

Mara, Janis. "IQ News: Earthlink, Sprint Go to Extreme." *Adweek*, September 11, 2000 (Lexis Nexis database).

Mariscal, George. "In the Wake of the Gulf War: Untying the Yellow Ribbon." *Cultural Critique* no. 19 (1991): 97–117.

Martin, Randy. "Derivative Wars." *Cultural Studies* 20, no. 4–5 (2006): 459–76.

McCandless, David. "Make Cheats, Not War." *Guardian*, May 22, 2003, 23.

McChesney, Robert. *Rich Media, Poor Democracy: Communication Politics in Dubious Times.* Urbana: University of Illinois Press, 1999.

McFeatters, Ann. "Laughter in a Time of War." *Pittsburgh Post-Gazette*, March 30, 2003. http://www.post-gazette.com/forum/col/20030330edann30p3.asp.

McLeroy, Carrie. "Army Experience Center Opens in Philadelphia." *Army.Mil/News*, September 2, 2008. http://www.army.mil/-news/2008/09/02/12072-army-experience-center-opens-in-philadelphia/.

McWhertor, Michael. "America's Army Deployed to Toy Aisles [Bureau of Licensing]." *Kotaku*, November 15, 2007. (Lexis Nexis database).

Medved, Michael. "Zap! Have Fun and Help Defeat Terrorists, Too." *USA Today*, October 30, 2001, 15A.

Melman, Seymour. *Pentagon Capitalism: The Political Economy of War.* New York,: McGraw-Hill, 1970.

Milbank, Dana. "Curtains Ordered for Media Coverage of Returning Coffins." *Washington Post*, October 21, 2003, A23.

———. "No Crawfishing from a Unique Vernacular." *Washington Post*, September 10, 2002, A13.

Miles, Donna. "Military, Hollywood Team up to Create Realism, Drama on Big Screen." *American Forces Press Service*, June 8, 2007. http://www.defenselink.mil/news/newsarticle.aspx?id=46352.

"Military Fears over Playstation2." *BBC NewsOnline, Asia-Pacific*, April 17, 2000. http://news.bbc.co.uk/1/low/world/asia-pacific/716237.stm.

"Military Recruiting: DoD Needs to Establish Objectives and Measures to Better Evaluate Advertising's Effectiveness." ed. United States General Accounting Office. Report to Senate and House Committees on Armed Services. Washington, DC: US Government Printing House, 2003.

Miller, Iain. "Decisive, Determined and Articulate. Is That Really My Bush?" *Independent*, May 9, 2004, 24–25.

Miller, Stanley A. "War Game: Army Deploys to L.A. To Capture the Attention of America's Gamers." *Milwaukee Journal Sentinel*, May 12, 2003, 1A.

Mills, C. Wright. *The Power Elite.* New York: Oxford University Press, 1956.

Montgomery, Lori. "Paying Tribute to the Chroniclers of War." *Washington Post*, October 2, 2003, B01.

Mueller, John. "The Iraq Syndrome." *Foreign Affairs* 84, no. 6 (2005). (Lexis Nexis database).

Murray, Stuart J. "Thanatopolitics: On the Use of Death for Mobilizing Political Life." *Polygraph* 18, (2006): 191–215.

Nadelhalft, Matthew. "Metawar: Sports and the Persian Gulf War." *Journal of American Culture* 16, no. 4 (1993): 25–33.

Nietzsche, Friedrich. *Beyond Good and Evil.* Trans. Walter Kaufmann. New York: Vintage Books, 1989.

"No 'Shock and Awe' for Sony." *CNN.com*, April 16, 2003. http://robots.cnn.com/2003/TECH/biztech/04/16/japan.sony.reut/index.html.

Norris, Margot. "Only the Guns Have Eyes: Military Censorship and the Body Count."

In *Seeing through the Media: The Persian Gulf War*, ed. Susan Jeffords and Lauren Rabinowitz, 285–300. New Brunswick, NJ: Rutgers University Press, 1994.

Obrien, Kathleen. "Most Wanted: Drilling Down/Television; the Other Reality." *New York Times*, March 31, 2003, C9.

Odelius, Dwight N. "These Games Provide Funky Fun, and One's Free." *Houston Chronicle*, December 25, 2003, 4.

O'Hagan, Steve. "Recruitment Hard Drive: The US Army Is the World's Biggest Games Developer, Pumping Billions into New Software." *Guardian*, June 19, 2004, 12.

Ohlmeyer, Don. "The Heroes of Desert Storm." 92 minutes: NBC, 1991.

Oldenburg, Don. "And Now, 'Rudy, the Ultimate Seal'." *Washington Post*, February 13, 2001, C4.

——— . "New Video War Games Give a Taste of Combat—for Fun." *Washington Post*, December 10, 2002, C1.

Olsen, Richard K. Jr. "Living above It All: The Liminal Fantasy of Sports Utility Vehicle Advertisements." In *Enviropop*, ed. Mark Meister and Phyllis Japp, 175 96. Westport, CT: Praeger Publishers, 2002.

"Operation / Series: Urban Warrior '99." Department of Defense. http://www.dodmedia.osd.mil/DVIC_View/Still_Details.cfm?SDAN=DMSD0002959&JPGPath=/Assets/2000/Marines/DM-SD-00–02959.JPG.

Orwell, George. *The Collected Essays, Journalism, & Letters, George Orwell*. Edited by Sonia Orwell and Ian Angus, vol. 4. Boston: David R. Godine, 2000.

Oser, Kris. "Big Guns Fall in Line Behind Army's Adver-Game." *Advertising Age*, April 11, 2005, 83.

Owen, Rob. "Reporters Get Yanked by Brass and Bosses." *Pittsburg Post-Gazette*, April 1, 2003, A1.

Oxman, Steve. "War Games." *Daily Variety*, March 28, 2001, 24.

Packer, Jeremy. "Becoming Bombs: Mobilizing Mobility in the War on Terror." *Cultural Studies* 20, no. 4–5 (2006): 378–99.

Parks, Lisa. *Cultures in Orbit*. Durham, NC: Duke University Press, 2005.

Peck, Michael. "Battlefield Gamers." *Defense Technology International*, September 1, 2007, 12.

Petrozzello, Donna. "War on Terror, the TV Series." *Daily News*, February 21, 2002, 100.

Pikul, Corrie. "The Photoshopping of the President." *Salon.com*, July 1, 2004 (Lexis Nexis database).

Poniewozik, James, and Jess Cagle. "That's Militainment!" *CNN.com*, February 25, 2002. http://www.cnn.com/ALLPOLITICS/time/2002/03/04/militainment.html.

Preusch, Matthew. "Games: An Army of Fun." *Newsweek*, November 28, 2005, 8.

Prochaska, David. " 'Disappearing' Iraqis." *Public Culture* 4, no. 2 (1992): 89–92.

Prose, Francine. "Voting Democracy Off the Island." *Harper's*, March, 2004, 58–64.

Pursell, Carroll W. *The Military-Industrial Complex*. New York,: Harper & Row, 1972.

"Quest for Saddam: Die with Laughter as Action-Packed 3D Shooter Lets You Hunt Down the 'Butcher of Baghdad'." *Market Wire*, May 12, 2003 (Lexis Nexis database).

"Quotation of the Day." *New York Times*, September 7, 2002, A2.

Rasmussen, Karen, and Sharon Downey. "Dialectical Disorientation in Vietnam War Films: Subversion of the Mythology of War." *Quarterly Journal of Speech* 77, (1991): 176–95.

Rasor, Dina, and Robert Bauman. *Betraying Our Troops: The Destructive Results of Privatizing War*. New York: Palgrave Macmillan, 2007.

Ratan, Suneel. "War Games Come Marching In." *Wired*, December 9, 2003. http://
www.wired.com/news/games/0,2101,61515,00.html.

"Raytheon Sarcos Exoskeleton Robotic Suit Linked to Iron Man Superhero." *PR
Newswire*, May 2, 2008 (Lexis Nexis database).

Reagan, Ronald. "Remarks on Presenting the Medal of Honor to Master Sergeant
Roy P. Benavidez." *Ronald Reagan Presidential Library*, February 24, 1981. http://
www.reagan.utexas.edu/archives/speeches/1981/22481d.htm.

———. "Remarks During a Visit to Walt Disney World's Epcot Center near Orlando,
Florida." *Ronald Reagan Presidential Library*, March 8, 1983. http://
www.reagan.utexas.edu/archives/speeches/1983/30883a.htm.

Regan, Patrick M. "War Toys, War Movies, and the Militarization of the United States,
1900–1985." *Journal of Peace Research* 31, no. 1 (1994): 45–58.

Rentschler, Eric. *The Ministry of Illusion: Nazi Cinema and Its Afterlife*. Cambridge, MA:
Harvard University Press, 1996.

"Residents Dispute Idea That Bomber Suspect Lived Amid Sympathizers." *Grand Rapids
Press*, June 2, 2003, A5.

Rhoden, William C. "Sports of the Times; Metaphors, Realities and Football." *New
York Times*, January 29, 2003, D1.

Rid, Thomas. *War and Media Operations: The U.S. Military and the Press from Vietnam to Iraq*.
New York: Routledge, 2007.

Riddell, Rob. "Doom Goes to War." *Wired*, May 4, 1997. http://wired.com/wired/
archive/5.04/ff_doom.html.

Robb, David L. *Operation Hollywood: How the Pentagon Shapes and Censors the Movies*.
New York: Prometheus Books, 2004.

Roberts, Chuck. *CNN Headline News*, March 20, 2003 (Lexis Nexis database).

Roberts, Les, Riyadh Lafta, Richard Garfield, Jamal Khudhairi, and Gilbert Burnham.
"Mortality before and after the 2003 Invasion of Iraq: Cluster Sample Survey."
Lancet 364, no. 9448 (2004): 1857–64.

Robinson, Piers. *The CNN Effect: The Myth of News, Foreign Policy and Intervention*.
New York: Routledge, 2002.

Roeper, Richard. "Nothing Is So Sacred It Can't Be Marketed." *Chicago Sun-Times*,
December 3, 2001, 11.

———. "TV Reporters Lack Sense to Come in out of the Rain." *Chicago Sun-Times*,
September 22, 2003, 11.

Rogers, Rick. "Video Game Brings the Fight to the Marines." *San Diego Union-Tribune*,
June 3, 2005, A1.

Romano, Allison. "New Fox Net Dubbed 'Fuel'." *Broadcasting and Cable*, April 14,
2003, 33.

Rosen, Steven. *Testing the Theory of the Military-Industrial Complex*. Lexington, MA:
Lexington Books, 1973.

Rumsfeld, Donald. "A New Kind of War." *New York Times*, September 27, 2001,
A21.

———. "Transforming the Military." *Foreign Affairs* 81, no. 3 (2002), 20–32.

Saletan, William. "War Is Halo." *Slate Magazine*, July 22, 2008. http://
www.slate.com/id/2195751.

Saltzman, Marc. "Army Enlists Simulation to Help Tackle Terrorists." *USA Today*,
October 2, 2001, 3D.

———. "Army Gives New Meaning to War Games—on a PC." *USA Today Online*,

May 2, 2002. http://www.usatoday.com/tech/techreviews/2002/4/22/army-game.htm.

Sandomir, Richard. "The Decline and Fall of Sports Ratings." *New York Times*, September 10, 2003, D1.

Scahill, Jeremy. "Blood Is Thicker Than Blackwater." *The Nation* (2006), http://www.thenation.com/doc/20060508/scahill.

——. *Blackwater: The Rise of the World's Most Powerful Mercenary Army*. New York: Nation Books, 2007.

——. "Bush's Mercenaries Thrive in Iraq." *Toronto Star*, January 29, 2007, A13.

Scanlon, Jennifer. "'Your Flag Decal Won't Get You into Heaven Anymore': U.S. Consumers, Wal-Mart, and the Commodification of Patriotism." In *The Selling of 9/11: How a National Tragedy Became a Commodity*, ed. Dana Heller, 174–99. New York: Palgrave Macmillan, 2005.

Scarry, Elaine. *The Body in Pain: The Making and Unmaking of the World*. New York: Oxford University Press, 1985.

——. "Watching and Authorizing the Gulf War." In *Media Spectacles*, ed. Marjorie Garber, Jann Matlock and Rebecca L. Walkowitz, 57–73. New York: Routledge, 1993.

Schechter, Danny. "Independent Press Was a Target in Iraq." *Television Week*, February 28, 2005, 8.

Schiesel, Seth. "Facing the Horrors of Distant Battlefields with a TV and Console." *New York Times*, March 19, 2008, E3.

Schleiner, Anne-Marie. "Cracking the Maze Online Exhibit: Game Plug-Ins and Patches as Hacker Art." *Switch* no. 12 (1999). http://switch.sjsu.edu/nextswitch/switch_engine/front/front.php?

Schmitt, Eric, and Thom Shanker. "A Nation Challenged: Body Count; Taliban and Qaeda Death Toll in Mountain Battle Is a Mystery." *New York Times*, March 14, 2002, A1.

Scodari, Christine. "Operation Desert Storm As 'Wargames': Sport, War and Media Intertextuality." *Journal of American Culture* 16, no. 1 (1993): 1–5.

"*Seattle Times* Tech News Column," *Seattle Times*, April 21, 2003, C2.

Segrave, Jeffrey O. "The Sports Metaphor in American Cultural Discourse." *Culture, Sport, and Society* 3, no. 1 (2000): 48–60.

"Series Eyes U.S. Military." *Montreal Gazette*, February 22, 2002, D11.

Seward, Zachary M. "Internet Hunting Nipped in Bud." *Seattle Times*, August 12, 2007, A9.

Shachtman, Noah. "Army Sets up New Office of Video Games." *Wired*, December 12, 2007. http://www.wired.com/dangerroom/2007/12/armys-new-offic.

Shafer, Jack. "Sacking Arnett for the Wrong Reason." *Slate*, March 31, 2003. http://www.slate.com/id/2080947.

Shapiro, Jerome F. *Atomic Bomb Cinema: The Apocalyptic Imagination on Film*. New York: Routledge, 2002.

Shelton, General Henry H. *Joint Vision 2020*. Washington, DC: US Government Printing Office, 2000.

Shugar, Scott. "Operation Desert Store: First the Air War, Then the Ground War, Now the Marketing Campaign." *Los Angeles Times*, September 29, 1991, 18.

Shulman, Robin. "Terror-Themed Game Suspended; Iraqi-Born Artist Asserts Censorship after Exhibit Is Shut Down." *Washington Post*, March 8, 2008, A3.

Silberman, Steve. "The War Room." *Wired*, September 2004. http://www.wired.com/wired/archive/12.09/warroom_pr.html.

Silliman, Stephen W. "The 'Old West' in the Middle East: U.S. Military Metaphors in Real and Imagined Indian Country." *American Anthropologist* 110, no. 2 (2008): 237–47.

Silver, Marc, and Betsy Streisand. "Hollywood at War." *U.S. News and World Report*, March 11, 2002, 76.

Sims, Josh. "When Reality Is Just an Illusion." *Independent*, March 29, 2004, 4–5.

Sindrich, Jackie. "Topps Turns Attack into Trading Cards." *San Diego Union-Tribune*, November 9, 2001.

Singer, Peter W. *Corporate Warriors: The Rise of the Privatized Military Industry*, Cornell Studies in Security Affairs. Ithaca, NY: Cornell University Press, 2003.

Sisk, Richard. "70% of Troops Want out—Poll." *Daily News*, March 1, 2006, 10.

Slotek, Jim. "Making War Look Good: Behind Enemy Lines Director Admits the Camera Exaggerates." *Toronto Sun*, December 3, 2001, 38.

Sloyan, Patrick. "The War You Won't See: Why the Bush Administration Plans to Restrict Coverage of Gulf Combat." *Washington Post*, January 13, 1991, C2.

——— . "What Bodies?" *The Digital Journalist*, November 2002. http://www. digitaljournalist.org/issue0211/sloyan.html.

——— . "What Bodies?" In *The Iraq War Reader: History, Documents, Opinions*, ed. Michael L. Sifry and Christopher Cerf, 129–34. New York: Touchstone Books, 2003.

Small, William J. "The Gulf War: Mass Media Coverage and Restraints." In *The 1,000 Hour War: Communication in the Gulf*, ed. Thomas A. McCain and Leonard Shyles, 3–18. Westport, CT: Greenwood Press, 1994.

Snider, Mike. "Spies Will Learn Craft Via Games." *USA Today*, June 16, 2005, 5D.

Snyder, R. Claire. *Citizen-Soldiers and Manly Warriors: Military Service and Gender in the Civic Republic Tradition*. Lanham, MD: Rowman & Littlefield Publishers, 1999.

Solomon, Norman. *War Made Easy: How Presidents and Pundits Keep Spinning Us to Death*. Hoboken, NJ: John Wiley, 2005.

Sontag, Susan. *On Photography*. New York: Farrar, Straus, and Giroux, 1977.

——— . *Regarding the Pain of Others*. New York: Farrar Straus and Giroux, 2003.

"Sony Drops 'Shock and Awe' for Playstation Games." *USA Today Online*, April 16, 2003. http://www.usatoday.com/tech/world/iraq/2003-04-16-shock-sony_x.htm.

Stacy, Greg. "Atrocity Becomes Art at OCCCA's 'Just How Does a Patriot Act?' Show." *OC Weekly*, October 16, 2008 (Lexis Nexis database).

Stahl, Roger. "A Clockwork War: Rhetorics of Time in a Time of Terror." *Quarterly Journal of Speech* 94, no. 1 (2007): 73–99.

Stam, Robert. "Mobilizing Fictions: The Gulf War, the Media, and the Recruitment of the Spectator." *Public Culture* 4, no. 2 (1992): 101–26.

Stauber, John C., and Sheldon Rampton. *Toxic Sludge Is Good for You: Lies, Damn Lies, and the Public Relations Industry*. Monroe, ME: Common Courage Press, 1995.

Stockman, Farah. "On the Internet, Betting on Hussein's Fate Is Heavy, Cyberspace Wagering Seen as Good Predictor." *Boston Globe*, March 11, 2003, B1.

Stone, Andrea. "Lights, Cameras Get Ready for War." *USA Today*, March 10, 2003, 3D.

Stossel, Scott. "Sports: War Games." *The American Prospect*, November 19, 2001. http://www.prospect.org/cs/articles?articleId=5978.

"Surfing the Wave." *Sports Marketing*, November 19, 2001, 14.

Susman, Tina. "Military Wins with Recruiting Game." *Newsday*, October 29, 2003, A7.

Susteren, Greta Van, and Steve Harrigan. "The Waterboarding Experience." *Fox on the Record with Greta van Susteren*, November 3, 2006 (Lexis Nexis database).

Swanson, Stevenson. "Iraqi Artist Claims 'Censorship'." *Chicago Tribune*, March 11, 2008, 3.

Tamrat, Hanna. "Hornet Hosts 'Fear Factor'." *Inside Bay Area*, July 16, 2006 (Lexis Nexis database).

Thomas, Tanja, and Fabian Verchow. "Banal Militarism and the Culture of War." In *Bring 'Em On: Media and Politics in the Iraq War*, ed. Lee Artz and Yahya R. Kamalipour, 23–36. Lanham, MD: Rowman & Littlefield Publishers, 2005.

Tierney, Mike. "Fox Now the Big Dog in Cable News—and Growing." *Atlanta Journal-Constitution*, May 9, 2005, 1A.

Tomlinson, Joe. *The Ultimate Encyclopedia of Extreme Sports*. London: Carleton, 1996.

Trimmer, Dave. "Tapping New Market: Team to Compete as 'Army of One'." *Spokesman Review*, July 5, 2004, C1.

"Trust in Federal Government, 1958–2004." American National Election Studies, http://www.electionstudies.org/nesguide/toptable/tab5a_1.htm.

Tulis, Jeffrey. *The Rhetorical Presidency*. Princeton, NJ: Princeton University Press, 1987.

Turse, Nick. *The Complex: How the Military Invades Our Everyday Lives*. New York: Metropolitan Books, 2008.

"TV & Movie Film Production Opportunities." USS Hornet Museum. http://www.hornetevents.com/film/index.html.

Tyson, Ann Scott. "New US Strategy: 'Lily Pad' Bases." *Christian Science Monitor*, August 10, 2004, 6.

Umstead, Thomas. "New ESPN Service Goes to Extremes." *Multichannel News*, April 29, 2002, 3.

"United We Stand." http://www.0100101110101101.org/home/unitedwestand/story.html.

"United We Stand." http://www.unitedwestandmovie.com/.

"U.S. Pilot O'Grady Sues Film-Makers." *Montreal Gazette*, August 21, 2002, F7.

"U.S. to Air Own Military News, Pentagon Wants More Control of Iraq, Afghanistan Reports." *Seattle Post-Intelligencer*, February 28, 2004, A4.

Vallis, Mary. "In Texas, a Mouse Can Kill a Deer; Web Site Would Give Hunters an Online Shot at Animals." *Chicago Sun-Times*, November 19, 2004, 46.

Vargas, Jose Antonio. "Way Radical, Dude; Now Playing: Video Games with an Islamist Twist." *Washington Post*, October 9, 2006, C1.

Veblen, Thorstein. *The Theory of the Leisure Class*. Boston: Houghton Mifflin, 1973.

"Velvet Strike Flamer Gallery." http://www.opensorcery.net/velvet-strike/mailgallery.html.

Verhey, Jeffrey. *The Spirit of 1914: Militarism, Myth, and Mobilization in Germany*. Cambridge: Cambridge University Press, 2000.

Verniere, Jim. "Excruciating: Diesel-Powered 'xXx' Results in Spontaneous Combustion." *Boston Globe*, August 9, 2002, S5.

Vinh, Tan. "Sporting Events Offer 'Gold Mine' for Army Recruiters." *Seattle Times*, July 25, 2005, B1.

Virilio, Paul. *War and Cinema: The Logistics of Perception*. Trans. Patrick Camiller. New York: Verso, 1989.

The Art of the Motor. Trans. Julie Rose. Minneapolis, MN: University of Minnesota Press, 1995.

——— . *Open Sky*. Trans. Julie Rose. New York: Verso, 1997.

——— . *Desert Screen: War at the Speed of Light*. Trans. Michael Degener. New York: Continuum, 2002.

Virilio, Paul, and Sylvere Lotringer. *Pure War*. Trans. Mark Polizotti. New York: Semiotexte, 1983.

von Sternberg, Bob. "The Pentagon Gives Reporters Front Seats but Not Free Reign." *Star Tribune*, March 7, 2003, 1A.

Wadhams, Nick. "Online Games Increasingly a Place for Protest, Social Activism." *Associated Press*, February 6, 2003 (Lexis Nexis database).

"Wafaa Bilal Sits in Small Room with a Paint Ball Gun While Visitors to His Web Site Take Shots at Him." *CBS News*, May 31, 2007 (Lexis Nexis database).

Walker, Andy. "U.S. Army Scores Hit in Kinder, Gentler War Games." *Toronto Star*, May 19, 2003, D1.

Walker, Dave. "Listen up, Maggots! The Drill Instructors Are the Real Stars in 'Boot Camp'—and Don't You Forget It." *Times-Picayune*, April 10, 2001, 1.

Walker, William. "So Many Fears for Such a Beautiful Afternoon." *Toronto Star*, November 17, 2002, B3.

Wallensteen, Peter, Johan Galtung, and Carlos Portales. *Global Militarization*. Boulder, CO: Westview Press, 1985.

Waxman, Sharon. "Thinking Outside the Tank; California's Institute for Creative Technologies Puts Tinseltown Talent to Work on Military Defense." *Washington Post*, May 7, 2003, C1.

Weaver, Jane. "Advertising for the Army." *MSN News*, March 13, 2003. https://www.msnbc.com/news/884250.asp.

"Web-Only TV Channel Launches for Extreme Sport Market." *New Media Age*, June 26, 2003, 4.

Weber, David. "Iraq Doctors Say Lynch Didn't Suffer Sex Assault." *Boston Herald*, November 8, 2003, 6.

Weschler, Lawrence. "Valkyries over Iraq." *Harper's*, November 2005, 65–77.

West, Gary. "Fort Worth Game Tries to Put Fun Back into the Bowls." *Fort Worth Star-Telegram*, December 22, 2006 (Lexis Nexis database).

Wetta, Frank J., and Martin A. Novelli. " 'Now a Major Motion Picture': War Films and Hollywood's New Patriotism." *Journal of Military History* 67, no. 3 (2003): 861–82.

Wheaton, Belinda. *Understanding Lifestyle Sports: Consumption, Identity, and Difference*. New York: Routledge, 2004.

White, Josh. "It's a Video Game, and an Army Recruiter." *Washington Post*, May 27, 2005, A25.

Wilkinson, Jack. "March Madness: NCAA: Show Must Go On." *Atlanta Journal and Constitution*, March 19, 2003, 1C.

Wilson, Peter. "Iraq Inquest." *Australian*, April 8, 2004, 20.

Winkler, Allan M. *The Politics of Propaganda: The Office of War Information, 1942–1945*. New Haven, CT: Yale University Press, 1978.

Wood, David. "Operation Makeover; Military Gets Real; Survival Themes Aim to Jazz Up Image." *New Orleans Times-Picayune*, April 1, 2001, 29.

Woolley, Wayne. "From 'Army of One' to Army of Fun." *New Orleans Times-Picayune*, September 7, 2003, 26.

——— . "Military Goes High-Tech to Spread 'Good News'." *Star-Ledger*, July 23, 2007, 1.

" 'xXx'treme Action Blurs Good, Evil, Fuels Diesel's Unlikely Hero." *Milwaukee Journal Sentinel*, August 9, 2002, 4E.

Yarmolinsky, Adam. *The Military Establishment; Its Impacts on American Society*. 1st edn. New York: Harper & Row, 1971.

Yin, Sandra. "Going to Extremes." *American Demographics*, June 2001, 26.

Young, Elise. "Talk of a Military Draft Has New Significance: Proposal to Require Service Alters Outlook for Some Youths." *Seattle Times*, February 2, 2003, A16.

Zirin, Dave, and John Cox. "Hey Guys, It's Just a Game." *The Nation*, June 20, 2006. http://www.thenation.com/doc/20060703/zirin.

Žižek, Slavoj. *Welcome to the Desert of the Real!: Five Essays on September 11 and Related Dates*. New York: Verso, 2002.

——— . "Passion: Regular or Decaf?" *In These Times*, March 29, 2004, 24.

Zmuda, Natalie. "Are the Army's New Marketing Tactics a Little Too Kid-Friendly?" *Advertising Age*, September 8, 2008, 1.

Index